MÉTRO STOP PARIS

MÉTRO STOP
PARIS

AN UNDERGROUND HISTORY OF THE CITY OF LIGHT

 GREGOR DALLAS

WALKER & COMPANY

NEW YORK

Published by Walker Publishing Company, Inc., New York
Distributed to the trade by Macmillan

All papers used by Walker & Company are natural, recyclable products
made from wood grown in well-managed forests. The manufacturing
processes conform to the environmental regulations of the country of origin.

Library of Congress Cataloging-in-Publication Data

Dallas, Gregor.
Métro stop Paris : underground tales from the City of Light / by Gregor Dallas.
p. cm.
ISBN-10: 0-8027-1695-4 (alk. paper)
ISBN-13: 978-0-8027-1695-8 (alk. paper)
1. Paris (France)—Description and travel.   2. Paris (France)—History.
3. Subways—France—Paris—Anecdotes.   I. Title.

DC707.D18   2008
914.43610484—dc22
2008001271

Visit Walker & Company's Web site at www.walkerbooks.com

First U.S. Edition 2008

1 3 5 7 9 10 8 6 4 2

Typeset by Westchester Book Group
Printed in the United States of America by Quebecor World Fairfield

To my mother,
Marjorie Eileen Dallas,
in fond memory

Numéro 336 — PRIX DU NUMÉRO : 40 CENTIMES — 19 Juin 1886

A. ROBIDA
RÉDACTEUR EN CHEF

La Caricature

JOURNAL
HEBDOMADAIRE

Abonnements d'un an : Paris et Départements : 20 francs. — Union postale : 25 francs. — Trois mois : 6 francs. — Bureaux : 7, rue du Croissant.

L'Embellissement de Paris par le Métropolitain. — par A. ROBIDA

La vue de Paris si jolie, augmentée juste au moment de l'Exposition de 1889, montre quels tréssors de beauté le Métropolitain bien conçu, peut apporter aux perspectives de la grande ville, quelles admirables transformations il peut opérer, et cela, seraient-il utile d'ajouter d'une façon ingénieuse et pittoresque des monuments qui, jusqu'à ce jour n'ont pu se servir à rien.

THOUGHTS FOR THE TRIP

Métro. n. m. (1891; de *métropolitain*). Chemin de fer à traction électrique, partiellement ou totalement souterrain, qui dessert les differents quartiers d'une capitale (notamment Paris) ou d'une grande ville.

Petit Robert 1

Ask a few Parisians: each has his Paris. Each has his Parises, one might say, insomuch as Paris is multiple, changing, contradictory . . .

Paris: le Guide Vert de Michelin

A QUIET REVOLUTION is taking place in the capitals of Europe. Walk through some of the streets of Chelsea, in west London, and all you will hear is French, whereas the main language on Rue de Rivoli, in central Paris, seems to be English. There are quarters in Rome where you will hear French, English and German—anything, it seems, but Italian. And these are not tourists you hear; they are the permanent, working residents from all over Europe. With 250,000 French residents in London, the French are right to claim that London is now the fifth French-speaking city in the world. In the same way, Paris is a major English-speaking city; one estimate puts the number of English speakers in the greater Paris region at 300,000 (there are no official statistics because census takers in the European Union are not allowed to record national origin). Every weekend, aeroplanes and trains are filled with the weekly commuters travelling between London and Paris. And every weekday, in the evening, you will find—cycling along the quays of the Seine, strolling in the boulevards and chatting in the cafés—the English, so excited to discover their new city.

This quiet revolution has occurred in the last five years. I have witnessed it myself in the expansion of professional associations, publications, political meetings and the number of social events aimed at English speakers in Paris. Old national myths are crumbling. Old national barriers are collapsing. Despite what politicians and the popular press may say, Europe, as a cultural, political and economic entity, is waking up. The old Europe *des patries* has gone, and it will never return.

This necessarily changes what one looks for in a "tourist guide." The "tourists" are no longer the same. Many of them will be permanent residents, seeking to deepen their knowledge of their new city. And for the majority of those travelling for pleasure, this will not be their first visit—they will want to know more than just the names and the dates of construction of the principal monuments. And even if they are first-time visitors, they will have read about the city, they will have seen it on television, and they will know what the place looks like. What they seek is the defining character of the town.

What gives Paris her character is not just her buildings, most of which are no more than two hundred years old, but also her rich history that goes back over two thousand years. There are many histories of Paris, but they won't fit in a pocket or a travelling sack. The following pages are designed for the new kind of tourist; it is a thinker's guide to Paris, made up of what Émile Zola—whom we will encounter in these pages—called "slices of life," little vignettes drawn from Paris's rich two-thousand year-history. I will take the traveller through the cheapest and most convenient system of transport: the city's underground, or "métro" as it is known in Paris, and stop at certain key stations where we will observe a building, a street, a statue, a tombstone or some other landmark that will spark off a story that tells us a lot about the character of the city. There are almost three hundred stations in Paris's sprawling métro system, not counting the express RER. I have selected just twelve.

A good friend of mine suggested that I make my selection by taking just one line—Line No. 1, because it crossed the centre of Paris—and tell my stories one station after the other. There are two reasons why this proved impossible. In the first place, it would have created a very disjointed sequence of tales. Secondly, it would have been utterly unhistorical. A brief history of the métro will explain why.

Paris got its underground train service relatively late. The first line opened in 1900, while London had trains rolling beneath its streets in the 1860s, and New York's elevated rapid transit service dated from 1870. But the idea of a *métropolitain* railway system linking Paris's districts—or *quartiers*—goes back to 1845, when it was proposed to link the Gare de Lyon to the Gare du Nord by a narrow-gauge rail that would slide trains freely down a slope in one direction and haul them up by cables in the other. London and New York adopted steam trains. Paris's urban geography made the problem of evacuating the steam and coal fumes a difficult one. Many alternatives to steam were considered. It was proposed to make wagons in the form of pistons, propelled by compressed air like an air gun; they would be shot into the stations by force of inertia. An aquatic project had wagons floating by way of underground canals. A futuristic monorail system of "trains without wheels" was tested in Lyon in the 1870s. But it was only with the approach of the Universal Exposition of 1900 that heads got together to propose the practical solution: an underground system of trains driven by "electric traction."

The initial plan, presented in 1895, faithfully reflected the historic contours of the city: a circular line and two diagonal lines running north-south and east-west. The north-south axis would have paralleled the city's ancient long-haul trade, an axis that dominated traffic patterns until long after the French Revolution. The east-west axis would follow the main trend of traffic in the twentieth century. And the circular line would obey patterns set by centuries of urban fortification, reflected in the city's great boulevards.

But those contours soon disappeared with the actual construction. The circular métro was never built; for many years the *Petite Ceinture*—a steam track laid in the mid-nineteenth century—acted as a poor substitute, and by the late 1930s only a small western section was still operating. As for the initial plan for a north-south axis, it encountered the stiff opposition of the Institut de France, under which it was supposed to pass. The forty "immortals" of the Académie

Française, whose job it was to decide what was and what was not French, could not countenance hollow ground beneath their solid feet. The first north–south line was thus distorted by two oblique turns under the Seine. The technical problem of building watertight *caissons* under the river caused further delays. Work only began on the winding north–south Line No. 4 in 1905; historically speaking, it corresponded to nothing.

Meanwhile, Line No. 1 had been opened in April 1900, on time for the Exposition. Its east–west orientation still dominates today's métro system, which, though it reflects the movement of twentieth-century traffic, is not in any way a historical guide: the main axis of traffic, for over two thousand years, was north-south.

To guide the métrostopper through the main historical routes of Paris, I have selected five lines: No. 1, which takes one through the centre of Paris; No. 3, which carries one out to the important eastern station of Père Lachaise; No. 4, which follows many of the sites on the ancient north-south axis; No. 6, which comes about as close as one can to the southern half of Paris's former peripheral frontier; and the important diagonal line of No. 7, which again cuts through the centre of the city and leads out to the site of the old slaughterhouses of La Villette. The trip through these five lines will carry the métrostopper from the old southern entrance of the city at the Barrière d'Enfer, or Hell's Gate, to the northern Barrière Saint-Denis, infamous in the travel literature of peripatetic Englishmen; then westwards to the Trocadéro to discover the opening of the east-west axis, across to the artistic and literary quarters of Montparnasse and Saint-Germain-des-Prés, into the central districts of the Opéra, the Louvre and the Marais. I have added a few diversions out into the periphery once more; the reasons for this will become clear in the text.

Writing history is like travelling, one of my professors at UC Berkeley used to explain. The more history I wrote, the more I realized that history *is* travelling: if you don't see the places where the major events of the past occurred, you get lost in the abstractions, system-building and theories that have so distorted our view of the past over the last few decades. The Battle of Hastings took place in Sussex, on the English coast, not in Westphalia; some historians write history as if the events they describe could have occurred anywhere on the globe. Paris is a cultural entity, a civilization that has been moulded by the swing of the Seine and the hills that surround it. If you want to understand the eighteenth-century Enlightenment, you must wander around some of those *hôtels particuliers* in the Seventh Arrondissement and see with your own eyes where modern philosophy was born. It is quite a thrilling experience, and your views on Montesquieu, Diderot, Voltaire and Rousseau will never be the same again.

This goes for all aspects of Paris's history. As you emerge from each métro stop, look up those alleys, stare into those old shops, pass your hands over the stones in front of you, you will discover what Parisians call, rather pretentiously, the "genius" of their civilization. But there is something authentic about it. Over many years of walking in Paris, and of writing about the French, I have become convinced that its essential feature is a link that has developed in the Parisian mind between birth and creativity. Parisian civilization is not erotic, as one could describe the arts in Rome or Vienna, say; it comes from the womb, from the origins of life: it is the civilization of Otto Rank rather than of Sigmund Freud and its possible source is seventeenth-century Jansenism and that very French notion of *gloire*, which dominates the plays of Pierre Corneille.

Follow the sequence of stations I have outlined here and you will discover what I mean. The trip through Paris's underground takes you through a life cycle, beginning with death and ending with death. But in death there is of course rebirth: a very Parisian theme, I would say. If we first clamber down into the catacombs of Paris we soon realize how this theme opens up into the life of the city: its saints, its struggle for birth—and the rights of children—and the process by which art is born, in sculpture, in music, in cuisine, in literature and even in philosophy.

The first three chapters address themselves directly to the problems of physical death and birth in Paris. The chapters on Montparnasse, Saint-Germain and Porte de Clignancourt explore that magical link between the hidden memory of birth, artistic creation and belief systems. The chapters on Les Halles and Porte de la Villette follow the city's food orbit, from the "belly of the beast" in the centre out to the old slaughterhouses at the periphery. The final leg of the journey, from the Opéra through to the cemetery of Père Lachaise, will take you through a series of stories about power, its corrupting influence and its fantastic creative potential — the finale at Père Lachaise, I think, bears full witness to both.

Will the métrostopper agree with me? You could decide to stay at home and merely imagine Paris as the book carries you from one station to another; you may well imagine other things than I. But it really would be better to take that trip and look for yourself. What I have sketched above is of course unabashedly schematic; what you actually see could be something different. But at least I will have opened your eyes — the main task, after all is said and done, of the walking historian.

Gregor Dallas
Le Vieil Estrée
2007

CONTENTS

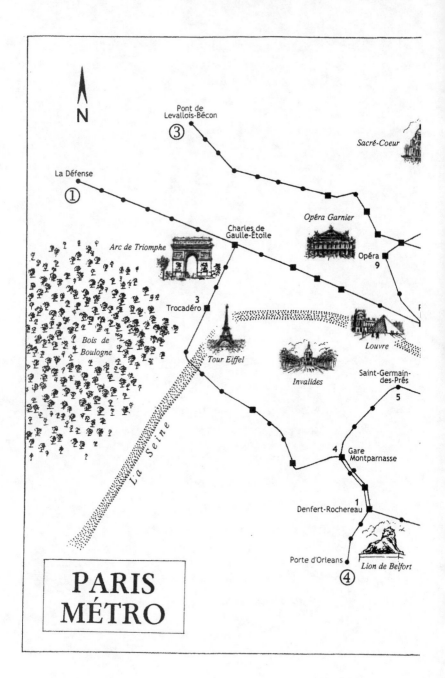

PARIS
MÉTRO

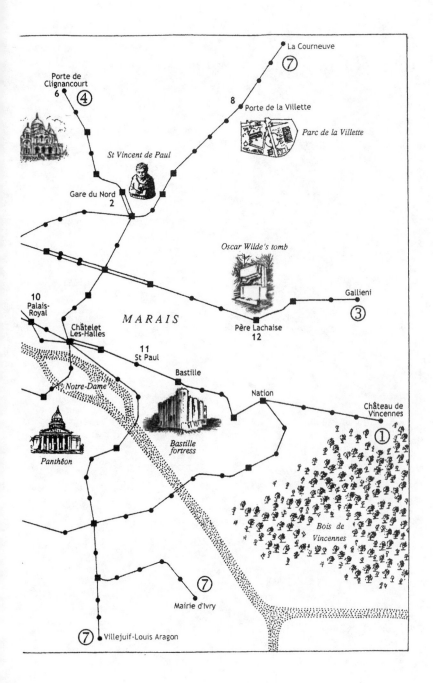

DENFERT-ROCHEREAU

THE BEST TIME to visit Métro stop No. 1, Denfert-Rochereau, is in the morning of Paris's first day at work, which for most people in Paris is on a Tuesday. Except for bankers, nobody in Paris works on Mondays because its citizens have been too busy enjoying themselves over the weekend. Throughout the provinces of France bankers work on Saturdays, but Paris has for the last thousand years always wanted to be different from the provinces—which is why bankers in Paris work on Mondays instead of Saturdays. Civil servants, on the other hand, do not like to work on the first day of the week—which is why all the National Museums, to the annoyance of foreign travellers, are always closed on Tuesdays. So pick a Wednesday. Everything will be open at Denfert-Rochereau on Wednesday.

A visit to the Catacombs of Paris awaits; that is, if you do not get lost. The map in the underground is based on a terror-control theory designed to mislead an enemy alien; following those directions will lead you to two locked green doors marked *privé*. The two oldest buildings in the square date back to the mid-1780s, just when everything happened here at Place Denfert-Rochereau. The only piece of decor is in the architraves below the roof, full of dancing Greek maidens, save the central figure. Who is that? An allegory of Life or of Death? This place was once called Hell.

Nobody knows exactly why they named that street running north the Rue d'Enfer, Hell Street; or the square itself the Barrière d'Enfer, Hell's Gate. Some writers believe it was a popular distortion of *Via Inferiora*, the old Roman road that ran southwards to Orléans. "*Enfer*" only appeared on the maps in the 1560s, at the beginning of the Religious Wars; but, like most place names, the term was probably used by a lot

of people before that. "Hell," at any rate, turned out to be the right name for this place.

The two buildings on the south side of the square are remnants of Claude Ledoux's tollgates that pierced the Farmers General Wall of 1784–87.* Most of the tollgates were destroyed by city rebels who liked neither the tolls nor the way they were being walled in or out of their national capital. "*Le mur murant Paris rend Paris murmurant,*" it was famously said of the Farmers General Wall, one of the most hated pieces of masonry in all of Paris; in the popular mind of the 1780s it competed with the Bastille as a symbol of arbitrary authority. Indeed, it was the spontaneous attack on the barriers and wall during the weekend of 12 July 1789 by bands armed with kitchen knives and clubs that prepared Paris for the fatal riot of 14 July and the surrender of the Bastille. Forty of the fifty-four *barrières* built around the city were destroyed in the space of two days. But they forgot about those two buildings standing in a place called Hell, for nobody lived in Hell.

Yet only a hundred years earlier this desolate place was designated by the most powerful of all France's kings, Louis XIV, to be not just the centre of his national capital, but the centre of the entire world. The King had been visiting his cousin, the Duc d'Orléans, at the Luxembourg Palace, when he looked out on to the vast empty prairie to the south and thought to himself that more was required here than lush royal gardens; what was needed was a vast monument, something to attract the eye. It so happened that the King's astronomers were at that time lobbying for an observatory to study the stars that sparkled above the kingdom; the King's chief stargazer, Giovanni Cassini, wanted the Observatoire built on one of the hills outside the city. But he missed the point. All the King could see was the wasteland to the south of the Luxembourg Palace, a place called Hell that had to be filled. So in 1676

---

* The Farmers General Wall was a toll barrier around the City of Paris, administered by the "Farmers General," a privileged group of sixty tax collectors nominated by the king's Ministry of Finance, who held a "farm" or "lease" on the royal state revenues. They enriched themselves through commissions on the taxes they collected on the king's behalf. Their association went back to the thirteenth century and they were eventually abolished by the Constituent Assembly in 1790.

the King, by royal decree, announced that this spot was the centre of the world and ordered that the Observatoire be built here. You can see it through the trees two hundred yards to your right.

But the whole world failed to be convinced by the science of Louis XIV, nor did it accept the idea—argued by most residents here—that Paris was the centre of the universe. It was eventually through the little English naval village of Greenwich that 0° longitude was drawn. Hell Street was thus pushed 2°21' into the eastern hemisphere—nowhere.

The Parisians took their revenge through a little play on words that would lull the foreign visitor into thinking that he was not really in Hell. It was Frédéric Bartholdi, best known for his Statue of Liberty in the waters of New York Harbor, who was responsible for that unapt, misplaced lion sitting uncomfortably in the middle of the square. He built an even larger version at Belfort, not far from where he was born amidst the mountains of eastern France, in commemoration of the brave resistance put up by Colonel Denfert-Rochereau during a winter campaign against the Prussians in 1870–71. The French lost, which is why the lion's head is facing westwards; it is turning its back on wicked Prussia. So that is why the square is called Denfert-Rochereau? Do not be mistaken. The Parisians are sometimes better at word games than we English speakers: "Colonel Denfert" rhymes so nicely with "d'Enfer," "Hell."

How, in fact, could Hell's Gate be the centre of anything? Nobody lived here. In the early 1800s it was the most frightening, deserted part of Paris. All you could see was that gate, and the one next to it, Jack's Gate, or the Barrière Saint-Jacques. Travellers from the south had no other choice but to pass through one or other of those two gates, though they did so at their own risk and peril. One of Balzac's old characters in the revolution of 1848 remarks that the area is "deserted by eight o'clock in the evening and robbery is the least of the dangers one encounters there." One could be robbed here, one could be raped and murdered here, and if one was really down on one's luck one could even be guillotined at Hell's Gate.

Everyone passed through Hell: the traders, the tourists, the pilgrims, the soldiers, the savers of souls, the heretics and even the dead.

When the administrators of death decided in 1830 that capital punishment could no longer be performed in central Paris, they moved the guillotine down here. Up to then the traditional site of executions had been the Grève (the word meant river bank). The Grève in Paris was a promontory of mud which stuck out like a huge black tongue into the Seine before the medieval Hôtel de Ville, or Town Hall, to the north side of the Île de la Cité; ships pulled up to the shore, or they moored at wooden posts in the river; bodies hanged from the gibbets on the black, slippery bank. Public executions had been royal days of festival. A famous example was on 2 March 1757 when Robert-François Damiens, who had attempted to kill the King, was quartered before an enthusiastic crowd by six horses "not accustomed to drawing." The operation took over an hour. Steel pincers a foot and a half long, built especially for the occasion, failed to tear away the arms and the legs; the patient, in his torment, cried out, "Pardon, my God! Pardon, Lord!" Finally Samson, the executioner, "drew out a knife from his pocket and cut the body at the thighs instead of severing the legs at the joints; the four horses gave a tug and carried off the two thighs."

The Paris public in the eighteenth century was delighted at that sort of thing. But with the July Revolution of 1830 the spectacle of public death changed. Damiens' torment had begun at two o'clock in the afternoon under the full light of the sun, at the city's busiest point and against the historical backdrop of the town hall, the cathedral of Notre-Dame, the Saint-Jacques tower and, most symbolic of all, the nearby Palais de Justice. And then, in July 1830, King Charles X was thrown out of the country. In the violence of that event, several dozen workers had been killed on the Grève. The popular sentiment spread through the city that the Grève had somehow been "purified" by their blood: it would no longer be possible to execute "common murderers" on this now sacred site. Executions in Paris were shifted south down the road to Hell.

The last executions on the Grève, under the reign of Charles X, had provided an extra motive for the move. The public beheading of Daumas-Dupin on 3 December 1829 had caused such a riot that it may be considered an augur of the revolution to come. The execution a few months earlier of three men responsible for the murder of the concierge at the Hôtel Vaucanson had not gone well either. One of the prisoners had taunted the crowd with a song:

Nous sommes trois bandits ici
Sortis de la forêt du Bondi.
Tas de vile canaille!
Pendant que vous nous regardez victimer,
Nos amis chez vous font ripaille.
Vous feriez mieux d'aller travailler,
Tas de vile canaille!
Pour vous acheter des souliers.*

But the move south of the guillotine was also a cause for scandal. Victor Hugo expressed the problem in a preface he wrote for his novel *Le Dernier Jour d'un condamné* (*The Last Day of a Condemned Man*), published in 1832. He described the inauguration of the guillotine at the Barrière Saint-Jacques with the execution, at eight o'clock in the morning—"barely dawn"—on 3 February 1832, of a certain Désandrieux. A few beggar children gathered on a pile of stones after noticing the guillotine being set up. Désandrieux had been hauled from his cell out at Bicêtre, pushed into a windowless police wagon which carted him to the location where, "without giving the man time even to breathe, furtively, deceitfully, shamefully, they conjured away his head. That is what they call a solemn and public act of high justice. *Infâme dérision!*" For Hugo, as for many other citizens of Paris at the time, Désandrieux had been covered with shame by not being allowed the honour of facing the blade of the guillotine in the full light of day, before the crowd in the central Place de Grève. Instead, he was doomed to the obloquy of deserted Hell.

---

* "We are three bandits here, / Out of the Forest of Bondi. / Heap of foul rabble! / While you see us victimized / Our friends feast in your homes. / You would do better going to work, / Heap of foul rabble / To buy yourselves shoes."

Hugo lived to be photographed, and after photography came film. It is difficult to imagine how high justice on the Grève could have continued for very long. The removal of the guillotine down to the southernmost point of what was then known as the Faubourg Saint-Jacques was the first step in the direction of the total abolition of capital punishment which occurred in our own time. It was a very long period of transition. During Louis Philippe's reign, crowds of the curious would trundle down the Rue Saint-Jacques whenever rumours of an imminent execution spread. Thackeray, in his 1840 *Paris Sketchbook*, recorded one instant when the crowd gathered down at Hell's Gate to enjoy a gory spectacle: "Tipsy old women and men, shrieking, jabbering, gesticulating, as the French will do; parties swaggering, staggering forwards, arm in arm, reeling to and fro across the street, and yelling songs in chorus: hundreds of these were bound for the show, and we thought ourselves lucky in finding a vehicle to the execution place, at the Barrière d'Enfer." But the event was called off and a thousand "drunken devils" were forced to rely on their imagination for entertainment. Solemn high justice, many argued at the time, had been reduced to a conjuror's trick; death had been magically removed out of sight, southwards.

What happened to the guillotine was in fact just a sign of a broader movement of death in Paris. It was during the same revolutionary period, at the turn of the eighteenth and nineteenth centuries, that Paris's dead—all her dead—were carried from the centre of town to the lonely southern district of Hell. How that occurred is itself a tale of eighteenth-century conjurors.

THE DEAD HAD always followed the main roads. For several millennia Paris had lived from the long-haul trade provided by the twin north–south routes of Saint-Denis and Saint-Martin; the dead were buried to the sides of the routes in "*caemeteria*" or "cemeteries," the "places where one slept." With the development of Paris as the kingdom's capital, protective walls were built; the cemeteries followed in their shadow, spreading from the road sites to areas that snuggled up against the city's parapets and towers. Sainte-Geneviève, Saint-Benoît and Saint-Séverin guarded the southern approaches. But the greatest threat to the city came from the English invaders to the north. So the strongest defences also lay on the north side of town, hence the fortress of the old Louvre.* Hence also the huge cemetery on the north side, between the walls and the old traders' route, *"La Grant Chaussée de Monsieur Saint-Denis."*

It was devoted to a church built nearly a thousand years ago and now no longer in existence, that of the Saints-Innocents. The Innocents catered to the dead of twenty parishes on the right bank of the city and was in operation for over six centuries. It came to resemble a huge municipal rubbish dump. Daily the Hôtel-Dieu, the town's main hospital on the Île de la Cité, brought in its pile of bodies, stripped naked by the nuns, who would sell off the rags to starving traders. The Châtelet dungeon added its bit, too. With an average life expectancy of twenty-two years, medieval and Renaissance Paris had a large demand for mass graves. The Innocents was quickly filled; the ground level itself rose several feet above that of the neighbouring road. Wandering dogs dug for food. Wandering beggars dug for jewellery.

Wandering minstrels, acrobats, lovers, jesters, bears and bear-baiters, mimes, divas and prostitutes were all attracted to this stinking place, for in the old days death and entertainment went together; they were a part of one world. King Philip Augustus (1180–1223), in his relish for walls, ordered the Innocents closed off: so the cemetery became a zone of enclosed entertainment and trade, which you can still find to this day—at the point where Les Halles meets Beaubourg on the Rue Saint-Denis. Behind today's Forum des Halles, along the southern side of Rue Berger runs an arcaded wall modelled after the notorious Charnier (Charnel House) des Innocents; it gives some notion of the

---

* The Bastille, further upstream, was constructed by Philip Augustus's great-grandson, Charles V, who in 1370 ordered a *"chastel Saint-Antoine"* put up to defend his unprotected Hôtel de Saint-Pol. His *Prévôt*—or governor—of Paris proved only too keen on the project, thereby earning himself enemies: he ended up as the first prisoner of the fortress.

size of the place as well as—with its prostitutes, drug addicts and police armed with truncheons—a feeling for its past atmosphere. But the dead have gone. In the 1790s the dead were expelled to a place called Hell.

In the centuries that followed Philip Augustus's enclosures, with plagues breaking out approximately every decade, the liveliness of the area increased in direct proportion to the smell of death. The famous *danse macabre*, the "Dance of Death," was invented on the soil of this charnel house in the fifteenth century. Abbé Valentin Dufour, writing at the time, described how the *danse macabre* encouraged *"les gens à dévocion . . . comme un mirouer salutaire pour toutes gens"*: it incited people to prayer by holding up a salutary mirror for everyone to look into. The Church was enthusiastic about it; the people were intrigued by it. The *danse macabre* at the cemetery of the Innocents was Paris's major gift to late medieval culture. It can be found in the paintings, the poetry and the music of the time. Ugliness combines with beauty, death beguiles youth. The engraver from Nuremberg, Albrecht Dürer, comes to mind, with his weird Late Gothic images—like that of the steadfast Christian soldier marching forward, his road strewn with skulls, while Death and the Devil tempt him aside. Or Jan Van Eyck's portrait of Jean Arnolfini, a very serious and ugly middle-aged businessman, with his teenage wife—the concave mirror hanging between them.

The *danse macabre* is the mix of the generations, the play of death with life, the transience of pleasure in the face of death, a titillating game between Eros and the Grim Reaper. In the instructions left by the aged *Ménagier de Paris*—or "Goodman of Paris" as this nameless late medieval Parisian bourgeois has come to be known—to his own adolescent wife, he advises that she "sing and dance full well and sweetly laugh and play and talk"; he wishes for her a life of gaiety bathed in "dancing and singing, wine and spices, and torches for the lighting." For a wealthy old man like the *Ménagier* acrobats would have done the dancing in his place. And the place where they danced could well have been the fetid neighbourhood of the Innocents, because the wealthy were just as likely to be there as the poor. As the Abbé Dufour put it, "death levels all conditions, it scythes out the old, but also the young." The nineteenth-century journalist Maxime du Camp remembered how "it was something for a bourgeois family to have his ancestors buried at the Cemetery of the Innocents." Some of the finest sepulchres in the city lined the road just there, next to the desks of the *écrivains publics*, who would write your love letters, the puppet show for the children and the tiny *réclusoirs*, into which adulterous women were walled with the blessing of the local curate. Nothing symbolized better the late medieval world's lively urban culture and its perverse play with death than the stinking fields of Paris's Innocents.

The dead were piled higher; the level of the fields mounted. Charles V in the early fourteenth century had a second cemetery wall built within the Innocents, parallel to the first and several yards from it. This created the effect of a walled trench into which the bodies could be thrown. Above was a tiled roof—though from that imperfect tiling exhaled stench and pestilence. The inner walls were styled in the form of Gothic arcades, within each of which was painted scenes of the *danse macabre*: a skeleton whirling around a young damsel in ecstasy, or a black-hooded gentleman with a scythe reaching out for another slim maiden.

The Wars of Religion, in the second half of the sixteenth century, which ended with a terrible siege of the city, brought more starvation, pestilence—and bodies to the Innocents. Louis XIII after 1610 did manage to extend his defensive walls westwards in order to protect his home in the Louvre, but the piles of dead to his north-east could expect no such relief; they just pressed themselves upwards and outwards. The graveyard was now about eight feet above the Rue Saint-Denis, and that was simply the ground level. The tiling of the roofs gave way, the walls cracked. One formal report estimated that the mass graves were "so rotten that a human body could be entirely consumed within nine days." The local inhabitants figured that only twenty-four hours were required; they were getting tired of the dancing.

It would be reckless to calculate exactly how many human beings ended up as remains in the rotting heap at the Innocents, though this was attempted by several in the two centuries which followed. The last gravedigger there claimed to have buried 90,000 bodies in thirty years. That was just after the great scandal of 30 May 1780: a brewer on Rue de la Lingerie descended into his two-storey cellar and got the shock of his life; he discovered not dozens, but hundreds of human bodies, in varying states of decomposition, lying there. Like many who served food and drink in the district, he had been wondering why the water in his wells was undrinkable, why his *galettes* gave off that fetid odour. Other cases like this had been recorded. But it was the scandal of Rue de la Lingerie, occurring just ten years after the first great smallpox epidemic, which wiped out one tenth of Paris's population and 90 per cent of all infants under nine months, that forced the city authorities to find a new solution for what to do with their dead.

Something radical happened in the last decades of the eighteenth century that altered attitudes towards death; it could be noticed in the changing style of public executions; it was reflected also in the new proposals regarding the accumulating piles of urban dead. The change seems to be linked to the fact that, despite all the epidemics, death itself was actually declining after the middle of the eighteenth century and would continue to do so from then on. As a result, Paris's population picked up rapidly after 1750, attaining 650,000 in 1790, three quarters of a million at the end of the Napoleonic Wars and its first million by 1850. That new million of Parisians, who could expect to live to the age of fifty or more, did not want to see or hear about death any more; they wanted to live. The culture of the *danse macabre* was gone and with it disappeared the Charnel House of the Innocents.

Nobody in Paris at the time of the Rue de la Lingerie scandal was aware that a political revolution was about to tear the kingdom apart. But the rapid increase in the number of printed pamphlets addressing the problem of what to do with the dead did demonstrate how fundamental was the shift in attitudes towards death. "The apparatus of death is terrible to behold," proclaims one of the pamphlets. "Its idea alone can poison life, its contemplation can shorten it. All who draw its image afflict us and displease us . . ." This is evidently not Dürer embracing the dead; it is a total rejection of death, a demand to hide it away. Even the mention of the "memory" of the dead requires an extended endnote on the paradox of reason and sentiment, with all the praise going to the former. The ancient Egyptians, the Greeks, and later the Romans kept their dead and their dying aside, the pamphlet goes on: "One never saw, I say, in the midst of their towns these appalling hospices of death, these asylums permanently exposing suffering humanity." The danger of constant exposure to death and to the dying is proved by the "pestilential diseases spread around by putrid and vile air."

For the anonymous author of the pamphlet, printed in London, the solution had to be found in "the hand of art." He meant this quite literally. Centuries of creative labour, the pamphleteer notes, had produced exquisite monuments in the capital. Now where did all that stone come from? Paris had been "countermined" everywhere; there were holes and caves which could easily be turned into "catacombs," as in ancient times. The "hand of art" had produced fabulous buildings on the surface of the town and great, unused caverns underground: let the "hand of art" store the piles of unwanted dead down there.*

The idea was popular among the *philosophes* and, after the Rue de la Lingerie affair, it spread fast among those who governed, although they did not like to talk about it in public. Louis Sébastien Mercier, the most famous of the late eighteenth-century pamphleteers, drew attention to Paris's huge network of underground stone quarries in his immensely popular *Tableaux de Paris*, whose twelve volumes provide us with the most extraordinary detail about the city's street life just before the Revolution. "These towers, these steeples, these vaulted temples," he meditated, "all these signs which say to the eye: what we see above ground must be lacking below." It was discovered that the whole outer area of Hell contained labyrinths of underground stone quarries. In 1784 three hundred yards of the Rue d'Enfer gave way and a gardener disappeared into the depths of nowhere. The idea began to spread: why not transfer all those bodies in the Innocents southwards to empty, undermined Hell?

After months of secret debate a royal edict of 3 April 1786 finally de-

---

* See Villedieu (a name invented, it seems, by the eighteenth-century cataloguer), *Projet de catacombes pour la ville de Paris, en adoptant à cet usage les Carrières qui se trouvent dans son enceinte que dans ses environs* (London, 1782). In *Histoire et descriptions de lieu*, tome 2, No. 2, Bibliothèque de l'Histoire de la Ville de Paris, cat. I1943.

cided the matter. The transfer would take place at night in the depths of winter. "Furtively, deceitfully, shamefully," as Hugo might have put it, they conjured away the dead from the centre of Paris down to this deserted spot in the south—along, indeed, the very same old north–south axis that the guillotine would take after the July Revolution of 1830.

In December 1786 convoys of carts and wagons set out for Hell, rattling across the poorly paved streets over the Pont au Change and the Pont Notre-Dame, through the narrow lanes of the Île de la Cité, and then down the two parallel streets of the Enfer and Saint-Jacques. The convoys were led by priests carrying torches and behind each convoy followed a municipal officer on horseback. Mercier records that the inhabitants in the neighbourhood of the Innocents "woke up, got out of their beds. One after another they appeared at their windows, half naked; others came out on the streets; the news spread; the young, the beautiful, gathered to gossip." What a contrast it made to the dead. It was Paris's last *danse macabre*. At the Barrière d'Enfer—the square where you stand—the dead of a Christian millennium were gathered in piles and carried down by labour gangs into the holes you will visit with your torch.

There were far more bodies than ever expected. The piles were immense. The job was exhausting—and expensive. In February 1787 the work was interrupted. But in late August and through to October that year the convoys of the dead began rolling once more. By this time the kingdom of Louis XVI was faced with a bill for the transportation of bodies amounting to over 279,000 livres—a bill which could not possibly be paid. The state was bankrupt and the country was entering the first phases of the French Revolution. It was at this point that the conjurors began to develop their plans.

Developments in the young science of chemistry, which had grown out of medieval alchemy, combined in many curious ways with the new culture of Revolution. Antoine de Lavoisier, who proved the law of the conservation of matter, would go to the guillotine for the income he drew from the Farmers General tax. The law of the conservation of matter would survive him and it would have a direct impact on what was next to be done with all those bodies now piling up in Hell.

A quarrel had developed over the question of "putrefaction," how

the flesh disappeared from the bone—a most topical subject in revolutionary Paris. The Hebrew word "Machabee," from which *macabre* as in
danse is thought to derive, did originally connote the process of body
rot. The eighteenth-century hypothesis of infection, thought to be due
to smells in the air, had its origin here. Minds began to turn on how,
chemically, one could speed up the process of rot and—in a project typical of the time—turn it into something beautiful. In the 1780s not only
Lavoisier, in the apothecary and gunpowder rooms of the Paris Arsenal,
was working hard on the problem. Also engaged on it was Dr. Michel
Augustin Thouret, a member of the Société Royale de Médecine and
friend of Benjamin Franklin, who claimed that bodies and earth, when
combined in the right proportions and heated up to the right temperature, could be converted into blocks of glass. This intriguing thought
led young revolutionary minds in Paris to propose that, following the
transfer of the bodies to the "catacombs" of Hell, cremation ovens be
built inside them so that on the surface would appear a huge solid pyramid of glass to the memory of the dead.

One can understand why historians of death—they do exist—
turned in horror when they rediscovered these ideas after the Second
World War. Philippe Ariès, one such historian, argued that these eighteenth-century men of the Enlightenment were the forerunners of
some of the worst twentieth-century attitudes towards death. They
created feelings of repugnance and disgust for death, pushing it away
from life, hiding it from life's pleasures—the beginnings of the consumer society. Death, he wrote, was "ensavaged." He quotes the Marquis de Sade's terrible ideas about nature destroying in order to create;
that death only exists "figuratively and without reality"; the body loses
all meaning. Modern sadism is thus born. Modern totalitarian plans of
mass cremation for the purposes of hiding death already seem present.

Ariès certainly had a point. Contemporary civilization does shun
death, consigning it to the sick and the old—two groups which were
better integrated in a culture that would not shun the face of suffering
or turn away from the biological reality of death. When the authorities
of Paris transported the guillotine down to Hell's Gate their main intention was certainly to hide death from the crowds of the morbidly

curious. How much more so was this the case with this earlier mass removal of the dead from the centre of town to the hidden caverns beneath the Barrière d'Enfer.

But perhaps we do need to look away from death. The kind of punishment inflicted on Robert-François Damiens on the Place de Grève would be intolerable today. Our view of justice has changed. No nation in Europe inflicts the death penalty, even for the most heinous of crimes, for the very sound reason that human justice is no longer considered infallible—and a death penalty cannot be reversed. The experience of two world wars has made us more modest. At the same time, it is true, we have pushed death into the background, beyond our daily preoccupations. As Ariès has argued, there is something unhealthy about this. But Paris's eighteenth-century hospices, her asylums and charnel houses—all open to the eyes and the noses of her citizens—would be wholly unacceptable in the prosperous urban life we enjoy today. Death has to be put aside.

That is a thought to bear in mind as one descends the staircase in the old eighteenth-century *barrière* at Place Denfert-Rochereau to view the catacombs of Paris. The skulls and crossbones of tens of thousands of Parisians who walked the streets of the city over the last two thousand years look so calm down there; indeed, the sight of their remains, displayed on row upon row of shelves, provides a very physical dimension to the human reality of this city's long history. There is just one little moment of trepidation, as one steps in at the entrance. Inscribed above the gate is a line of poetry from an eighteenth-century abbot, Jacques Delille: *"Arrête! C'est ici l'Empire de la Mort!"*—"This is the Empire of Death!"

1780   PARIS. — La Gare du Nord. — LL.

GARE DU NORD

IF HELL IS at the bottom of the map, then why not seek Heaven at the top, on the north side of town? On the land beneath this station trod one of the most celebrated Parisian saints, Vincent de Paul, the guide of lost children, the father of philanthropy, and one of the first teachers of modern philosophy—right here, where you gather your bags. And the story is an inspiring one. But it is also a tale of human failure, an example of what happens when noble ideas of charity are institutionalized. Above all, the story reveals what was, until very recent times, the terrifying experience of childhood for the majority of Parisians.

Historically, the entrance into Paris from the north via the old Roman road of Saint-Denis had never inspired thoughts of Heaven, nor did the Barrière Saint-Denis make one think for a moment of the Gates of Saint Peter. Travellers from the north were more frequently put in mind of another version of Hell. Graphic descriptions of what it was like to enter Paris through the Barrière Saint-Denis—today the site of the Gare du Nord—were given by Englishmen who took the trip at the end of the Napoleonic Wars when the Continent opened up for the first time in over ten years.

What made entrance into Paris from the north side so appalling was not, as at the Barrière d'Enfer, the emptiness of the land; it was the crowding. The whole of French rural civilization seemed to follow this route into town—wine wagons, hay carts and bullocks would line up at the gate. Chickens clucked and strutted in the alleys by Rue du Faubourg Saint-Denis; through the old stone arch of the carpenter's abode on the left you might see a goat tethered, or even a cow; pigs were raised by the *barrière*, perhaps distant descendants of the runaway pig that killed Louis VI's son and heir in 1131 on the Grand Pont of the Île de la Cité.

How it all smelled. The historian, Thomas Carlyle, in his lyrical description of Paris at the time of the Revolution, was obviously borrowing from his own experience in the 1830s and comparing this to the southern Scottish towns of his childhood: "Mud-Town of the Borderers (*Lutetia Parisiorum* or *Barisiorum*)." The good Reverend Norgate had passed by those gates at the time of the Emperor's abdication in 1814; he complained that from there and downwards into the town's centre all he smelt was "effluvia and foetish gases"—he eventually fled to the western suburbs, which as it turned out was a good move, one that would be followed over the next few decades by much of Paris, thereby opening up new vistas along an east–west axis.

English travellers in 1815 usually arrived in late evening; oil lamps strung across the street gave off a vague and demonic light—Paris's rebels hanged men from them: many travellers, with the gates behind them, felt closed in, terrified.

On a "Map of the City of Paris Drawn Geometrically According to the Best Sources . . . By Maire, Geographical Engineer, 1808," one can see what lay behind it. "What an immense enclosure within the walls of Paris!" is inscribed on the map, the exclamation mark included. "It is larger even than the garden of the Thuilleries to the west of the Louvre Palace." Most of this area, including what is now the Gare du Nord, consisted of pleasant orchards and vineyards. A garden of Eden? Not exactly. On the enclosure's southern perimeter lay the Hospice Saint-Lazare, a medieval leper colony.

Through the orchards and vines strolls a man with a sharp nose, a greying moustache and pointed beard—perspicacious and resolute: his eyes are narrow and a smile lights his face; he wears a priest's black tricorne and his clothes make a colourful sight. The nuns address him as "Monsieur Vincent"—his Christian name. It is May 1643. "The King is dead, long live the King!" And well they might cry it, for Louis XIV is not yet five.

"It is said that one seeks the Kingdom of God. So seek it, it is only a phrase. But it seems to me a good phrase," said Monsieur Vincent yesterday. "It means that we must continually aim at what is recommended us: work perpetually for the Kingdom of God and not remain in a state of laziness, of arrest. Pay attention to one's interior life and regulate it. And the exterior life is not designed for amusement." He had been talking to the new Council of Conscience, set up for the child king. He had angered some on the Council who wondered if he were turning Protestant, or about as bad, becoming one of those hated Jansenists from Port-Royal in the south side of the city — their Augustine heresies came from dangerous Holland. Monsieur Vincent insisted he would stand by the Most Christian Monarch for the reformed Catholic faith. Cardinal Mazarin, the King's First Minister — who, oddly for a cardinal, had never been a priest — had guessed he meant it, but he would remain suspicious for the rest of his life.

Care and action was the message Monsieur Vincent wanted to pass on to the King. It was a message for a child. *Enfanter* is another key word repeated in the fifteen volumes of his complete works. *Enfanter*, "to give birth" — a continual process, that of the interior life issuing forth into the exterior world: seek, seek, seek the grace of God, the love of God, *caritas* — charity. Prove its existence through works, act on its existence.

Monsieur Vincent's perpetual enterprise of charity can be traced to his roots, a peasant born a "Depaul" in the flat Landes of Gascony. His birth in 1581 occurred in the midst of a religious civil war, which is probably why he became such a man of action. As a child he dreamed of being a brave cavalier, like Cyrano de Bergerac; he had the same nose. But he became a priest instead, though a kind of cavalier priest. This was taken by some too literally. The story went around Paris that in the year 1607 he embarked from Spain to Rome in a fisherman's skiff for his ordination — around 800 sea miles. Barbary pirates captured him and carried him to Tunis where he was kept as a slave until he miraculously escaped a year later. Monsieur Vincent repeatedly said that it was a pack of lies. But the Parisians loved the tale because it seemed so like their favourite curé. That is undoubtedly why Louis Abelly wrote it all down in the first biography of Vincent de Paul, as he came to be known after his death in 1660. It could not possibly be true. It was a favourite literary genre. The most famous is told by Cervantes in the adventures of the Man of La Mancha, Don Quixote; Abelly's old French is an exact translation of Cervantes' old Spanish, published, it so happens, in 1607.

That Parisians should embrace Vincent de Paul as their own Don Quixote indicates the kind of man he was: a figure of brave deeds who was often criticized for his theatricality by his royal enemies. Monsieur Vincent's masses in the old leper colony of Saint-Lazare—the chapel lay on what is now Boulevard de Magenta—were celebrated before a congregation drawn from every section in life. Rich men, poor men, noble ladies and prostitutes, orphans and princes showered praises on him; they loved what they heard. Action, he preached, must be supported by one vital impulse, one single will; the question was how to keep it sacred, how to prove it came from the Kingdom of God. "It must be like a spring," he sang out in his musical voice, "that makes all the organs of the body tremble." Perpetual action, perpetual conversion—Saint Paul was his favourite apostle. "My God," exclaimed a man in the congregation, "*there's* a priest who says mass well: he must be a saint." And so he became.

Enfanter, care, action: Monsieur Vincent regarded his greatest achievement to be the establishment of the Daughters of Charity, those nuns we saw. Their mother house was created here in 1683. Their task was to bring aid and succour to foundling children.

There was a crying need for those Daughters. At the time Louis XIV succeeded to the throne, the wastrels of Paris had become such a common sight that people compared them to swarms of flies rising out of the dung and the dead. Seventeenth-century Paris was not unlike today's worst corners of Bucharest, or of Calcutta. Children robbed and killed. Their weapon was the sling, or *fronde* as it was known. Paris was a hotbed of violence, a violence that exploded into civil war five years after Louis' accession. Appropriately, they called the war the *Fronde*. It divided the royal family and the Church, it separated the Paris Parlement from the monarchy and, for five long years (1648–53), it split up Paris into warring factions. any of Monsieur Vincent's noble friends were among the rebels; he lost his position on the Council of Conscience, and his relations with the unordained Cardinal Mazarin became very strained.

The Daughters of Charity, nevertheless, continued their work on Paradise Street. They installed in their high wall a small revolving wooden door; *le tour* it was christened. Desperate young mothers would place their children there, ring the bell and then run away. That little door kept turning until 1863.

THE ABANDONMENT OF children was not invented in the seventeenth century. The earliest image we have of a Parisian face—discovered in 1878 by the archaeologist Eugène Toulouzé in a Roman cemetery behind the Port-Royal maternity hospital—is that of a child who may well have been abandoned; it was around a year old and mud, turned to concrete, had received an imprint of the dead infant's face. But the charitable mysticism of Saint Vincent de Paul was transmuted into the politics of Louis XIV, which in its turn would lead to a veritable industry of abandoned children by the time of the French Revolution. It was a good example of how—as a later Parisian, Charles Péguy, was to describe the process—*mystique* would slip into *politique*, and how *politique* would sink further down into the foulest, most repressive type of bureaucratic administration.

There is something terrible about the story. It is as if goodness could only become evil, as if a saint's charity was fated in "Mud Town" to develop within a generation into a source of selfishness and exploitation. Heaven would become Hell, hope would be turned into despair. The work of another churchman is worth noting here, one who developed a whole philosophy out of this very point. While the French capital was convulsed in unending cycles of violence in the name of a better world, an English vicar looked across the Channel from his quiet parish of Albury in Surrey and wrote, in 1799: "The increase of population is necessarily limited by the means of subsistence," and the "superior power of population is repressed, and the actual population kept equal to the means of subsistence by misery and vice."

The Reverend Thomas Malthus was not impressed by Parisian claims for the perfectibility of man. "Passion between the sexes" was the key to the degenerate process on God's earth. "It appears that a society constituted according to the most beautiful form that imagination can conceive," Malthus claimed, "would, from the inevitable laws of nature and not from any original depravity of man, in a very short period, degenerate into a society constructed upon a plan not essentially different from that which prevails in every known State at present." Or as the Parisian song of the 1930s went, *"Plus ça change, plus c'est la même chose"*— "The more it changes, the more it stays the same." All your charities will come to nought: within thirty years you will be back in "Mud Town." It turned out to be a fairly accurate prediction. "Towards the extinction of the passion between the sexes, no observable progress whatever has hitherto been made," noted the solemn vicar of Albury.

Such thoughts made Malthus very unpopular among "progressive" circles at the time; in the nineteenth century he was laughed off as the founder of the "dismal science," economics. But was he in fact so dismal? In the final, grandiose chapter of his *Principle of Population as it Affects the Future Improvement of Society* one finds in the Reverend Thomas the smile of Monsieur Vincent. "Evil exists in the world, not to create despair, but activity," he concluded. And he quoted Shakespeare:

> Hope springs eternal in the human breast,
> Man never is, but always to be blest.

"We are not patiently to submit to it, but to exert ourselves to avoid it," thought Malthus. That same emphasis on perpetual activity had coloured the philosophy of Vincent de Paul. And it would be the mark of the very Parisian philosophy of existentialism in the twentieth century.

BETWEEN VINCENT DE Paul's death in 1660, the same year Louis XIV took personal control of the monarchy, and the French Revolution of 1789, the population of Paris doubled; the strain on charitable work for unwanted children had perhaps quadrupled, though no statistics are available. The worst was yet to come. *Le tour* kept turning.

The saint's buoyant mysticism had been converted into earnest politics during his lifetime. A royal decree of 1656 established the Hôpital Général, a vast administration designed to control all works connected with the sick, the mad, the poor, the disabled—along with orphans and foundlings. Conforming to the novel concerns with hygiene and clean city air, hospitals in principle were pushed out of the city centre and ambitious building projects were started, such as La Salpêtrière near the old gunpowder warehouse of Faubourg Saint-Victor, or the hospital out in distant Bicêtre (named after another English churchman, the Bishop of Winchester who had been a landowner there). Louis' kingdom in Paris was, after the anarchy of the *Fronde*, gaining control of local government. As the hospitals were moved eastwards, so the wealth and the *gloire* of government was moved westwards into the virtually uninhabited spaces of Saint-Germain, the Invalides and, on the Right Bank, beyond the Tuileries out to the Trocadéro: the modern east–west axis of Paris was being born.

The works of charity were thus dispersed under the panoply of the *Grand Monarque*'s administration. It made France strong and Paris unique, not just in the way in which it siphoned off political power to the centre, but also, most significantly, in the way it treated its children. Childcare became one of the chief preoccupations of the Hôpital Général. Under Louis XIV, *le tour* spread to Rue Saint-Victor in Bicêtre and Rue Neuve-Notre-Dame in Paris, just a few paces from the cathedral and, conveniently, right opposite the maternity wards of the Hôtel-Dieu, the one major hospital to remain in the city centre.

Paris's grim *tours* became poles of attraction, not simply for the city but for the whole Paris basin and beyond into the Île de France, southwards into the Loire Country and the Nivernais, westwards into Normandy and, along with Louis' wars and refugees, eastwards into Champagne, Lorraine and Alsace. Child-dumping became a national industry.

Following the mercantilist tradition established by Louis' finance minister, Jean-Baptiste Colbert, the industry was regulated over the course of the eighteenth century. Child abandonment was an accepted fact. The Hôpital Général even recommended two methods for ridding oneself of unwanted offspring. *Exposition*, or "exposure," was the most popular, one that continued on into the nineteenth century. The child would be left in a public place like a market or a well-frequented street, sometimes with a note attached. Here is a typical police report, dated 10 May 1840, for the Fifth Arrondissement Commissariat (today's Eighth):

> Declaration of Monsieur and Madame X, fruit merchants living in Paris, who brought to our bureau a little girl aged six to eight months whom they found abandoned and exposed on the pavement of Rue Duphot, in front of No. 4, at nine o'clock in the morning, when they were going to collect provisions at the Halle; they brought also a packet of baby wear belonging to the child who, because of the care she required, was sent to the foundling hospital, along with the packet found beside her. No paper was found on her or in the packet, and despite the enquiry conducted, neither the mother nor the perpetrator of this *exposition* has yet been identified.

The second method of abandonment was through the *tour*. In the eighteenth century midwives and *meneurs*, that is, intermediaries of Paris's thriving wet-nursing industry, would often for a pittance perform the task for parents. Royal decrees provided financial help to the *hospices dépositoires*, and they also attempted to control the transportation and "care" that these abandoned infants were subjected to in rural hovels as far afield as Brittany and Burgundy. Money would be, in theory, paid to the *père de famille*, not the wet-nurse herself, until the child was aged twelve, when boys were expected to support themselves, either as agricultural workers or as apprentices in some trade. In towns, particularly Paris, they usually ended up in orphanages, lunatic asylums or old-age hospitals.

The Hospice Saint-Vincent-de-Paul was administered by the Daughters of Charity and had its own rules: boys were returned from the wet-nurse at twelve to be placed as apprentices; girls came back at fifteen. In July 1793 abandoned children were nationalized; they became, as in the national hymn, "*enfants de la patrie*," wards of the state. Religious congregations were banned and, by Napoleonic decree of

1811, the depositing of abandoned children was centralized in the Hospice de la Seine, which set up headquarters down in Hell, the Rue d'Enfer. Vincent de Paul's Daughters of Charity returned with the Restoration of 1815 and it was they who "manned" the station in Hell Street through the nineteenth century. That squeaking wooden cylinder never stopped turning.

"During the day," wrote the novelist Alphonse Esquiros in 1847, "nothing about the Hospice of Foundling Children appears out of the ordinary. Its functions only begin at the hour of darkness and of crime." We know at midnight Hell Street was deserted. A single light filters from behind a curtained window in the distance, the only sign of life: "Here is Charity at work! The quiet clink of a bell alerts your ear; the sound of the wooden cylinder in the wall; a woman covered in a shawl, her head hidden under a black veil, slides by you in the shadows. It is done, the secret abandonment is accomplished: a poor newborn child has just fallen into the pit of Charity . . ."

CHARITY HAD FALLEN to Hell. The population of Paris had risen to its first million. The Swiss banker Jacques Necker—forever remembered for his handling of the financial crisis of 1788–89—reported for the year 1784, during his first spell at the Ministry of Finance, that the number of abandoned children surviving in Paris had reached 40,000. That was nothing compared with the bleak figures of the decades to come. By 1820, when Louis XVIII ruled France from the Tuileries Palace, a total of over 100,000 children had been "exposed" in the King's capital or swivelled through the *tour*. By the Revolution of 1848 the number had risen to a grim 130,000. From then on it very gradually declined. When the Franco-Prussian War broke out in the summer of 1870 it was down to a mere 100,000 again.

The *tour* would continue to function until well into the second half of the nineteenth century. The campaign to abolish it was as vicious as the campaign against slavery; indeed, it had the same origin. "Just as Rome had its slaves' war, who can assure France she will not have her foundlings' war?" asked the philanthropist Louis Desloges in 1854, exasperated at over two decades of fruitless effort. It was the Duc de La Rochefoucauld-Liancourt who founded the Société de la Morale Chrétienne in 1821, uniting a hundred French peers; their aim was to finance a campaign to extinguish poverty, provide elementary instruction for all, abolish slavery, abolish the death penalty—and suppress the *tour*. Consistent with the teaching of Saint Vincent de Paul, the Society set up *Comités d'Action* for each project. But the Society almost fell to pieces over what to do in the presence of that damnable swinging *tour*.

With the Revolution the *tour* had been taken over by the centralized Administration des Hospices de la Seine which made Louis XIV's army of bureaucrats within the Hôpital Général look like a gentlemen's club. "The displacements, conducted with prudence and precaution, are without notable inconvenience for the children thus transplanted," was the Administration's nice reply to the growing foundlings scandal during Louis Philippe's reign. One of the moral dilemmas in the debate was who to defend: the mother or the child?

Alphonse Lamartine, revolutionary and poet, defended the mother. Her dignity had to be respected, her anonymity had to be maintained—he was an abolitionist over slavery, but he did not want to abolish Vincent de Paul's *tour*. Haven't these poor women suffered enough? "Have they not been exposed to rigour? pain? exile? barbarism? Ask those poverty-stricken mothers. Ask their lost children, who become suicidal at a precocious age." Lamartine's conscience was torn over the issue. He was so aware of the suffering of the children, too. He was appalled by the "almost funereal convoys" of "expatriated children" he saw on the nation's roads—long files of peasant nurses and lost babies with white faces. And one can understand why. It was a priggish group of "Economists" who cried out loudest for the *tour*'s abolition, not for humane reasons, but because it encouraged debauchery in Paris and was a heavy tax burden for the "honest men" of trade. In the debate on the *tour* it was not easy to differentiate between the good, the bad and the ugly.

Another major campaigner in the debate was Maxime du Camp, the journalist. He visited the reception bureau of the Hospice de Saint-Vincent-de-Paul down in Hell during the early 1850s. He described the dirty bits of paper found with the abandoned babies: "Please, protect it," "I cannot keep this child," "She has been baptized, her name is . . ." The centre, with its sick and lunatic children brought back from rural hovels, did not compare well with an American slavers' market. He cursed that *tour* as a type of deferred abortion.

The short Second Republic of 1848 attempted to suppress it, but even the most progressive people balked at this. In 1853 it was briefly suppressed—and then it was noted how *expositions* in the streets and markets rose. The Economists succeeded in reviving it in 1856, and *expositions* declined. It was abolished for good in 1863, the year Abraham Lincoln abolished slavery in the USA.

What prevented another rise in *expositions* was a policy of support for the mother, usually poor and single. Children were still brought in to the Hospice de Saint-Vincent-de-Paul—a practice that was formally ended only in 1901. Mothers were allowed, by virtue of a law of 1793, to give birth under the name X at the neighbouring maternity hospital of Port-Royal—a practice that formally ceased only under François Mitterrand's presidency in 1987.

SAINT VINCENT DE PAUL'S *tour* would never have sustained such enormous numbers of abandoned children had there not been a vast wet-nursing industry, another peculiarity of Paris and its dependent provinces. The industry was built on a complex division of labour. Men called *meneurs* travelled around France seeking wet-nurses who would cater to Paris's needs. In 1866 *half the children born in the city*, that is around 25,000 babies out of a total of 53,000 births, were nourished by mercantile breasts supplied by the outlying rural economy. "Trading on one's breasts has become a means of earning one's living," a report as late as 1898 noted.

Wet-nursing was the largest industry in Paris, driven over the centuries more by the supply of impoverished peasant women than by the demand for their breasts. King Jean, back in 1284, tried to protect these women from rapacious *meneurs*. Since then there had always been an ongoing battle between the advocates of a "free trade" that would work through private networks and those who wanted a tightly controlled state administration. The latter was always strong, but it never achieved a complete monopoly; indeed its very existence probably encouraged others to compete—they mutually nourished, if one may say, one another. Just as royalty in the eighteenth century tried to set down rules on the abandonment of children, so did it attempt to regularize the wet-nursing business. In the nineteenth century a central *Grand Bureau* was established on Rue Sainte-Apolline, about a hundred paces down from Rue du Paradis, where Saint Vincent de Paul's charitable works had begun. You can still see the building, just on the other side of the overhead métro that skirts the boulevards.

The division of labour rapidly developed. The wealthiest Parisians had their own connections and farmed out their children to the neighbouring countryside. It was the poor, under compulsion to work, who used the services of the Bureau. "The courtyard by the entry cannot contain all the nurses," wrote one witness in the 1820s. "They obstruct the street and risk the danger of being run over, and they do annoy the passers-by." "You often meet there old women of the most disgusting appearance," it was reported in the article on "Nurses" in the *Dictionnaire des Sciences médicales*, published in 1819. "Their withered breasts promise poor food for a child. They have been practising the trade for twenty or thirty years, their language is gross, and the rudeness of their manners can only give rise to the wildest alarm." One Director, Monsieur Pierret, confessed in 1829 to being on the verge of a nervous breakdown. He tells the awful story, unfortunately all too common, of a child being returned to her poor mother having been disfigured by burns—peasant households rarely possessed fire-guards. "I am the first to receive the reproaches of these saddened parents," he wrote. "I have myself a child being nursed in the country."

The *meneurs* were an uncouth lot, most of them starting out as wagon drivers, innkeepers, pimps or barbers (who doubled as surgeons): they knew where there was rural poverty and how they could get child-bearing women to abandon their homes and infants for Paris. Country doctors in the early nineteenth century reported how whole cantons and arrondissements were turned into female deserts. Doctor Monot, for example, reported in 1858 on the villages emptied in his own canton of Montsauche in the Nièvre because of women leaving for Paris; "a third of the women who have given birth here have left." Huge convoys for Paris were organized by *meneurs*; then after a month or so back they would trundle with Paris's babies. A letter from a certain Campaigne de Boissimène to the Minister of the Interior on 17 February 1808 describes how the women were "installed with their nurslings in small, poorly covered carts drawn by one or two nags . . . The poor children suffered the impossible." Pay was irregular, indeed it often as not never came through. "I have never travelled on the roads of the Perche," read a report of 1866, "without being overcome with emotion, seeing these huge *meneur*'s wagons in which nurses and nurslings returning from Paris are piled in pellmell like animals returning from market. This revolting vehicle is known aptly as a *Purgatory*."

One may well ask what kind of population grew up in Paris where one in ten of its children had been abandoned and over half of them had been surrendered to poor mercantile wet-nurses. Patrick Süskind's cult novel, *Perfume*, has its historical inaccuracies—most notably among its early eighteenth-century characters who manage to count in French francs. But the tale he tells of his murderer hero, Jean-Baptiste Grenouille, abandoned at infancy and put out to wet-nurses, contains more than a grain of the terrible truth. Historians today often mock the fears contemporaries expressed of "the mob" and the "dangerous classes." But historians do not have to walk the streets of Paris in the days when they were lit by oil and gas lamps—if lit at all. And they do not have to face the scream of the mobs in the revolutions of 1789, 1830 and 1848, which could be blood-curdling; nor have they sat amongst the kind of crowds that gathered for a nice drawn-out public execution. Paris was not simply picaresque; it was fetid and savage—a condition the good Saint Vincent de Paul had tried desperately to improve.

The scale of the wet-nursing business was unique to Paris, though Marseille did at one point in the eighteenth century manage to overtake the capital. In 1866, three years after the abolition of the *tour*, Napoleon III's Minister of Public Instruction, Victor Duruy, set up a Commission to investigate the matter. The reports that it presented were devastating. "Of the 20,000 children confided to women in the country, how many survive?" asked one Monsieur Brochard. "Nobody knows. Many nurses depart with a newborn and never return. We agree with Monsieur Boys de Loury: departure with a nurse is a form of conscription for infants. Little Parisians die without anybody noticing." When the Second Empire crumbled before Prussia's armies in 1870, complaints about France's peculiar institution became shrill. "In Belgium and Great Britain feeding by the mother is honoured," it was said. "Here we have the 'luxury of Administration' which has been deployed to create an industry out of wet-nursing."

It was no longer charity, it had gone beyond all control; it was child murder. In 1874 a major new law was passed at the instance of the Moderate Republican Théophile Roussel, himself a country doctor. Certificates were demanded from all nurses; committees of inspection were set up. The appalling mortality rates of infants did decline because the law, unlike any that had preceded it, was executed. Moreover, the wealthy of Paris were now taking their rural nurses into their own homes. But what really broke the vicious cycle was a campaign that encouraged mothers to feed their own children: "What unites all the best advantages for the newborn child?" ran the 1904 poster: *"LE LAIT DE SA MAMAN"*—Mother's Milk.

TROCADÉRO

AT MÉTRO STOP NO. 3, the Trocadéro, one emerges into what is, by common accord, the prettiest spot in Paris. The hill of Chaillot—the historic name of the place—is not the highest in Paris, but this view over the Seine, just where the river swings south-westwards, is un-equalled by any other. The Eiffel Tower is before us, the Champ de Mars is at our feet, the École Militaire lies beyond. In this delightful setting we shall consider a story of love, war—and psychoanalysis. It is a strange Parisian fact: in this city there are more practising Freudian psychoanalysts today than in any other city in the world, save Buenos Aires, Argentina.

What a beautiful view from a beautiful hill. The problem for cen-turies was that nobody knew what to do with it. There had been a con-vent here in the seventeenth century, but neglect had allowed it to fall into ruin. The same fate awaited the makeshift military barracks erected here during the Restoration. Napoleon III set up a terrace at the summit from where he could admire what progress his Prefect of the Seine, Baron Haussmann, was making in demolishing and remodel-ling the city. His uncle had planned in 1810 a vast palace for his son, the King of Rome. It would have been larger than Versailles and would have flattened most of the hill, a truly imperial project. Unfortunately, the forces of Europe were allied against him and he managed to do no more than pull down the shacks, dig a few holes and build some sections of the planned outer walls, which his successor promptly dismantled.

During the decades that followed a few intrepid hunters would clamber up the hill to kill a rabbit. In 1823 there was a mock battle and a firework display at the top to celebrate the Duc d'Angoulême's capture of the Spanish fort of Trocadero, a campaign that was already forgotten

by the end of the year; only the quaint Spanish name stuck. The poet
and writer Paul de Kock has described Sunday picnics he used to have
here with his family; they would sit in the grass and eat *pâté de veau froid*.
In the Musée Carnavalet hangs a delightful watercolour by Sigismond
Himely which shows a stone quarry on the edge of a field of rye; a visitor
sits contemplating a peasant girl on the back of an ass with baskets filled
with vegetables. And we are only a couple of miles from the centre of
Paris!

What eventually decided the fate of the Trocadéro was the westward movement of buildings and people, a movement that would cut
through the ancient north–south axis of Heaven and Hell and impose
the new east–west axis of the Louvre, the Concorde, the Champs-
Élysées, the Arc de Triomphe and La Défense—the Paris you and I
know, the Trocadéro you and I see.

One of the persons to enjoy the modern Trocadéro was Adolf
Hitler. "It was the dream of my life to be able to visit Paris," he said on
a sunny 28 June 1940. "I cannot say how happy I am that this dream
was realized today." A lightning campaign and the death of 150,000
men had made the trip possible. The Trocadéro, the outing lovingly
recorded on celluloid, was one of the highlights of the Führer's visit.

In the 1930s Nazi Germany developed an absolute fascination for
Paris. Paris—that is, the visual image of Paris—corresponded so well to
the Nazi ideal of spectacle and power, the "triumph of the will" to bor-
row the title of Leni Riefenstahl's famous film of the Nuremberg Rally.
Look at that terrace of the Trocadéro: it puts you in mind of Riefenstahl's Nuremberg, no? One does not have to possess enormous aesthetic sense to notice that the architecture and paintings of Italian
Futurists, French Surrealists, German Nazis and Russian Socialist Real-
ists all had something in common. Call it modernism, if you will. A single theme runs through them all, that of a Prometheus unchained, man
breaking out of the walls that had imprisoned him, man born again: the
triumph of the will, the creative burst. This virile message put Christian art on the defensive.

Paris responded in style to the new pagan times. Unable to be capital of the industrial world, she strove to be capital of the artistic world.

She was more than successful. Crowds had flocked to her World Expositions, all of them held at the foot of the Trocadéro. The Trocadéro was designed for these big shows. Thirty-two million people visited the 1889 Exposition, carrying home the little models of the new Eiffel Tower; fifty-one million came to Expo' 1900 — that is more than seventeen times the entire population of Paris, a figure that has only once been exceeded in the history of the world since (at Osaka, Japan, in 1970). As a result, many artists and literary figures decided to make a second home in Paris. Especially important among these aesthetic migrants were the British and, later, the Americans.

There was also the German component. How Berlin enjoyed watching Josephine Baker dance nude on their stages, singing *"Mon pays, c'est Paris."* German cabarets in the 1930s were filled with French song; Mistinguett and Maurice Chevalier had their imitators in Berlin. Huge choral groups and girly reviews made a nice complement, a mirror image, to the troops out on the streets in Berlin; but they were also an idealization of the Paris that Ludendorff's armies had not reached in 1918. At the end of the 1930s Goebbels's film industry produced *Bel Ami*, which showed Paris to be a welcoming place, a living spectacle of perpetual gaiety; in one scene, the song "The Harmonica Invites Us To Dance" is performed right in front of the Hôtel Meurice — just where General von Choltitz set up his headquarters in August 1944. Looking at the Trocadéro you can see how, with its terrace and the museums and theatres on either side, and the Champ de Mars beyond, it has been built for the big parade, the spectacular dance.

That was the culture Hitler represented. He arrived to an empty Paris in the early hours of 28 June 1940. He insisted on having two artists accompany him, his architect, Albert Speer, and his principal sculptor, Arno Breker. The accounts left by these two men closely corroborate each other. The filming of the event — high sweeping cameras which, every now and then, zoom into the Führer's black Mercedes with the two artists sitting behind him — come up to the highest Nazi standards. Every detail that demonstrates the triumphant will of the Führer, the beauty of the occasion, is brought to the fore. At one point the car passes a group of confused gendarmes (they are described by both Breker and Speer) who can think of nothing better to do than salute the Führer. The cameramen obviously like roundabouts; they give them a chance to show off their equipment. This is done with great *éclat* as Hitler is driven up to the terrace of the Trocadéro (though the car is actually driven the wrong way round the roundabout). On his approach a lone French worker, symbolic of the defeat, is observed in the corner of the frame.

SO THERE IS Hitler, there the palace, there the commanding hill. But the story that needs to be told on this pagan terrace, its stones devoted to the triumph of the will, is of a more human dimension; it is a story of love and passion that developed under the shadow of Hitler's dictatorship. Those stones on Trocadéro Hill contain the memories of a man and a woman who lived not far from here.

Dr. Otto Rank was one of the great heretics of the psychoanalytic movement. His writings about human will and the artistic act had got him into trouble with his master, Sigmund Freud, in Vienna. Rank claimed that the cause of human anxiety lay not in sex (the libido) but in the experience of birth. Replacing Freud's explanatory metaphor of the Oedipal myth with the metaphor of the expulsion from Paradise, he overthrew the patriarchal schema of the Freudians—the murder of the father and incest with the mother—with an idea that reinstated the mother-child bond as the model of all relations. "*Im gegenteil! Die Mutter!* On ze contrary, ze mozer!" Rank exclaimed to the American Psychoanalytical Association in Atlantic City when outlining his new book, *The Trauma of Birth*. This was in early June 1924 during his first trip overseas since the First World War. He was received as an emissary of Freud. "He was the very image of the scholarly German student," said Jessie Taft, who would become a much needed friend in the years to come.

At the time Rank also thought of himself as an emissary of Freud. But within months the discord was set in motion. Rank never really understood what had happened to him; he was Sigmund Freud's adopted son; since 1905 he had recorded the minutes of the weekly meetings in the Professor's house and taken long midnight strolls through Vienna's empty streets with him afterwards; he had been an instigator of the secret Committee which reviewed membership of the International Psychoanalytic Association and expelled recalcitrants; he was one of Freud's intimates, indeed his most intimate. In 1925 the tables were turned: it was "little Rank" who was under attack.

He was baffled. But the sniping went on for years. He was not a theoretician, he said. "I haven't anything to 'teach' and can't have any kind of a 'school'—not even an undogmatic one," he protested to Jessie Taft. The Americans, he said, were trying to create a "struggle to match my theory against the Freudian when I haven't got one." Rank's two central ideas, that a child's first anxiety was a consequence of birth and that therapy should be set a definite time limit, could certainly be traced back to Freud. The problem was one of emphasis. Those who minimized the role of the libido—Fliess, Jung, Adler and Rank—would be purged. The way this was done—through the public "revelations" of a dissenter's "neurosis"—bore a certain comparison to Nazi and Communist tactics.

The point is not made lightly; there really was a parallel. The rise and fall of psychoanalysis followed the same curve as that of the other great ideological poisons of the twentieth century. It reached its peak in the 1940s, then gradually fell off. Psychoanalysis, just like Communism, received a second wind in Paris with the student riots of 1968, only to collapse under its own weight in the decades that followed. One hundred years after its birth psychoanalysis has few strongholds left in the world; one is Paris.

The glory of Otto Rank is that he realized that something was fundamentally wrong with the movement as early as the 1920s, which is when he migrated to Paris. The therapist should be humble and not pretend that his knowledge was pure science; on the contrary, it was pure art. "I never try to cure," he once remarked. Instead he tried to confront the patient with his neurosis; help the patient realize that the source of his anxiety was the very source of his creativity. "Will therapy," as Rank called it, allowed the patient to realize his full potential as an integrated, creative being. Unlike Freudian analysis, which could go on forever, Rank limited therapy to six months; an "end-setting," claimed Rank, forced the patient to crystallize the inner will conflict. Like the artist who works within the borders of his canvas to enhance a portion of experience, like the poet who transcends his own complaint about the poverty of language, Rank sought, in the analytic hour, to seize the patient's love, anger, pain or joy and demonstrate that these were the very forces that made him creative. To Freud's claim that "the unexamined life is not worth living," Rank replied, "the uncreative life is not worth living." Rank was the "midwife," as he described himself, attending upon a "rebirth."

By 1926 it was no longer possible for Rank to continue practice in Vienna. There was a last painful scene at 19 Berggasse, where Rank had first met the Professor twenty-one years before. "So quits!" wrote Freud to his colleague in Budapest, Sandor Ferenczi (who was himself constantly subjected to Freud's personal slights). "On his final visit I saw no occasion for expressing my special tenderness; I was honest and hard. But he is gone now and we have to bury him."

Rank arrived in Paris that April. Psychoanalysis in Paris had already found a patron in the immensely wealthy Princess Marie Bonaparte, a direct descendant, as everybody knew, of Napoleon I's brother Lucien and a descendant also, through her Jewish mother, of the founder of Monte Carlo's gambling casino—as few people knew. "I went to Vienna in 1925 to undergo analysis by Professor Freud," as she put it. "I thus had the occasion to make the acquaintance of his family." Most practitioners in Paris before the Second World War were foreigners and their patients were also drawn largely from the artistic immigrant community. A therapist of special note was the Polish-born Eugénie Sokolnicka who, in the 1930s, became André Gide's analyst before she committed suicide. But it was Rank, working through the American community, who gave the movement a serious note. After several changes in residence, in the summer of 1927 he eventually acquired his magnificent corner apartment at 9, Rue Louis-Boilly, just opposite the impressionist Musée Marmottan and less than a quarter of a mile from the Trocadéro. How appropriate: Rank was the painter of souls and an impresario of human personality. American writers and artists flocked to his handsomely furnished consulting room. He charged them five dollars an hour, three times the going rate in New York.

❦

"I DON'T REMEMBER how I found out that Dr. Otto Rank was living in Paris, on the boulevard Suchet," wrote the American novelist Anaïs Nin in her journal on 7 November 1933. Slim, languid Anaïs Nin with her startling oriental eyes was nervous. "I impulsively decided to ring Rank's doorbell," she continues. "By sheer accident, it was he who opened the door. 'Yes?' he said in his harsh Viennese accent, wrapping the incisive, clean French word in a German crunch . . . He was small, dark skinned, round faced; but actually one saw nothing but the eyes, which were beautiful. Large, dark, fiery. With my obsession for choosing the traits which are beautiful or lovable, and wearing blinkers to cover what I do not admire or love, I singled out Rank's eyes to eclipse his homely teeth, his short body."

It was one of the encounters of the century, initiated within a few months of Hitler's rule in Germany, though few would know what actually transpired until the unexpurgated diaries of Anaïs Nin were published in the 1990s.

Anaïs Nin and Otto Rank made an improbable couple. Otto Rank was born "with hair complete," in April 1884, into Vienna's poor Jewish quarter of Leopoldstadt on the east side of the Donau Canal. He and his elder brother, Paul, both hated their father, Simon Rosenfeld, an artisan jeweller who was frequently drunk. Paul was put through law school while Otto worked in a machine shop until he met Freud in 1905. Rank's ideas about willpower and artistic creation were born out of his own isolated adolescence, spent at night reading Schopenhauer, Ibsen and Nietzsche—works that "brought him to the brinks of ecstasy and despair." Music, which Freud hated so much that he could not even support the presence of musicians in a café, was defined by Rank in his adolescent diary as "not the image of an idea but the image of will itself." He adopted his name from the "Dr. Rank" in Ibsen's *A Doll's House*, the sympathetic old man who befriended Nora. In private circles Rank also adopted the name "Huck" from Mark Twain's *Huckle-*

berry Finn; in contrast to Tom Sawyer, who pursued an elaborate, bookish strategy to free slaves, Huck was direct, emotional and practical with his pal Nigger Jim.

Briefly, there was nothing scientific about "Huck" Rank's upbringing. He was an artist to the core, and this showed in his first book, *The Artist*, completed before he was twenty-one. It so impressed Sigmund Freud that he was hired on the spot as his personal secretary; it was Freud who put him through the Gymnasium and University, ironically while Rank was already sending out directives to fellow psychoanalysts throughout the world.

Rank's poor health—he had suffered rheumatic fever as a child— had kept him away from Armageddon during his military service in the last years of the war. In 1917 he had been posted in Cracow, then in Austrian Galicia, where he met his beautiful and talented Jewish bride, Beata Tola. In 1919 she gave birth to their daughter, Helene. Beata would herself become an accomplished psychoanalyst. But she was no socialite and gradually, in the 1920s, she withdrew from Rank's life. She lived with her husband behind the Trocadéro at Rue Louis-Boilly. But in the autumn of 1933 they were on the point of divorce.

Could "Huck" be the sympathetic old man to Anaïs Nin? It was not exactly the role she sought in him. They came from such totally different worlds, though there was in Nin that soul—"an angel pattern externally while internally diabolical"—urging her to live her creations. Anaïs Nin was born in Paris in 1903 with a silver spoon in her mouth. Her father was a Spanish composer and playboy, Joaquin Nin, her mother a Danish singer, Rose Culmell. Just before the outbreak of war the mother and Anaïs's brothers moved out to New York because Joaquin had deserted the family for another woman. But it was Joaquin whom Anaïs loved, incestuously so. In the 1920s she was back in Paris. Around the father developed over the next two decades a network of husbands, lovers and occasional man friends that would include most of the American artistic community as well as wide sections of Parisian high society.

One might say that her life between the wars reads like a great Parisian novel; but actually her life *was* the great Parisian novel, for many of the American authors who followed her culled their books from the story of Anaïs Nin. "Draw a chart!" she told her lover Henry Miller who was working on a new novel. "We always attain beautiful heights, wrestling with the immense load of ramifications . . ." Yet it was all so complicated! Anaïs was in need of a psychoanalyst.

At the moment she rang Otto Rank's doorbell her network spread outwards from hot to cold like our bright solar system with its planets and circling moons. In the centre radiated the Father taking "joy out of his silly little cunt chasing"; Anaïs travelled between the planets but her life still depended on Father's warmth, a fact that she resented; she was determined "to make him suffer before he made me suffer."

Further afield revolved her husband, Hugh Guiler, a wealthy Bostonian who had married her in Havana, Cuba, when she was twenty; he worked for National City Bank in Paris and he provided his wife with homes: a sizeable house in Louveciennes, to the west of the city, and various apartments in Paris, according to the season. There was also his parents' home at Forest Hills, outside New York. Hugh commiserated with his Scottish friend, Donald Killgoer, about their spouses' infidelities; Anaïs knew that if she suddenly confessed everything, "Hugh would twist his hands, as Donald did, until the bones cracked, and rave as Donald did, and curse me, and try to kill me;" but Anaïs was not the confessing kind.

Further out still was one of the major planets, the Brooklyn refugee Henry Miller, a system all of its own. He was at this time "staying in a pimp-and-whore hotel in Montmartre" but he had just agreed "to move to whatever hotel I [Anaïs] chose." She found what she thought was a modern, attractive hotel—again behind the Trocadéro—at 26, Rue des Maronniers; she only later found out that it was very well known for "temporary alliances and well-kept mistresses;" but at least it was comfortable. Anaïs spent much of her energy trying to get Henry's first novel, *The Tropic of Cancer*, published; her chief link here was Rebecca West who kept a posh place in London and cultivated relations with the grand London literary agent A. D. Peters. But nobody seemed to appreciate Henry's efforts; Rebecca told Anaïs that she wrote better, and that is what Anaïs thought, too. Caresse Cosby, who ran a press in Paris, was also a promising link—particularly inviting because of her large property out at Ermenonville, Jean-Jacques Rousseau's old haunt about an hour's drive from Paris. Henry talked to himself as he tapped at his typewriter, "writing about dung, ulcers, chancres, disease. Why?" Henry was driving poor Anaïs to despair.

Other planets included a beloved cousin from Cuba, Eduardo Sanchez, an astrologer who spent a lot of time at the house in Louveciennes; Antonin Artaud, the actor and playwright who was another frequent guest at Louveciennes; Dr. René Allendy, who had made a faint-hearted attempt to psychoanalyse Anaïs in 1932; and a certain Mr. Turner, a businessman, in whom Anaïs seemed to have more than a passing interest. Louise de Vilmorin provided advice; Princess Natasha Troubetskoia lent her artist's studio for secret liaisons; Chana Orloff, the sculptor, provided similar services. Then into the whole system burst the asteroid, Dr. Otto Rank, the man of willpower, the artistic creator.

It was "impossible to analyse his way of analysing, because of its spontaneity, its unexpectedness, its daring, nimble opportunism." "There is a pre-Rank vision, and there is an after-Rank swimming." He had made her "swim in life," Nin wrote in her diary after two months of analysis. It was a mental adventure. After she had outlined her complicated system of relationships and alliances, Rank said, "I can't help you unless you break away from all of them, isolate yourself until you are calm." She slowed down her round of the planets, and she did get Henry to move from his down-and-out lodgings in Montmartre to Rue des Maronniers.

But what really changed her life was the discovery, in May 1934, that she was six weeks pregnant: "I know it is Henry's child, not Hugh's, and I must destroy it." She could not awake herself as an artist unless she did away with this child, because Henry was the child. Her pregnancy was a mark of failure: "When Henry and I have failed to bring forth works of art, we create a child." Having his child would at once destroy her love for Henry and break the tie with Hugh. But Rank's analysis on this point was telling. "When the neurotic woman gets cured, she becomes a woman," he said. "When the neurotic man gets cured, he becomes an artist. Let us see whether the woman or the artist will win out. For the moment you need to become a woman." There was the dilemma.

Her reaction was to create yet further complication. "On Tuesday I decided to become an analyst, to become independent." It was six months since her analysis had begun; Rank was "end-setting," forcing his patient to confront her inner will. She put on her new hyacinth blue dress and on the last day in May she rushed to Rank. "I couldn't talk. I got up from my chair, and I knelt before him and offered my mouth. He held me tightly, tightly; we couldn't speak." On 1 June 1934—there had been riots in the streets that spring but Anaïs Nin never noticed; Rank himself was the object of vicious attacks from America—Rank "dragged me toward the divan and we kissed savagely, drunkenly . . . I had not imagined his sensual accord." His hand thrust out. "I like the hardness. I like the animal thrust forward."

On 6 June she woke up after dreaming all night of an orgy with Henry. She went round to his bed and found him "depressed and desirous," and "I swallowed his sperm for the first time." Up she got, quickly powdered herself, and rushed off to Rank's. They kissed voraciously, she lay under him and kissed again; and "in our drunkenness I found myself drinking his sperm, too." With that tender operation completed, he threw himself once more over her, crying, "You! You! You!"

"Hugh tortures me, Henry uses me, Father is cruel; but I have the jewelled tower with Rank." 12 June 1934: "After this moment of darkness, I began to dream again. I was going to see Rank, to see Him; I was going to see Him, I wanted to see Him." Rank in fact got quite ill; on the day they planned a naughty weekend in Louveciennes he turned up at the agreed café pale in the face and speechless. Nin offered to come round to his Boilly apartment, and there she tucked him into bed. The naughty weekend occurred the following week, but was somewhat cooled by the prospect of Hugh turning up early in the morning. Rank needed a sexual education: "Too swift, he is too swift, and so unaware of the woman's response." The gardens outside were snowed with withered blossoms.

Henry was moved out to Mother's apartment, also in the Seizième.

Rank was having difficulties making financial ends meet; there was the possibility that he might have to do something drastic, like move to America—Jessie Taft had contacts. Rank was however making headway that summer with the English-language Psychological Centre he had set up with Dr. Harry Bone and his colleague, a Dr. Frankenstein, at the Cité Universitaire, just south of Hell's Square. Between orgiastic feasts with Anaïs, Rank managed to get a successful seminar running, attended by fifteen American female schoolteachers and three male writers. Anaïs came along but found the discussions to be "pragmatic, dull, like all American craft talk." Rank managed to stand above it all, making brilliant and dangerous talk about Freud. "There are two Ranks," Nin observed; "Rank the philosopher and psychologist, and Rank the human being." She knew what she needed, "the power of love. It is what I want. I want wine."

Rank's "end-setting" was getting rather intense. His finances still didn't look good. He knew that if he went to America to teach he would also be moving among his very worst enemies, the members of the American Psychoanalytic Association. Jessie Taft offered the prospect of the Pennsylvania School of Social Work in Philadelphia and a practice in New York; the APA had a hold on all the positions at Harvard, Yale, and the main universities in New York. "I'm falling in love with your books. Are you jealous?" asked Nin. "That depends how far they take you away from me," he replied. Or again: "I have finished my creation without you, I can love you as a woman"—just a woman.

All the while Nin was carrying this child, an unwanted child. Her taut breasts were full of milk, bitter milk; every morning she looked down at her rounded white stomach. Abortion was illegal—though that in itself was no problem; she could find the *sages-femmes*, the midwives, as well as a good German doctor, through the astrological people who revolved round her cousin Eduardo Sanchez. But the *sages-femmes* were having trouble with their instruments; Anaïs Nin's pelvis was too small for an effective operation; the German doctor told Nin that if she were to give birth it would require a Caesarean. Nin hesitated and delayed. In late August she was carrying a foetus of six months. Rank was away in London laying plans for what looked like an increasingly probable departure for the United States. Henry was at her mother's apartment, sulking in his jealousy.

On the evening of 29 August 1934 Anaïs Nin was in Rank's empty apartment, alone, awaiting the arrival the next morning of the terrifying German abortionist and his *sages-femmes*; alone for her last night with her child.

She told the child: "You should be glad not to be thrust into this black world in which even the greatest joys are tainted with pain, in which we are slaves to material forces." The child replied by kicking against her womb. The room was dark, just as dark as her child's little room. "So full of energy, oh, my child, my half-created child that I will thrust back into the *néant* again. Back into the paradise of nonbeing." All the child represented at this moment was a future, a future that Anaïs did not want. "You are the abdication," she whispered to her child. "I live in the present, with men who are closer to death. I want men, not a future extension of myself into a branch." The child again kicked and stirred in response.

"You ought to die before knowing light or pain or cold. You ought to die in warmth and darkness. You ought to die because you are fatherless." Anaïs sighed to her child, telling it of the solar system she had created. Not a true father was there. First there was the Sun, Joaquin Nin, "it was he who fathered me . . ." She wasn't going to go through all that a second time, "I should be an orphan again." Then there was the war: "I wept for all the wounds inflicted." Then a thousand injustices: "I struggled to return life, to re-create hope." Then there was Hugh. Well, he was taking care of her—all those apartments! "Now, if you came, you would take him for a father and this little ghost would never let me go"—what would be left of me? Then there was Henry: "This man is not a father; he is a child, he is the artist . . . There is no end to his needs . . . He is my child and he would hate you." There was then Rank. Rank could be a father. But how could Rank be both an artist and a father? It would be his death. "*There is no father on earth*. The father is this shadow of God the Father . . . This shadow you would worship and seek to touch, dreaming day and night of its warmth, the shadow of a magic father which is nowhere to be found: it would be better if you died inside me, quietly, in the warmth and in the darkness."

The fourteen pages Anaïs Nin devoted to her abortion, under the date 29 August 1934, are the most extraordinary of her entire multi-volume unexpurgated diary. They are the most powerful, with a tension far more gripping than the thousand plus pages detailing her sexual exploits. To whom is she addressing this diary entry? Her dying child? Her sadistic German doctor? The violent, ugly *sages-femmes*, worthy of the Bureau Général on Rue Sainte-Apolline. Her diary? God the Father? The style is religious, the mood one of ecstasy, like that of a seventeenth-century saint. One is not even sure where she is or who knows what, who knows whom. "Hugh drove us to the *clinique*." So Hugh was eventually told? There is no other reference in the diary to such a major event. Who is *us*? Was she really introduced to the German doctor as "Princess Aubergine"? The name seems a little ridiculous. And where is this *clinique*? There are many *cliniques* in the Seizième, hidden behind the public spectacle of the Trocadéro.

We cannot even picture where she first meets the German doctor. At Rank's apartment? At the *clinique*? "While he operates we talk about the persecution of the Jews in Berlin. I help him wash the instruments." Anaïs wears the ring Rank gave her, the ring that Freud gave Rank, the ring that symbolizes the alliance of the secret psychoanalytic Committee Rank helped set up in Vienna in 1911, the Committee that eventually purged him. In his most famous photograph one sees Rank at thirty-four—the last year of the war—seated authoritatively, well dressed, staring out of his horn-rimmed spectacles, while holding high the right hand which sports Freud's secret ring.

Anaïs is shaved and prepared for the major operation. She is resigned, yet terrified of the anaesthetic. Anxiety. The high birth trauma begins.

The German doctor has the face of a woman, his eyes protruding with anger and fear. For two hours she makes violent efforts, the child inside her too big, the veins inside swelling with the strain. "Push! Push with all your strength!" yell the gaggle of women. One of them bangs down on her stomach. "Push! Push!" With all her strength? She has none left. She has nowhere to put her bent legs.

"Push! Push!" Her bones are cracking. A curtain is torn, bare light bulbs seem everywhere, heads, heads, heads hung with the lamps, a chorus of screaming voices, the words turning as on a badly wound phonograph disc; the doctor is in a frenzy, he wants to kill; the women all laugh—there is no more bandage! No more bloody bandage! They wash instruments. They talk. They talk. "Please hold my legs! Please hold my legs! Please hold my legs! PLEASE HOLD MY LEGS!" They start again. "Push! Push!" The bare lamp is shining white. "It sucks me into space." "Push! Push!" The ice in the veins, the cracking of bones, this pushing into blackness.

The German takes hold of some long, medieval type of instrument and thrusts it into her. A long animal howl: "That will make her push." He smiles to the *sage-femme*. "If you do that again I won't push. Don't you dare do that again! Don't you dare!" The doctor bends down to look. She's dying. The child's dying. The doctor is baffled, furious. He wants to take a knife. "*Let me alone!*" Is that its head? "I want to die in its grasp." The ice. The doctor takes up his long instrument again. "Don't you dare! Don't you dare! Leave me alone all of you!" The *sage-femme* places her fat knees on the stomach. "I push into this tunnel, I bite my lips, my eyes, blood, blood." "Push! It is coming! Push! It is coming!" "For God's sake, don't sit up, don't move!" "Show me the child!" The *sages-femmes* force her down. "Show it to me!" The doctor holds it up: a small, diminutive man, but it is a little girl, perfectly made, glistening with the water of Nin's womb. "A dead creation, my first dead creation."

Anaïs then experiences what must be described as a mystical vision. She had, as she puts it, abdicated one kind of motherhood for the sake of a higher one. Nature had shaped her body for passion alone, for the love of man. The child, such a primitive connection with the earth, had been cast off, thrown aside. She had killed the child, she had sustained the lover. "Man the father I do not trust. I do not want man as father. I stand by man the lover and creator." She sat on the operating table, looking at "that little Indian," the dead child. It was a penis, "swimming in my overabundant honey."

Then appeared the planets. Hugh came to her bedside; she wept.
Henry and Eduardo; Henry and Hugh; poor old Henry had been suffering stomach pains all night. Henry and Eduardo again. They all passed
by as if in a dream. Then in came Rank at eleven o'clock, just back from
London; "We said very little." But it had been Rank who provided the
vision, the trauma of birth, the "end-setting."

And end-setting it was. In four weeks Rank was gone. He would
take the ship for Baltimore from Le Havre. "Dr. and Mrs. Rank" spent
the night together in Rouen, then he left.

But the end-setting proved a drawn-out business, as bad as any in
Freudian psychoanalysis. Nin did not let Rank disappear so easily; in
December 1934 she followed him out to New York, where the old
passion was revived. But, ironically, her departure for New York ultimately strengthened her tie with Henry who, madly jealous, turned up
on a pier in New York in January.

Gradually her love for Rank turned into physical revulsion. Writers
on the affair, leaning on the censored versions of the Nin diary, have
said that for Nin it was always "Rank." This is not so. When Rank set
himself up in America in late 1934 he became known to his friends as
"Huck," thanks to Rank's rereading of Mark Twain, this time in English: he saw that "Huck" was the embodiment of the "roguish boy"
that Freud had characterized him as being at the moment of their rupture in 1926; he was a fun-loving, spontaneous artist. Huck bought
black panties and bras for Anaïs and, during their naughty nights in Atlantic City and at the Barbizon-Plaza in New York, they played Huck
and Puck together, Huck sometimes dressing up as Puck and vice
versa—the meaning of the psychoanalytic rhyme on the words being all
too obvious; in Harlem they danced with the Negroes, which Huck was
convinced every patient in analysis should do. But Anaïs yearned for
Henry and not Huck, especially after Henry's arrival in New York.

The sex games with Huck frankly disgusted her. Henry of course was
only too eager to help her along that route: "Oh, the ugliness, the vulgarity," said Henry. "A most unprepossessing guy." One of Nin's women
friends wrote to her, "I saw an ugly little man with bad teeth." On meeting him in Pennsylvania Station as he returned from his teaching post in

Philadelphia, Nin noted in her diary: "I dreaded the moment when he would kiss me. I eluded it." She hated the bad breath, the perspiration.

Huck could not accept Anaïs's lies, the *mensonge vital*; he would not—unlike Father, Hugh and Henry—believe them. "Twice now a black pall came over Huck," Anaïs noted in May. "His depressions are terrible and like an animal's. He lies there sighing, collapsed, with an earth-colored face, with a breath like death. Death all over his face." It only made Anaïs angry.

In June she boarded the boat for France; Henry followed that autumn. "No one will ever come so near to me, to my soul and being," Anaïs wrote in her farewell note to the greatest beast in her life. "I just wanted you to know." "Where will I meet Rank again?" she wondered, sitting by the petal-strewn lawn of Louveciennes. "At the Café du Rond Point, where we met on our way to the room? At Villa Seurat, while walking with Henry, or carrying Henry's market bag? Paris is like a second-rate fair."

The political situation was getting increasingly uncomfortable and Rank, in New York, made more and more references to it. "Times are difficult all over the world," he had written to Jessie Taft while still in France: "people in America have no money to come over and besides Europe seems to be threatened by war!" In a postscript he added: "Jung has gone overtly 'Nazi' and propagates now a 'Germanic' psychology against the 'Jewish.'" It was perfectly true, and is a fact deliberately overlooked by Jung scholars. Carl Jung took over the presidency of Berlin's New German Society for Psychotherapy and used it shamelessly to disseminate his own Aryan ideas. Yet in 1936 he received an honorary doctorate at the Harvard Tercentenary celebration and, a year later, he received another honorary doctorate at Oxford. Hitler marched into Vienna in 1938 and Freud, through the aid of the British psychoanalyst Ernest Jones, marched out. At the age of eighty-two he still had his sense of humour. Signing the paper required by the authorities certifying that he had been properly treated, he wrote: "I can heartily recommend the Gestapo to anyone."

Psychoanalytic politics also got increasingly vicious. There were no honorary doctorates for Rank. He had shocked colleagues in Washington for an International Congress on Mental Hygiene by announcing that there was no single psychological truth and that psychoanalysis could never be a science. In his book, *Art and the Artist*, which is probably his best, he took the idea further by claiming that the creative impulse had to be put directly at the service of individual personality, unique for each man. At the peak of life, he said, we confront the vale of death; one is most aware of finiteness at moments of great joy. If art is the loan, he taught, death is the repayment. He repeated a childhood theme he had pinched from Schopenhauer: one must will a *yes* to the *must* — an idea not far from Blaise Pascal's "thinking reed" bending to the wind.

It was not a very satisfactory analysis for the scientific Freudians, who shrouded everything in the unprovable unconscious, refusing to recognize physical birth trauma in the formation of human personality (an exterior and thus measurable phenomenon). A. A. Brill had taken control of the New York Psychoanalytic Society from which he excluded all lay analysts, such as Rank. The Boston Psychoanalytic Society threw out the Rankians after 1929. The Americans may have been selective in their comments about Freud — hadn't he said after his one visit to the United States that "America is a gigantic error?" — but by 1930 the main faculties of the East Coast were run by orthodox Freudians. For Rank the worst insult came when Erich Fromm, a young psychoanalyst of high standing in New York, published in the May 1939 issue of *Psychiatry* an article that argued that the philosophy of "will therapy" was fascistic, akin to the authoritarian ideologies of Mussolini and Hitler with its "concept of the necessity of submission and sacrifice." The vast majority of American psychoanalysts agreed with Fromm, whose books remained required reading in university curricula until the 1970s. The rumour went around that Rank was "sick, sick, sick."

And so it seemed. Neither Freud nor his adopted son would survive the new war more than a few weeks. Freud's death had been expected. After another gruelling experience of surgery which cut out most of his lower jaw, Freud took an overdose of morphine on 23 September 1939 and died in his new, pretty English home. Rank had been having trouble with his kidneys, liver, gall bladder and had had major dental surgery — "you may wonder what is left," he quipped to Jessie Taft, "the good old colon . . . had been troubling me years ago . . . I know I am sick." His eyes were giving up, but here he had been lucky to find a second pair in the person of Miss Estelle Buel, a Swiss American who had become his secretary—and in July 1939 his second wife. They had driven leisurely across the country and had decided on a new life in California. But that was not to be. Back in New York in mid-October he wrote once more to Jessie Taft: "I remember the old story of the man whose execution was set for Monday morning and who on his way to the gallows remarked, 'This week does not begin too well!' " On Friday, 28 October, while dining out with Estelle, he complained of a sore throat; the fever rose; he was admitted to hospital; his daughter Helene was there, as was Estelle. Death came at 8.30 that Monday morning, after he had breathed a last word in German: "*Komisch*" (comical? strange? peculiar?—Rank, fifty-five years old, carried the joke to his grave).

Anaïs, in Paris, cured her disenchantment with Henry by involvement with a Peruvian, Gonzalo Moré, who wooed her in Spanish. But the war caught up with her, too. She returned with a thousand other artist migrants to New York. "Now I see that the extraordinary was in my own vision," which of course was what Paris had been for them all. It was February 1940 and Nin was renting an apartment on Washington Square West. "I thought about Otto Rank, and wondered how he was." So she called: "When I telephoned this morning I could not believe the voice that told me he had died of a throat infection." She could not believe it "because of his vitality and love of life." "Did Rank die not knowing perhaps how much or how deep was his gift, how vivid his human presence?"

Hitler's armies were on the move that May: Holland, Belgium, France: "Impossible to think of anything else, to feel anything else." The machines had taken over. Paris was empty when the Führer arrived under the morning sun for his show at the Trocadéro, the Eiffel Tower shrouded in mist before him and the modern grey walls of the Trocadéro rising on either side—like the thighs of a woman giving birth.

MONTPARNASSE

AT THE EXIT of Métro stop No. 4, Montparnasse, silvery escalators seem to climb into nowhere, their glazed-eyed passengers looking all astonished; bare grey concrete walls reach upwards into space; the floors of the wide corridors are so shiny that you will be afraid to tread on them for fear of falling; and the whole area is enclosed by great glass panels supported by steel. Step outside and there is a kind of medieval fair, a *cour des miracles*, fit for Fellini. A barrel-organ is playing as children jump on the merry-go-round and the fast-food shop serves *Popcorn*, *Crêpes* and *Barbes à Papa*—lord knows what the *Boissons* are. On one side are the *écrivains publics*, described by Louis Sébastien Mercier in his "pictures" of eighteenth-century Paris: they write love letters for your loved one, business letters for your tax inspector and curt letters for your *avocat* if you are seeking a divorce. They come from another age when few knew how to read and write—the mirror of our times. Not a block from here, in a narrow, rural street, there once lived a sculptor whose extraordinary work stretched, like the station at Montparnasse, as much into the past as it reached forward into the future.

Paris was divided up into twenty *quartiers* in 1702; the boundaries have shifted several times since then, but the number has always remained twenty. But the veritable *quartiers* of Paris, as opposed to the administrative *arrondissements*, are something else. From the heights of the black skyscraper is a very clear view of what these natural, living *quartiers* actually are. The old Latin Quarter of the university, to the north-east, is obviously one. The Marais, on the opposite bank of the Seine, stands out as another. The wealthy Seizième, stretching out from the Trocadéro, forms an evident *quartier*; as does the Septième on the Left Bank with its two main poles of attraction, the Eiffel Tower

and the Invalides. The Americans who came to live in Paris in the 1920s came to the area at your feet, Montparnasse, and called it "The Quarter"—they lived in the "pimp-and-prostitute hotels" of Le Madison, Le Royal, Le Foyat and the Hôtel de Nice. They enjoyed the jazz in the cafés of the Dôme, the Coupole, the Select and the Closerie des Lilas. "A good many of my friends camped in Montparnasse," wrote Silvia Beach, owner of the American bookshop Shakespeare and Company. "They had only to cross the Luxembourg Gardens." And that surely is the point: Montparnasse is not, and never has been, a real *quartier*.

The area of Montparnasse, the Quatorzième Arrondissement, is divided into two distinct sections: one is basically an extension of the old Latin Quarter, the other is built up on the rural fields that stretched down to Hell, the old Barrière d'Enfer. The north-eastern zone, lying around the Carrefour Vavin—the intersection of the Boulevard Raspail and the Boulevard du Montparnasse—is merely a prolongation through the Luxembourg Gardens of the Latin Quarter, where Sylvia Beach kept shop; indeed, Montparnasse was created by students expelled from the university by Catherine de Medici in the sixteenth century. The remainder of the Quatorzième was, up until the First World War, largely open country.

A remarkable amount of what the Americans—the "Crowd" as they called themselves—saw in the 1920s is still standing. The old Gare Montparnasse, which was located on what is now a large square in front of the tower, has obviously made way for this outdated vision of the future constructed in concrete, glass and steel. But what the eyes of 2001 actually see is not very different from what was here in 1901. At the turn of the last century the built-up zone of the Carrefour Vavin was poorly lit at night, even along the major boulevards. Down Boulevard du Montparnasse from the station through to the crossroads of Avenue de l'Observatoire there would have been a few glimmers of light like beacons on a deserted moorland. Those of the Dôme, a café on the Carrefour Vavin, would have lit up the corner of the Boulevard du Montparnasse and the narrow Rue Delambre, which was a hideout for rag pickers and tramps; the few shops along that street were lit by acetylene lamps. La Closerie des Lilas, further on, was lit by bright white globes which made it seem a haven from the menacing darkness that surrounded it.

It was here, in the spring of 1905, that the poets Paul Fort and André Salmon launched their review, *Vers et Prose*, involving readings and popular music, a modest start to the legendary café life which exploded with the arrival of the Americans after the First World War. Why did the Americans—Ernest Hemingway, John Rodrigo Dos Passos, Robert MacAlmon, Kay Boyle, to mention the most famous—appear in such numbers? The decline of the franc against the dollar made living in Montparnasse very cheap and an ideal escape from their Prohibitionist homeland. They liked to call themselves the "Lost Generation," the disillusioned victims of the war, though few of them had served under the flag during the war and many of them became household names in their twenties. "I can't think of a generation less deserving of this name," admitted Sylvia Beach.

Beyond "The Quarter" the second, rural Montparnasse spread southwards. There was a bird market by the municipal cemetery on Boulevard Edgar-Quinet. Poor immigrants from Brittany, many of whom could not speak French, populated the area; it remains to this day a "Little Brittany." Nearby, in the food markets, animal trainers played with their singing dogs and dancing goats, sword swallowers and fire-eaters attracted a gaggle of giggling children—the same sort of crowd you find today in front of the Gare Montparnasse. Fields stretched all the way down to the Fortifications. Every day along the provincial roads herds of mules and goats would be driven up and down to the Luxembourg Gardens; one old herdsman was famous in the quarter for his goat cheeses that he flogged from door to door. The houses had a quaint, pastoral look and each one of them had their stables.

It was the stables that attracted the artists. The old artists' colony at Montmartre was getting expensive and overcrowded; Montparnasse's stables, which lost their purpose as the car replaced the horse, were easily converted into art studios. New technology was having an effect here, too. Photography was forcing painters to explore new styles and this revolution in the plastic arts would eventually feed into music and literature: Montparnasse was where the world's Modernism was born.

It is ironic that the man who invented Modernism should have made his home among the goats and herdsmen of this old rural Montparnasse. He was never seen in the cafés of the Carrefour Vavin. Neither Sylvia Beach nor Ernest Hemingway mentioned him in their memoirs of "The Quarter." Antoine Bourdelle lived in another universe—and it was he who, with his antique visions, changed the way we look at the world.

BORN IN 1861, he was of the first generation of artists to be raised since childhood in the civilization of photographs—mountains of photographs that are today preserved in the archives of the Musée Bourdelle, his former studio. The building is barely a hundred yards from that railway station with its outdated vision of the future. Follow the underground passage to Place Bienvenüe—another of those Parisian jokes*—and you will come out in an area that displays every form of architecture invented since the eighteenth century. Rue Antoine Bourdelle, the former Impasse du Maine, is just a few paces down on your left.

Before you go into the museum, have your lunch—Parisian bangers and mash—at the little rural bistro at the end of the street; you will love the girl who serves you while the general atmosphere will make you think you are in some isolated café on the limestone plateaux of south-western France. In the museum a number of Bourdelle's photographs are on display. You can see how he learned to sculpt from photographs taken in faraway Athens, Florence, Rome,

---

* Paris's first métro line, from Porte Maillot to Porte de Vincennes, was built within seventeen months and was opened on 19 July 1900, in time for the World Exposition. The director of works was the Breton engineer Fulgence Bienvenüe, whose surname lends a traditional French word of welcome to travellers arriving at the Gare Montparnasse.

and even in the jungles of India and South East Asia; Bourdelle's collection is like that of an exotic explorer. You discover how he photographed his male and female models, and distorted them into fantastic shapes: every major movement of the young twentieth century—Expressionism, Cubism, Futurism, Picasso and Matisse—is to be found in Bourdelle's creative interpretations of his huge photograph collection.

Bourdelle has a photograph of the poet Jules Tellier. To model his bust he examines the photo and, he reports in a letter of 1905, "I pick up the clay with my naked soul and make the profiles of this face move." You can see how he photographed himself at work. You will discover the enormous amount of preparation he put into each statue, some of them taking ten years or more to complete. Above all, these photographs give you an idea of the smell, sound and sight of his studio when the twentieth century dawned—wooden turntables rotate on iron wheels, pulleys creak as a statue is hauled into place, the dust of marble settles on the parquet flooring, in a corner you can see Bourdelle in his indigo blue costume labouring away at a detail in his statuary; students in white blouses try their hands amid piles of decorative stone; and who is that young woman model looking so contemporary but born over a century ago? You want to touch her. Bourdelle did not drink; he did not go to the cafés. He had two wives, but he does not seem to have been a womanizer. Bourdelle just worked, and worked, and worked.

Cutting stone was in his veins. "Four gods taught me everything," he wrote. His father was a carpenter who kept an imposing house overlooking the River Tarn at Montauban. "From him I acquired the sense of architecture," said the son. It was the most important feature of his work, whose construction he was always contrasting to the individual, momentary passions cast by his master, Auguste Rodin. Rodin's *Gate of Hell* "is not made to be used as a gate," complained Bourdelle. Everything Bourdelle designed stood, like his father's solid home, on sound foundations. "Architecture is the interior of sculpture, and its form, to be worth something, must simply extend from it," taught Bourdelle. Giacometti and Matisse counted among his pupils.

His second god was an uncle, a "Herculean stonemason" from

whom he learned "to listen to the rock" and follow its direction and turns "according to the advice of the stone itself." For Bourdelle had the greatest "respect for the beautiful material" and, in this, resembled Michelangelo, who, by just looking at a rock, could see the statue within it. "What I mean by sculpture is what one obtains by removing something," Michelangelo had written in a statement Bourdelle liked to quote. The photographs of Michelangelo's works, many dating from the 1870s, in Bourdelle's collection prove what an influence the Italian was: it accorded so well with the music of his stonemason uncle. Matisse would call it the "colour" of the stone.

The two other deities in Bourdelle's pantheon were his grandfathers. There was a weaver on his mother's side who introduced him to the fabric of colour; this is found in the many hundreds of paintings and sketches Bourdelle made when preparing the field for his sculptures. Among the most exquisite were his watercolours of centaurs— half human, half horse: dancing, fighting, dying, coupling and praying—obvious precursors of Matisse's dancers and of the Cubists' compositions of movement and surfaces. On the father's side was a goat herder. The family came from the Causses, a dry rugged plateau to the north of Montauban where the rocks were interspersed with box hedge and juniper and the principal inhabitants were goats. Bourdelle's work would remain a reflection of his childhood sight of rocks sculpted by the wind; the goat tracks through the rough land organized "my capricious thoughts and threaded them together as one." Rodin's work lacked that kind of structure; Bourdelle's work grew out of the unified world of the south-western peasant, a world of ancient pathways and solid architecture which he brought to the city as a student of the École des Beaux-Arts in 1884. He set himself up in the rural quarter of Montparnasse, among the goatherds, at 16, Impasse du Maine, and remained there for the rest of his life.

"I am like Socrates," he told the students who used to gather in his studio, "I give you birth through your soul." He was the kind of sculptor who would have pleased Dr. Otto Rank—indeed, Rank would have seen Bourdelle's work in the theatres he attended. He would not have seen Bourdelle's *Aphrodite or the Birth of Beauty*, a 1924 coloured stucco composition which decorated the Opera House of Marseille—here one can recognize, as in many of the photographs he took of his works, the head of Bourdelle himself rising above the dancers who attend the delivery. But Rank used to go to the Théâtre des Champs-Élysées, where there was a display of Bourdelle masterpieces. "Oh, my sweet bacchanalia of earth," writes Bourdelle on the birth of his sculpture in 1910, "I have taken in my hands a little of your trembling flesh, removed from your side. I knead it, impatiently, I mould it at night, I mould it into my dreams, this piece of the clay's flesh . . ." Bourdelle was so sensual. He believed that every one of his sculptures carried an inner *élan*—he was consciously Bergsonian. He could capture, like Rodin, one critical moment. But he went further than Rodin by following the eyes of his peasant ancestors out into an architectural landscape of universal, eternal truths. This is what opened the way to the Modernists of Montparnasse.

Bourdelle was, in less than two years, exasperated by the neoclassicism of the École des Beaux-Arts, on Rue Bonaparte. "I have had enough! I can't understand anything about all these systems of prizes and competitions," he wrote in early 1886 to his master, Alexandre Falguière—an academic sculptor whose dull *République triomphante* crowned the Arc de Triomphe in 1886. For more than a decade Bourdelle eked out a living on Impasse du Maine, producing some fabulous though generally unremarked works for Paris's art salons. After the shock of his mother's death in 1888 he started producing his lifetime series of Beethoven busts—*Beethoven with Long Hair*, *Beethoven with Short Hair*, *The Mask of Tragedy* and so on—which had only the vaguest reference to Beethoven's physical appearance; they were designed to show the tumult of the composer within. "Music and sculpture are the same thing," explained Bourdelle, who thought of himself as a suffering Beethoven of sculpture. With a few of his friends, including his neighbour, the old Communard Jules Dalou, he exhibited in the cellar of La Closerie des Lilas in 1891 where he met the poet Paul Verlaine, "staggering drunk, dressed in rags, his neck wrapped in a huge red scarf"; his eyes were like those of "the changing skies of autumn where the clouds are swept along by the wind": Bourdelle would attempt to sculpt those clouds in stone.

This was just before he was engaged by Rodin in 1893 to be his *praticien*, a job that could go so far as executing the Master's work. Bourdelle reshaped Rodin's *Bourgeois de Calais* and he transposed to marble or stone several of Rodin's famous works, such as *Le Purgatoire* and *Orphée*. In some cases he had contributed to the conception of the statue; it was, for instance, Bourdelle who recommended to Rodin that his statue of Balzac, which was erected at the Carrefour Vavin in Montparnasse, be draped in a vast cloak—a favourite Bourdelle technique for suggesting movement: Bourdelle's collection of photographs include several of himself, his wife and various models dressed up in sheets. Rodin had opened the breach with the academic neoclassicists of the École des Beaux-Arts by bringing life and an intensity of passion to his statues through a play of light and shadow. Bourdelle widened the gap yet further by providing an architecture of angular surfaces, furrowed grooves and lines that would shoot out in a way that would convey both solidity and action.

One evident mark on his work absent from Rodin's sculptures is the great tragedy of the early twentieth century—war. War is the dark shadow behind all the Modernists of Montparnasse. But the curious thing about this war culture is that it actually pre-dated the war. Nature imitates art, argued Oscar Wilde, an *habitué* of the Paris salons of the 1880s and 90s. Which came first, the imagination or the fact? In the case of First World War art, it is a pertinent question. Expressionism, Cubism, Surrealism, Futurism and the other movements that we so often associate with the post-war years can already be found in Montparnasse in the years before the First World War, and particularly in Bourdelle's work. One obvious reason is that there were factors working on these movements that had nothing to do with the war—photography is the most striking example. But at a profounder level there can be found in the modern revolt against neoclassical form and its fascination with primitivism a radical aggressiveness that prefigured the war: the inhibitions of the Victorian age were dropped. Paris of the great Expositions had never shared the confidence that London had enjoyed; her industry was not as strong and she had already been crushed in one German war back in 1870. The horrors that Bourdelle's

Parnassian neighbour Dalou had lived through that year had no parallel in Britain. So in Paris the modern revolt joined with anguish—a *mal*, as the future war leader Georges Clemenceau put it, "that gnaws at us."

In 1893, the year he started work as Rodin's *praticien*, Bourdelle received a commission from his home town, Montauban, to build a memorial for the local boys who had died in the Franco-Prussian War of 1870–71. It became an epic project: its graphic depiction of violence and death would inspire many of the war memorials that would be scattered through France after 1918; no French town square had ever seen anything like it before, which is why, when it was eventually erected in 1902, there was a tremendous scandal. The famous review *Art Décoratif* labelled it "Hottentot art" and criticized it for defying the laws of anatomy; for the art critic in the *Petit Journal* it was a large pile of bronze that seemed to have been pulled from under the ground by archaeologists, "having been bizarrely deformed within the entrails of the earth."

For the untrained eye it had the look of chaos. From no single angle could one view the whole collection of screaming heads, bent torsos and contortions of death. But nobody who passes through Montauban will ever forget it. Those serpentine human forms are worth pondering. Bourdelle had spent a decade working on the details, gradually building them up on a pivot that turned on a naked warrior whose outstretched left arm, it is true, defies the laws of anatomy—though photographs show that Bourdelle used his own left arm as a model. His screaming heads show the influence of medieval gargoyles and foreshadow the paintings of Edvard Munch.

The principle of isolating detail for study went back to the Italian Renaissance but, then, the purpose was simply to perfect the part as an element of the integral whole. Bourdelle, working with his primitive Kodak camera, sought the autonomy of the detail; he often photographed his pieces at night, using experimental lighting—a technique that had been used by Rodin in his studios at Meudon. Bourdelle has recorded the fantastic shapes produced by the camera under these conditions. Pablo Picasso practised a similar technique in the 1940s, with wartime acetylene lamps, in collaboration with the Surrealist photographer Brassaï. The method could have impressive results. One series of photographs shows Bourdelle piling his screaming heads on top of each other to study their effects. The result, in the monument at Montauban, was Bourdelle's peculiar gift to Modernism; needless to say, this was not a technique that could have been applied by the neoclassicists of sixteenth-century Florence.

Bourdelle worked frequently with themes drawn from Greek antiquity because he found in them, not the static models of harmony taught at the art schools, but an architecture that could frame his wildest fantasies of action and movement. Another pre-war statue that according to his critics again defied medical laws was *Heracles Archer*, which was first put on exhibition in 1910: the figure's outstretched, twisted left leg is supported on a vertical rock while his right is bent under the weight of his body, which leans back almost vertically to pull an invisible string of the bow, his muscular left and right arms perfect reflections of the positioning of his two legs. Nobody could have imagined it at the time, but photographs again demonstrate that Bourdelle had been working with a living model, the athletic Commandant Doyen-Parigot, who managed, in a series of what must have been painful fifteen-minute sessions, to contort his body into that of the ancient archer. In the background one notices the stone profile of Bourdelle's naked warrior of Montauban.

Heracles Archer made Bourdelle France's most celebrated sculptor next to Rodin. The *Archer* was the very image of man born out of kneaded clay, simultaneously erotic and primitive. Studies made in clay show how, over the years, the sculpted figure lost all resemblance to Commandant Doyen-Parigot and increasingly came to resemble the cannibal birds Heracles was required to murder by the shores of Lake Stymphalis. One can imagine Heracles—Latin Hercules—emerging for his kill from the kind of singing primal forest that Bourdelle's Parisian contemporary, the Douanier Henri Rousseau, liked to paint. It brilliantly synthesized the spirit of art in the French capital on the eve of the First World War: form, movement, *élan*.

A wealthy financier named Gabriel Thomas bought the *Archer* at the Salon of 1910 where it was exhibited and he immediately consulted

Bourdelle on a pet project he had been toying with since 1906. Thomas was the director of Paris's wax museum, the Musée Grévin on Boulevard Montmartre, and president of the Eiffel Tower Society. Like many of the wealthy men of his day, he was a man of immense culture and learning; his desire was to set up a modern theatre on the Champs-Élysées that would startle the public both in its appearance and with the productions performed within it. Thomas had a Wagnerian project in mind, one that united all the arts, one that would revolutionize perceptions. In the first decade of the twentieth century it was thought that dance, rather than opera, was the medium by which this could be achieved. "In the ballet," wrote one of Paris's leading critics, Alexandre Benois, "I would point to the elemental mixture of visual and aural impressions; in the ballet is attained the ideal of the *Gesamtkunstwerk* about which Wagner dreamed and about which every artistically gifted person dreams." When Thomas gazed upon the nimble *Heracles Archer* he realized he had found the man who would decorate his theatre.

For the project's realization, Thomas had set up a real estate company with Gabriel Astruc, a flamboyant Parisian impresario whose love of foreigners proved stronger than French nationalists' hatred of them. Astruc crowded Paris's pre-war stages with the ablest foreign artists in the world: Wanda Landowska and Artur Rubinstein from Poland; Enrico Caruso, Arturo Toscanini, Lina Cavalieri and Titta Ruffo from Italy; Negro spiritual singers from the United States; and most significant of them all, Serge Diaghilev's dancers from Tsarist Russia. But the question was to purchase a suitable plot on which to build the theatre. Nothing could be found on the Champs-Élysées and, in the end, land on the still rural Avenue Montaigne was acquired by the company, though the name of the theatre remained unchanged; that is why the Théâtre des Champs-Élysées is, curiously, by the Place de l'Alma on the Seine and not on the Champs-Élysées.

Thomas and Astruc had financial backing from the great artistic philanthropists of the age, like William K. Vanderbilt, J. P. Morgan and John J. Astor, along with the moral as well as financial support of Otto H. Kahn of the New York Opera. For architectural ideas they leant upon the Belgian, Henry Van de Velde, who was then based in Weimar, where he was spreading his gospel of simplicity in form and decor—it was around Van de Velde that the German *Werkbund* and the *Bauhaus* movements were born. "Ornament is a crime!" said Adolf Loos. War was declared on architectural ostentation, a campaign that was aided by another critical pre-war technological development, the invention of reinforced concrete. The masters in Paris were the Brothers Perret—Auguste, Gustave and Claude—who had erected in 1903 the city's first concrete block of flats on Rue Franklin, behind the Trocadéro. It would be no exaggeration to say that here is to be found the origin of the matchbox functionalism that has since ruined urban landscapes around the world. Its saving feature was the thorough artistry of its origins; the Théâtre des Champs-Élysées makes a very pretty matchbox—thanks largely to the work of Bourdelle.

Thomas and Van de Velde came round to his studio on Impasse du Maine on 30 November 1910 to show him the Perret plan for the theatre. Could he sketch on to the plan the figures he intended to sculpt for the theatre's façades? There was a board meeting the next day. "I got to work at six o'clock in the evening," he wrote to his second wife, Cléopâtre. "I made six little projects in clay, six little models. After dinner, I finished them, and then I took up my crayons and brushes. I drew the main lines with a bad crayon, using an old broken ruler. I had no square. Instead I used a square of cardboard. All the same I did all the reliefs and then a plan of the whole façade. I even managed to correct the defects. The sky was blue when I went to bed; it was morning." The board was delighted with the results. Thomas reportedly wept.

"The wall itself," Bourdelle told his students, recollecting the image of birth through matter, "should appear to stimulate the human images while at the same time maintaining its surface, its flat light as a wall." Bourdelle worked painfully in his studio on his solid marble friezes, sticking rigorously to the rectangular plans of the Brothers Perret—to the point that the figures were shaped into the square shape of the stone. It was an extraordinary achievement, given the energetic theme he had picked: "On the call of the god Apollo the muses run from all points of the horizon." The harmony between a serene but dominant Apollo in the centre of the frieze and the running muses to right and

left could only be achieved by a sense of perspective imposed by differ-
ing figure sizes, Apollo being the largest. Most sculptors would have let
Apollo's figure determine the layout of the rest. Bourdelle did the reverse: he concentrated on draped runners, thus drawing the eye to their
movement, while Apollo and his attendants—theoretically too large
for the central stone in the frieze—were turned in physically impossible contortions that were typical of Bourdelle's modern style: the architectural rule came first in his sculpture; the problem of physical
reality was relegated to a distant second. The result is to create a dynamism that is missing from all neoclassical sculpture.

He worked on the same principle in the three framed reliefs above
the theatre's entrance—reliefs framed by the bodies in movement:
naked Tragedy stretches her arms out horizontally to a vertical sword,
her head thrown back so that her long hair falls in the same vertical direction; the violinist and piper form a perfect counterpoise, the former
curved over her instrument in a manner which, though anatomically
impossible, gives sound to her instrument; heads are turned sideways
and drapes follow the movement of the bent legs in Dance that obviously has little to do with ancient ritual, but everything to do with the
violent modern performance one is expected to find inside the theatre. The figures were based on drawings Bourdelle had made of the
Polish dancer Vaslav Nijinsky and the well-known American Isadora
Duncan.

Bourdelle had become fascinated by Isadora Duncan's draped displays on stage. He watched the performances mesmerized—only later
at night and in the early mornings would he sketch his first impressions. "But look, just look," he said to his wife one evening. "Don't you
see that she is dancing Death? I see Death even in her veils which seem
so like shrouds." That same evening they watched the artists depart in
a black motor car that resembled, to Bourdelle's eye, a coffin. A few
hours later the same car fell in the Seine, killing Isadora's two children
and their governess. The play of life and death, a *danse macabre*, informed the entire display that Bourdelle prepared outside and inside
the Théâtre des Champs-Élysées, which opened just one year before
the outbreak of the First World War.

The coincidence between Bourdelle's art and this great European
tragedy proved to be yet more extraordinary. In its opening season of
spring 1913 the theatre lived up to all the scandal that Thomas and
Astruc expected of it. Lights were projected on to Bourdelle's white
friezes on the opening night, 30 March, at which extracts from
Berlioz's opera on Florence's god of sculpture, *Benvenuto Cellini*, and
Weber's rousing piece of German romanticism, *Der Freischütz*, were
performed. Battle lines were drawn when a 120-manned orchestra performed on 29 May Igor Stravinsky's new *Rite of Spring*. To piercing vio-
lins and thundering percussion Nijinsky led Diaghilev's Russian Ballet
in a shocking *danse macabre* during which the chosen sacrificial virgin
danced herself to death.

"An extraordinary, ferocious thing," said Claude Debussy of the performance. "One might call it primitive music with every modern conve-
nience." The booing and whistling was so loud that Gertrude Stein
reported: "We could hear nothing . . . one literally could not, throughout the whole performance, hear the sound of music"—which was quite
something considering the demonstrable fact that she was not present.
The press dismissed Nijinsky as "a sort of Attila of the dance" and *Le Figaro* went so far as to describe the evening as "a border incident whose
gravity the government should not underestimate." Cultural historians
have pointed to this performance of Stravinsky's *Rite of Spring* as the
precursor to Europe's post-war culture.

Bourdelle's own involvement in the theatre did not end with his
dramatic friezes. All through the summer and autumn of 1913 he was
engaged in painting the glorious frescoes which decorate the first floor
of the atrium. During an interlude, or even during the performance if
the music is too loud, a member of the audience can come out to the
quietness of the theatre's iron staircase and contemplate Bourdelle's
mythological beasts. The subject of the series once again revolves
around that quintessentially Parisian obsession, the Dance of Death.

According to the legend, Heracles defeated the centaurs in the Battle of Pholoë. The last centaur was condemned by Prometheus to an
eternal dying because he was immortal, like the gods. But this was simply an excuse for Bourdelle to follow his own fantasy. As one follows

the series of frescoes through, one sees emerging in brilliant colours—with all the distortions and contortions so characteristic of the sculptor—a tragedy of Christian proportions, just six months before the outbreak of war. Amidst a forest of trees the last centaur dies with his arms outstretched in the form of a crucifix.

Then, one month before the war, in July 1914, Bourdelle exhibited what is commonly recognized as his greatest piece of sculpture, *The Dying Centaur*. It is the man, a Herculean figure naked to the hips, who dies while the surviving beast of a horse remains strong, firm and forceful on its rock—but headless: that was Bourdelle's message to the world in the summer of 1914. It may be said that this one statue signals the beginning of Modernism in Montparnasse. Why, Bourdelle was asked, does the centaur die? "He dies like all the gods," the master replied, "because no one believes in him any more."

SAINT-GERMAIN-DES-PRÉS

IN THE TWENTIETH CENTURY, belief became the central issue. "Every minute of the day I ask myself what I could be in the eyes of God," Jean-Paul Sartre puts in the mouth of a character in his play *Le Diable et le bon dieu* (*The Devil and the Good Lord*). "Now I know the answer: nothing. God does not see me, God does not hear me, God does not know me." Sartre did not take his atheism lightly. He devoted a large part of his most important philosophical work, *L'Être et le néant* (*Being and Nothingness*), to the problem of God and at one point, like Bourdelle, compared belief in God to a belief in the centaur: "To say that the centaur does not exist," he wrote, "is by no means to say that it is not possible." In a famous lecture on "Existentialism" which he gave at the end of the second war he began with the God problem, stating that his aim was not to demonstrate that God did not exist, but rather to show that "even if God existed that would change nothing." Man, with a consciousness which gave him total freedom of choice, projected himself as God: that was the principal argument of the sage of Saint-Germain-des-Prés.

Sartre is not popular today. "Unhappy 100!" chimed the *Times Literary Supplement* at the centenary of his birth in 2005. "Sartre's philosophy was never very coherent and means nothing now; his novels are unreadable" crowed Paul Johnson in the *Literary Review*. Comments in the French press were not much better. Memories are bitter because of Sartre's slide into Communism and the extreme left which began—one can give it a date—in 1952, around six months after the première of *Le Diable et le bon dieu*. The image many have of Sartre is that of an old man haranguing a few workers from the top of a barrel outside the Renault factory at Boulogne-Billancourt, or of him

distributing a Maoist rag in Rue Daguerre, near Place Denfert-Rochereau, or of his mad defence on television of the Baader-Meinhof terrorist band.

Before 1952 Sartre was an individualist. The closest he came to recognizing collective action in *Being and Nothingness*, published in 1943, was—appropriately for us—in his example of commuters in the métro. Down in the métro in 1943 the traveller would look into the wan faces of other commuters and wonder silently what was their story—their broken families, their deported loved ones, their lost soldier. The last métro before the midnight curfew became a morbid ritual in occupied Paris, yet another kind of *danse macabre*. Only here there were no partners. All was performed in solitude. Sartre evoked the rhythm produced by striding commuters in the passageways, comparing it to the "cadenced march of soldiers," the "rhythmic work of a crew" (he had served on the front and had been a prisoner of war) or "dancers on the stage:" "the rhythm to which I give birth is born in connection with me and laterally as collective rhythm . . . It is finally *our rhythm*." But that is as far as he was willing to go; before 1952 Sartre's interest was focused on the free individual, necessarily finding himself in conflict with the freedom of others. In his métro example the signposts are all projected at *me*; "I am *aimed at*": "I avail myself of the opening marked 'Exit' and go through it." Sartre climbs the steps, with his mind still free; he turns home, *alone*. It is the hour of silent curfew throughout most of Sartre's hefty philosophical tome. How then could he subsequently align himself with the collectivist Communists? How was it possible?

Saint-Germain-des-Prés is the closest-knit, cosiest *quartier* and also one of the oldest in Paris. True, the boulevard itself has, like all of Haussmann's thoroughfares, cut a blind swathe right through the heart of the historic *quartier*: ancient buildings have literally had their northern half sliced off in order to make way for the boulevard. But people cross the boulevard as if the boulevard did not exist—it is the one spot in Paris where pedestrians have priority over the cars, and so it was in Sartre's day. On the north side of the boulevard are the cafés Deux Magots and the Flore, on the south side, opposite, is the Brasserie Lipp. The marketplace on the south side—it is one of the few examples of Napoleonic architecture in Paris, square and uninteresting—is on the site of a fair that had been held here since at least the early Middle Ages. The twelfth-century abbey tower ascends to the north, defying the clouds, and establishing a powerful point of stability for the community that surrounds it. In the abbey's interior you will find the original display of Gothic coloured sacred stone: pillars of red and gold, and a high starry ceiling that are enough to challenge the thoughts of any doubter of God. On the south wall are inscribed the names of near five hundred parishioners *morts pour la France* in the war of 1914–18, and well over a hundred *morts pour la France—soldats, résistants, déportés, fusillés, victimes civiles* in the war of 1939–45.

Religion, fair and festival were what kept Germanopratins (as the happy residents are known) together for so many centuries. Trade was vigorous in the Middle Ages and Renaissance because outside the city walls of King Philip Augustus (which followed the current Rue de Seine) one escaped the city's taxes. The abbey's farmlands provided fruit and vegetables, while the clerics encouraged the spread of books, paintings and engravings; there was plenty of music performed in the streets. Most of the abbey properties were destroyed during the French Revolution, but the market remained, as did the books, the paintings, and even the music.

War left its imprint. Because Saint-Germain was outside the city walls, Viking marauders were allowed to run amok in the abbey and its surroundings; in the fourteenth century it was the turn of the English. The near total destruction of the abbey during the Revolution was in response to a war with the rest of Europe that didn't seem to be going too well. But it was the last two world wars that most affected what one finds today in Saint-Germain.

Speak of Saint-Germain-des-Prés to a Parisian and his eyes will go misty and his hands rotate as he conjures up images of intellectuals regaling themselves in cafés, of jazz bands pounding out all night in the cellars, of painters, actors and actresses joining hands with famous writers in the late 1940s and early 50s—one long, gigantic party after the Second World War. Yet there had been an earlier celebration. "The great epoch of Saint-Germain-des-Prés was *before* the war," says the painter and actor Roger Edgar Gillet, who turned twenty at the Liberation. Before the war you could find great writers like Roger Martin du Gard, André Gide and François Mauriac having coffee in the Deux Magots. The Flore next door was considered a bit of a pit; many of its clients were Poles, who are still today an important minority in the quarter. The main bookstore then was across the street at the Divan, run by Monsieur Martineau, who suffered from a chronic ulcer. Others preferred the pretty young owner of Champion, down the road by the Seine. Yes, those were serious days born out of the poetry and disillusionment of the First World War. Then, with the Occupation, writers and artists closed in on themselves. "And they liberated themselves," Gillet goes on. "Yes," he ruminates, "after the war, came *the explosion.*"

Sartre himself thought the critical change occurred during the war itself. This was when the move was made by the intellectuals from Montparnasse to Saint-Germain-des-Prés; and it was during the Occupation that the Flore triumphed over the Deux Magots. Sartre said, "Montmartre became a forbidden place because: (1) it was cold at the Dôme; (2) the grey mice of Boulevard Raspail arrived lugging sachets of tea, pots of butter and jam, and white bread: it was intolerable; (3) the Metro Vavin was closed." Paul Boubal, the new owner of the Flore, installed a pot-bellied coal stove and, just as important, a telephone. German soldiers and collaborators frequented the Deux Magots; they rarely made an appearance at the Flore. During the last winter of the Occupation people passed mornings, afternoons and evenings in Boubal's Flore; one lady spent two to three hours in the toilets every day. Sartre thought, "Either she's got enteritis, or she's reading compromising papers." Boubal became King of the Quarter, ran several dubious financial affairs, threw prostitutes out of his café and, with the Liberation, convinced trumpeter Boris Vian that he was going to run for Prime Minister.

In 1942 Boubal noticed a little man arrive every day at opening, leave at midday and return in the afternoons to stay until closing time. He would always be accompanied by an attractive but very serious-looking young lady and they would spend their time scribbling at different tables. This went on for months. One day the telephone rang to ask for Monsieur Sartre. Boubal knew a man called Sartre and he was not there. The caller insisted that he was, so Boubal announced the name. Up got the little man: "I am Monsieur Sartre." The telephone calls became so numerous that Boubal put a special line through to Sartre's coffee table.

Boubal was witness to the making of *Being and Northingness* and Sartre's *roman-fleuve, Les Chemins de la liberté (The Roads to Freedom)*. By the time Sartre had got to his first plays—*Huis clos (No Exit)* was put on at the Théâtre du Vieux-Colombier at the time of the Normandy landings—he was so well known that he took to hiding in the Café Pont-Royal in the distant Septième Arrondissement. Within weeks the term "existentialist" was being applied to the cafés, the restaurants, the jazz cellars and all the mad youth, the *zazous*, crowding into an ecstatic, liberated Saint-Germain-des-Prés.

What was an existentialist? The popular weekly *Samedi Soir* ran an article in May 1947 on the troglodytes of Saint-Germain that defined an existentialist as one who stayed in a hotel for a month and didn't pay the bill. When the manager says he will seize his bags the existentialist clambers up the steps on all fours and puts on as many shirts and trousers as he can and slinks off to another hotel. After several months he has only one pair of trousers left, he can't sleep, so he spends his nights in the Bar Vert on Rue Jacob, writing on the lavatory and telephone cabin walls existentialist graffiti . . . And so the article goes on. Parisians remained poor for a long time after the war; conditions were worse in 1947—when there were a series of Communist-led strikes—than they had been at the war's end. People stayed in the cafés because they were warm, they ate in the little restaurants because there was nowhere else one could find food, and photographs of *zazous* dancing to the jazz bands with trousers held up by string show that the description in *Samedi Soir* contained a grain of truth. People often looked ragged and dirty (though the women maintained an aura of Parisian chic that had astonished American GIs when they arrived in 1944). Sartre himself was seen, the four seasons round, wearing the same dirty woollen sweater. The historian Alistair Horne recalls meeting him shortly after the war: "Smelling like a goat, he rather set the tone. If ever there was a philosopher guilty of the sin Socrates was accused of, being a false corrupter of youth, Sartre seemed to be it." Part of this may have been just appearance (I myself met Sartre, years later, in the Rotonde—he was dressed in a dark blue suit and did not smell like a goat): at the École Normale Supérieure right-wing students were known as "the Clean" while the left-wingers were called "the Dirty"; Sartre was one of the Dirty, putting on plays that shocked the Director and hammering out, to the delight even of the Clean, American jazz on the piano. Even when Sartre started earning big money he stayed in a hotel; it was considered "bourgeois" to live in anything as comfortable as a three-room flat. In the last years of the war Sartre kept lodgings in the Louisiane, on Rue de Seine, one of the "pimp-and-prostitute hotels" where Henry Miller lived in the 1930s.*

In the cafés, the existentialist "family" sat at separate tables from the "*bande à Prévert*" and would rarely even be seen in the same locale as members of the Communist "cell." Part of the Germanopratin legend is that spirits were so jubilant around those little tables that all social and political barriers vanished. "An extreme leftist would talk with an unconditional Gaullist, a Catholic with an anticlerical or a Jew," recalled Daniel Gélin. "The only thing *de rigueur* was tolerance." Claude Mauriac, a Catholic, remembered a truly surrealist scene on the terrace of the Deux Magots one warm evening in June 1946. André Breton, former surrealist and arch-Communist, was surrounded by his old disciples when Antonin Artaud, who had been thrown out of the Party, walked by: "he gave a very low bow and Breton bowed even lower; it was from below the coffee tables that they eventually started talking: a most amiable chat."

All those imbibers at Saint-Germain would have told you they were "anti-Fascists," but the term was getting a little worn around the edges— even in 1945. Sartre described the atmosphere in the Flore during the Occupation: "The permanent clientele was composed of absolutely closed groups . . . It was like an English club. People would come in, recognizing

---

* The hotel still stands at the sharp intersection of Rue de Buci and Rue de Seine, to the side and above a bountiful fruit and vegetable shop. It even houses a genuine writer, an Egyptian, who has been living there for over fifty years.

everybody; each one knew down to the slightest detail the private life of his neighbour; but between groups one never said '*bonjour*.'" There was always the fear of *mouches* (flies) and *corbeaux* (crows)—spies. Most of those present would have been party to what Jean Cassou, critic and veteran anti-Fascist, called the *refus absurde*, an absurd refusal to accept the fact of occupation, though often counter to self-interest. But that was hardly enough to create a community of interest; each one stood on his guard. Here were the essential ingredients of the existential mind.

Étienne Antonetti, a teenager who danced in the cellars of the Liberation, who loved Juliette Gréco in her slinky black dresses, and enjoyed being in the company of Camus, Sartre and Picasso, thought there was something about being an "existentialist," even if he did not read *Being and Nothingness* at the time: "Our two *maîtres à penser*, Sartre and Camus, brought, each in their manner, a kind of direction, a moral sense to life, and that really marked me, yes. That 'liberty of choice which determines the individual,' that was a part of me, I practised it."

One should not underestimate the huge impact of Sartre's thought on his age. Sartre's initial understanding of freedom was drawn on two forms of being, the chaos of the universe of objects (the *en-soi*) and the structured consciousness of man (the *pour-soi*) which perceives this universe and constantly yearns to colmprehend it. In contrast to the German phenomenology of G. W. F. Hegel, Edmund Husserl and Martin Heidegger, the *pour-soi* in Sartre's schema never arrives at its end, which ideally would be a "higher" synthesis in the form of an *en-soi-pour-soi*: God. Instead the *pour-soi* is destined to fail in its goal through an unavoidable process of self-negation; as Sartre explained, "man is doomed to be free," though that freedom can never be complete. In a critical chapter on "The Situation" Sartre outlined the limitations which consciousness was constantly running up against: the place I inhabit, my past, my environment (even when changing place), my neighbour and my death—Sartre quotes André Malraux's terrifying comment that "death transforms life [determined by my choices] into destiny [my past as perceived only by others]."

Being and Nothingness is at times baffling. But persistence is rewarded by a privileged look into the mind of a genius. There are not many writers who have demonstrated such an array of talents as Sartre; he wrote a great philosophical work, a first-rate play (*Huis clos*), a splendid novel (*La Nausée*) and a wonderful work of autobiography (*Les Mots*)—and he produced a lot else besides. His experience as a novelist and a playwright allowed him to provide graphic examples as demonstrations of his formidable philosophical theories. *Being and Nothingness* is filled with inkpots, cups, coffee tables, waiters in a rush, suspicious strangers, spies, anonymous crowds, oppressive police forces, anti-Semites, sadists, resisters and an anticipated liberation. It is above all a philosophical work born out of the German occupation of Paris: the reader finds Sartre working at the Café de Flore or in the confines of his hotel room; there are shortages and absences; one discovers the impotence of an isolated civilian; one shares with him his despair, his hopes, his search for meaningful acts; his disappointment in the face of the constant annihilation of his will.

To demonstrate how freedom is born not out of its end goal but from its initial negation—"that the practical conception of freedom is wholly negative"—Sartre takes the example of the curfew: "Remove the prohibition to circulate in the streets after the curfew, and what meaning can there be for me to have the freedom . . . to take a walk at night?" It is the negation of freedom which makes one conscious of freedom. That "surging forth," that *birth* within the *pour-soi*, the "original choice," the doomed effort to transcend the *pour-soi* of human consciousness into the *en-soi* of the objects about us always begins with a negation, with a threatened annihilation of the subject. The mountain outside the window is a colourful part of the landscape during a summer holiday in the Alps until the idea is born in one's consciousness to climb it: then the mountain becomes a challenge, a nightmare, a life-threatening object. This inkpot in front of me is *not* a coffee cup—it is through that "not" that human consciousness distinguishes one object from the other and imposes order on the chaotic universe.

But in young Sartre, during the Occupation, that order is never complete, it is frustrated. The fact of frustration creates an existential anguish, a fear of the void and a desire to escape the choices before us. Man escapes the terrifying choices laid before him by putting on a mask of conformity, by living in "bad faith" with his *pour-soi*, his consciousness. Sartre is very cruel here, and utterly uncompromising. A man suffers from an inferiority complex because he wants to be inferior. A woman behaves as if being exploited because that is the easy way out of her physical condition. A Jew in occupied Paris behaves as a Jew; a worker takes himself to be a worker. But it can be otherwise. In a toughly worded passage—remember this was published in 1943— Sartre laid out the kind of choice facing the individual endowed with freedom, whatever his environment. "The most atrocious situations of war, the worst tortures do not create an inhuman state of affairs," he wrote: "there are no inhuman situations; it is only through fear, through flight and through recourse to superstitious forms of conduct that I decide that conditions are inhuman; but this decision is itself human and in thus acting I bear the total responsibility for my deeds." Acts performed out of fear, evasion or the resort to religion were for young Sartre made in bad faith. One had to take the bitter pill and embrace the situation, alone. Sartre appealed in print, in 1943, for "engagement" to an "authentic" freedom, a commitment to resistance. He contrasted the "partisans of liberty" to the determinists who believed that man's consciousness and his choices were conditioned by something beyond his control—for the Marxists by the economic regime, for the Freudians by the unconscious, for the Christians by God. Sartre's idea of "engagement," as he expressed it in the 1940s, was not simply political; it lay at the base of the individual's whole project of life. The freedom for which man strived, in a universe without God, was the only absolute capable of generating a system of values and of providing his being with meaning. But, though promised in the concluding paragraphs of *Being and Nothingness*, the work on an existentialist value system never got written; events instead would push Sartre, disastrously, down a more collectivist, political path of engagement.

THE CAFÉ—JUST like the métro—provided an excellent example of how limited a collective consciousness, the *nous-sujet*, was. The sense of togetherness in these cafés was a Germanopratin legend that did not have much foundation in fact. *Being and Nothingness* gives a striking example of what café life was actually like. Sartre is sitting on the terrace of his café observing other clients while they observe him "in the most banal kind of conflict with the Other." Then suddenly on the street opposite a vélo-taxi collides with a delivery tricycle: "*we* watch the event, *we* take part in it;" temporarily—like the commuters in the métro—one is engaged in the "we." The Sartrean "family," Christians and Communists alike, all participate, but once the event is over they return to their coffee and silence.

The abbey was right next to the principal cafés; it marked the central point of the Germanopratin community. Parallel to the boulevard ran the narrow street of Rue Jacob, with its clubs, its restaurants and publishing houses. Virtually opposite the Échelle de Jacob was a small provincial house with a tree in front of it: the house is still there, looking as provincial as ever, and the tree now reaches beyond the roof. In 1946 the editors Paul Flamand and Jean Bardet set up the new publishing firm of Le Seuil here; the top floor became the headquarters of the widely read Catholic journal *Esprit*. Just down the road was the Éitions Gallimard; its top floor was occupied by Sartre's new journal, *Les Temps Modernes*, founded in autumn 1945. Christians and existentialists formed a mirror image of each other, and not just in stone.

A series of events going back to the Dreyfus Affair in the 1890s had isolated practising Christians in France from the political and social mainstream. The republican separation of Church and state in 1905 had meant they could expect no support from the state, and the papal ban in 1926 on Action Française—mouthpiece of the extreme right with which the French Church had been identified—suggested that Christianity could not risk political affiliation. Many of the Catholic elite avoided the bitter choice Pope Pius XI presented them: they formally submitted themselves to the ban while secretly flouting it, the kind of hesitancy that made them easy targets for the atheist charge of "bad faith." The novelist Georges Bernanos maintained his political allegiance to Action Française and thus deprived himself of the holy communion for years.

Then there were the converts. Since the late nineteenth century a number of intellectuals, in the face of rapid de-Christianization, had converted to the Catholic faith. Some of these conversions were dramatic, such as that of the poet Paul Claudel in Notre Dame Cathedral on Christmas Day, 1886, or of Charles Péguy on the eve of the First World War. "What am I?" the philosopher Jacques Maritain, co-founder of *Esprit*, wrote to his friend Jean Cocteau. "A convert. A man God has turned inside out like a glove." Sartre himself was fascinated by the process of conversion—there are so many references to it in *Being and Nothingness* that one wonders if he was not tempted to take the step himself (Albert Schweitzer was, after all, his uncle). Many of the converts were the children of mixed family backgrounds: Catholics married to Jews, or Protestants living with Catholics (such as in Sartre's family). All these people had taken, in the face of adverse opinion, a definite choice that would influence what Sartre called their "life project." And all of them, as a result of the historical dilemma of Christianity at that moment, were men stranded alone with their conscience—a very existential situation.

All this demonstrates a complicity between Sartrean and Christian thought, and it did not stop there: the very origin of existential philosophy in France was Christian.

Gabriel Marcel was one of the converts, though his acceptance into the Church was hardly dramatic. The Catholic novelist, François Mauriac, wrote to him one day, pointing out what a lot they had in common. "Why aren't you one of us?" asked Mauriac, so "one of us" he became. The two dramatic events in his life were the death of his Jewish mother when he was four, which put his whole life in a "desert universe," and the First World War when, too weak to fight, he served with the Red Cross's information bureau: every day he would see relatives of men missing in action so that "every index card became a heart-rending personal appeal." Born in 1886, Gabriel Marcel was sixteen years older than Sartre. His life was marked by the empty and the absurd. This influenced the philosophy he developed, in fragments, during the years that followed the First World War.

His biographer M. M. Davy called him the "itinerant philosopher"; he travelled a lot and, although he passed his *agrégation* in philosophy at the tender age of twenty, he never held a teaching post. He lived in a flat in that significant frontier-land between the Luxembourg Gardens and the Sorbonne, an area which, though beyond the formal limits of the Sixième Arrondissement, was considered one of the "protectorates" of Saint-Germain-des-Prés in the heyday of the Germanopratin empire. What interested Marcel in his empty universe was the human relationship. He used his talents in music to express the unexpressible features of that relationship; and, like Sartre, he wrote for the theatre as a means of demonstrating the central role played by the "*moi*" and the "*toi*." His first major philosophical work, *Être et avoir* (*Being and Having*), which he began at the end of the Great War and completed in 1933 (to be finally published in 1935), anticipated Sartre's ontology by a whole generation. The themes of Marcel's thought are recognizably Sartre's.

Marcel by the 1930s had, after the experience of the Great War, the rise of new brutal dictatorships, the disorientation of the Church and the weak response of Europe's democracies, become convinced that his world—the "broken world" he called it in one of his plays—had been emptied of humanity; it was like a watch which ceased to tell the time, or a body whose heart had stopped beating: things seemed to go on as before, but there was nothing inside; the world had lost its soul. During the Occupation he wrote a series of essays that were published in 1945 as *Homo Viator*, or "Man the Traveller"—unlike Sartre, Marcel did not manage to get his works past the Vichy censors. His message was a clear call to "engagement." "The true patriot cannot believe in the death of his country," he wrote, "he does not even consider he has *the right* to believe it."

But for Marcel the Liberation of 1944–45 was no cause for celebration. In *Les Hommes contre l'humain* (*Men against Humanity*) he described the world that emerged from the war as even more "dehumanized" than it had been in the 1930s. He had no sympathy for the ideology of Resistance that conducted purges on suspected collaborators, he did not join the ranks of anti-imperialists and de-colonizers, he disliked the ruling post-war penchant for "the spirit of abstraction" and warned against becoming the "vassals" of organized political allegiance. As the leading proponent of what by now was known as "Christian Existentialism,"

Marcel took Sartre's *Being and Nothingness* to task for taking—with its *pour-soi* and *en-soi*—a step backwards into dualism; Sartre, he thought, was artificially separating thought into idealistic and materialistic domains and risked falling into the trap of pure materialism. These comments were published in 1951, shortly before Sartre slid, irredeemably, into the extreme left.

THE MATERIALIST TEMPTATION for Sartre—as Marcel perceived it—lay just around the corner from the Café de Flore, on the Rue Saint-Benoît. Communist journalists used to meet in the Montana and neighbouring cafés; formal meetings of the Germanopratin "cell," no. 722, took place in the nearby Salle de Géographie on Boulevard Saint-Germain, after which the elite of the Party would withdraw for an encounter at No. 5, Rue Saint-Benoît (it was the district of saints), in the flat of Marguerite Duras, then a slim brunette author with a bark. It was the relations Sartre had with the Communists, along with divisions in his own "existentialist" camp, that drove him over the brink in 1952.

The Communists were themselves divided by the developing Cold War, which by 1948 was getting very hot. "If the Red Army Occupied France What Would You Do?" asked the political weekly *Carrefour*. In interviews, members of the French Communist Party turned the question round, "Why not the American army?" Anti-Americanism reached fever pitch amongst Communists and fellow-travellers. One Communist paper, *Action*, began a serious campaign against Coca-Cola, warning that it was "a drug liable to provoke violence." Communist frenzy could be turned on its own people, sometimes in quite ludicrous circumstances. Marguerite Duras and six of her friends were expelled from the Party in 1949 because of a conversation in the Café Bonaparte during which Laurent Mannoni, journalist at *Ce Soir*, described Laurent Casanova, editor of *La Nouvelle Critique* and patron of Communist intellectuals, as a "*Grand Mac*," a pimp. Jorge Semprun, active in another journal, reported this to the Central Committee and, as a result, earned a reputation as a *mouchard*. The affair was still being heatedly discussed on French television fifty years later.

Expulsion from the Party was, for a Communist militant, like the break-up of a marriage or the loss of a close relative. The sociologist Edgar Morin, who had joined the Party at the end of the war, has spoken of the "great warmth of comrades, the wonderful feeling that radiates from the words '*c'est un copain*,' '*je suis un copain*.'" Communist camaraderie was an adolescent game that married well with the jazz culture of Saint-Germain; but its somewhat murderous "anti-Fascist" rhetoric makes hard reading today. Many of the participants—two of Marguerite Duras' husbands, for example—had spent time in Nazi concentration camps. Communists tended to survive. A Communist network inside the camps placed comrades in relatively safe administrative positions— both Jorge Semprun and the Italian author Primo Levi have described the cruel logic behind this. As a result Communist resisters in France tended to survive. Well might the French Communist Party of the post-war years boast of the "75,000 *fusillés*": most of the 40,000 resisters executed by the Nazis were in fact not Communist—they had been denounced to the Nazis by the Communists.

The subject of concentration camps was a particularly sensitive one after 1945 and a major cause of division among comrades and fellow-travellers—not the Nazi camps, but the Soviet ones. Sartre was dragged into the debate.

The whole quarrel began when a Soviet defector to the United States, Victor Kravchenko, published in 1947 a French translation of his *I Chose Freedom*. The Communist-run *Les Lettres Françaises* accused the book of being written by anti-Soviet specialists in US intelligence. Parts of the original English version, it was true, had been subject to intrusive editing in order to make it "fit for the American reader," but that Kravchenko was its author could never be doubted. Kravchenko filed a double suit for criminal libel against *Les Lettres Françaises* and came over to Paris to push his case through. When he appeared, in January 1949, in the Salle de Géographie at the opening of the trial the world press was present. The intellectuals of Saint-Germain-des-Prés had never had such coverage before. The Soviet Union flew in a fleet of witnesses, including Kravchenko's former wife; but they did the Communist cause no good. "What I did, I did for the whole world, for all free people," said Kravchenko and, supported by devastating testimony on the barbarity of Soviet camps, he won his case.

For the Communists of Saint-Germain, worse was to follow. In November 1949 a left-wing Socialist who had himself done time in the Nazi camps, David Rousset, published in the conservative *Figaro Littéraire* an "Appeal for the constitution of a committee of enquiry into the Soviet camps." The camps, reported Rousset, "are placed under the direction of sections of the Ministry of Foreign Affairs which carry the name Gulag." Rousset had not fully grasped the complexity of Soviet camp administration, but this was the first time the term "Gulag" was used in the West.

It caused an uproar within the Germanopratin community of deportees, represented by a Communist front organization called the "National Federation of Deportees, Internees, Resisters and Patriots" (FNDIRP) under Pierre Daix, a pure Stalinist who was in large measure responsible for the expulsions of Marguerite Duras and friends. Emergency meetings of Cell 722 were held, insults were exchanged; Duras' ex-husband, Robert Antelme, claimed that the alienation of workers under "capitalism" was just as inhuman as the Soviet Union's concentration camps. He deplored the anti-Communist tone of Rousset's article. Antelme's position was endorsed by Sartre in his *Temps Modernes*. Rousset filed a suit for libel; Daix and his director at *Les Lettres Françaises* were fined as a result of graphic court testimony on the horrors in Soviet camps. The Communists of Saint-Germain were quite evidently living in "bad faith."

WITHIN TWO YEARS, Sartre was behind them. Every Sunday afternoon in the late 1940s there would be an editorial meeting, in the Gallimard building, of *Les Temps Modernes*. Most of the young present were either Party members or fellow-travellers, despite a vicious Communist campaign against Sartre—"the hyena," the impenitent individualist, the "disciple of the Nazi Heidegger" and the inventor of a philosophical system that was both "nauseating and putrid." Sartre had a soft spot for the young, especially young women—and it may have been this that was the cause of his slide leftwards.

When asked how he managed to handle so many "contingent loves" at the same time, Sartre admitted that he had to resort to lying. In the more important political domain he lied, too. The ridiculous positions he took as a "public man" after 1952 naturally caused people to wonder about *his* responsibility as a writer and *his* philosophy of engagement, liberty, authenticity and freedom of choice. Was man really as radically free as Sartre had initially insisted? Or was his behaviour determined by deep, hidden forces beyond his control? If the latter were true, Sartre's whole philosophical system crumbled.

Most influential on Sartre's political position was his assistant editor at *Les Temps Modernes*, the Sorbonne professor of philosophy, Maurice Merleau-Ponty. Merleau-Ponty lived on Rue Jacob and, though the author of the most cerebral, abstract works, had an enormous sense of fun; he was the only philosopher in Saint-Germain to dance with the girls in the jazz clubs—the others used to cogitate in a dark corner with their friends, half-hidden by a pall of cigarette smoke. In stark contrast to his behaviour, Merleau-Ponty's philosophy was sombre, ambiguous and empty of any hope of discovering the secret of the chaotic universe in which he lived—a reflection of his unhappy, if privileged, childhood. Merleau-Ponty's sentences ran on forever; one could never be sure whether priority should go to the well-camouflaged main phrase or the multiple qualifications that enveloped it. He rejected Sartre's division of being into the *pour-soi* and the *en-soi*, which he thought too close to Descartes' duality of mind and body to be comfortable, and instead he offered the reader the idea of a "body subject" that combined the spiritual and the material—in this sense he was closer to the Christian thought of Gabriel Marcel than Sartre. But there was no religious faith in Merleau-Ponty to act as guide; just the self-organization of the thinking subject, an "*en-être*," which the American intellectual historian H. Stuart Hughes translated as "being with it." It was a philosophy full of doubt, the forerunner of that of today's cultural relativists. Indeed,

Merleau-Ponty spoke in his last major work, before he was struck down by a heart attack at the age of fifty-three in 1961, of writing a "relativism beyond relativism." By that time he had withdrawn from political activity entirely and had retreated into a study of the problem of perception.

But in the late 1940s he, and not Sartre (or Albert Camus), was the driving force in the politics of Saint-Germain's existentialists. The book that gave him political leadership was *Humanisme et terreur*, an apology for Soviet terrorism published in 1947. Juliette Gréco described an enjoyable evening spent with him, drinking punch and dancing: "He accompanied Jujube [as Gréco described herself] to her door and then returned home to his *Humanisme et terreur*." Sartre affirmed the importance of Merleau-Ponty's political influence in the obituary he wrote for *Les Temps Modernes* in 1961: "He was my guide; it was *Humanisme et terreur* which made me take my step. This little book, so dense, opened up both method and object: it was the snap of the fingers that pulled me out of inactivity."

The book advocated a "Marxism of expectant waiting," one that would give the Soviet Union the benefit of the doubt, an "understanding without adherence and of free examination without belittling"—in other words, a blank cheque, a refusal to accept the anti-Communism of the American camp while taking advantage of the margin of safety in European events that would allow one to remain neutral and thus save the peace. Typical of his relativistic stance, Merleau-Ponty compared French and British "terror" in their colonies with Stalin's crimes, which needed to be "understood." Merleau-Ponty argued that Soviet leaders were more honest than those of the West in admitting to their own terrorist practices. By the mid-1950s he deeply regretted having written this perverse little book.

On 25 June 1950 North Korean troops, with the encouragement of the governments in Moscow and Peking, invaded South Korea. Merleau-Ponty recognized that the Soviet Union was the principal aggressor, as did Sartre's other wayward collaborator Albert Camus, whose last illusions about the nature of Soviet Communism had been destroyed by the evidence of the Soviet concentration camps. Sartre, on the other hand, joined the majority of left-wing intellectuals in accusing the United States of warmongering.

Merleau-Ponty's subsequent drift into relativism and metaphysics had been anticipated in his earlier writings, which were not exactly a ringing endorsement of commitment. As for Camus, he had never been a philosopher; he is remembered today for his novels — *L'Étranger* (*The Outsider*), *La Peste* (*The Plague*), *La Chute* (*The Fall*) — not his essays. *L'Homme révolté* (*The Rebel*), published in a critical year for Sartre, 1951, which contained some marvellous portraits of Marx and Lenin, and with comments even more incisive on the Marquis de Sade, Nietzsche and the French Surrealists, was analytically weak: all it argued was that, faced with the savage, formless movement of history, man should endeavour to respect human life and remain moderate. Sartre, in his stinging criticism of the book the following summer, rightly pointed out that Camus was attempting to have the best of both worlds, the ethics of the violent rebel and personal happiness; this kind of ambiguity could not be endorsed by the philosopher of "engagement," existential Sartre. "Friendship can become totalitarian," wrote Sartre, and he accused Camus of pursuing "only literature"; Sartre broke with Camus for good. For a couple of years Camus withdrew from writing altogether, concentrating instead on the production of his plays. He then seemed to be moving in the direction of intensive literary creation when his career was tragically cut short by a motor accident near Sens in January 1960.

From a strictly philosophical point of view, Camus' story is marginal. As for Merleau-Ponty, he had marginalized himself by pursuing a purely relativistic strain of thought that committed him to nothing. In contrast to both Camus and Merleau-Ponty, Sartre had set himself a clear choice: the wrong choice. He plunged into it with gusto.

By the time the Korean War broke out he was living under a punishing regime of political activity, playwriting, journalism and a night-time reading of the works of Karl Marx — not to mention his complex love affairs. He was smoking two packets of unfiltered Boyards, drinking coffee and tea by the litre, and chewing up to twenty pills of corydrane — a popular 1950s mixture of aspirin and amphetamines — every day. Simone de

Beauvoir, his companion, recorded in her diary that he did not sleep for three nights out of the week, and when he did decide to go to bed he gulped down half a bottle of whisky and four or five sleeping pills. To arrive at this point of clear choice Sartre was, as he graphically put it himself, "breaking the bones in my head."

In *Being and Nothingness* Sartre described the futility of man's efforts fully to apprehend himself and his surroundings in terms of Henri Poincaré's sphere, in which the temperature decreased as one moved from the centre towards the surface. Try as they might, individual beings could never reach the surface because the lowering of temperature produced in them a continually increasing contraction: "they tend," wrote Sartre, "to become infinitely flat proportionately to their approaching their goal, and because of this fact they are separated from the surface by an infinite distance." The surface was the *être-en-soi*, the *autrui*, the Other—a living being always beyond reach.

Pushed to its logical limit this Other was, in the way Sartre described human consciousness, the omnipresence of God, an unrealizable ideal towards which man was constantly striving, though always falling short. If he did not push himself to his limits, man would fall by the wayside in "bad faith," and reduce himself to acting out the role that the Other's presence wanted him to be: a "waiter," a "worker," a "slave," a "Jew," even a "writer." Though he could never reach that unattainable surface, man had to strive to do so; in Sartre it was a process of continual birth within oneself, a surging forth, a transcendence from oneself to the Other, and ultimately an impossible "conversion"—an image which was repeated throughout his great philosophical work. In his wartime play, *Huis clos*, he showed the cost of not striving towards the unattainable—in the form of three people, a male coward, a female narcissist and a lesbian, who had to live eternity together: "Hell is other people," remarks one of the characters. "I did not mean to say that our relations with others are always poisonous," elaborated Sartre in an interview in 1965. "I wanted to say that if our relations with others are warped and tainted, then the Other can only be hell." Man had to make an open choice and swallow the bitter pill, otherwise he was damned.

So in 1952, Sartre swallowed the bitter pill. For years he had been groping from a position of aggressive neutrality—a "socialist" Europe which stood outside the influence of the two superpowers—to one of complete cooperation with the Communists. On the Soviet camps, Sartre clung to Merleau-Ponty's Soviet apology of 1947 that capitalism had committed as many evils as those of Stalin's regime. On social policy he argued that the Communist Party most clearly represented the interests of the "proletariat"—a term that he and other intellectuals used with careless abandon to mean any group that appeared poor and exploited. "It is impossible to take an anti-Communist position without being against the proletariat," he explained glibly in 1951. But it was the Soviet Union's Peace Movement, which had been gathering momentum since its first congress held in Wroclaw in Poland in 1948, that eventually brought Sartre with so many other Western intellectuals round to the Communist camp.

Peace was the old dream of Paris's Liberation; the call for peace was a sure magnet for a Germanopratin who had lived through those dramatic months of transition. In *La Douleur*, Marguerite Duras recorded her impressions of the end of April 1945, shortly after her ex-husband, Robert Antelme, returned from a German camp: "Paris lights up at night. The Place Saint-Germain-des-Prés is illuminated as if by headlights. The Deux Magots is jam-packed. It is too cold for people to sit on the terrace. But the little restaurants are also crammed. I walk outside. Peace seems imminent. I return home in a rush. Pursued by peace."

Ah, peace! Picasso drew his famous dove for the Communist-sponsored World Congress of Partisans of Peace, held in April 1949 in Paris's Salle Pleyel. Ah, peace! Sartre still hesitated at that time, not least because of the foul language the Communist press was deploying against him. It was the Korean War which decided him, not least the American bombing of North Korea. Ah, peace! Many in Paris were awaiting a nuclear war, instigated by the United States. Ah, peace! In a long essay, "The Communists and the Peace," which was published in *Les Temps Modernes* during the summer of 1952 (at the time of his break with Camus and Merleau-Ponty), Sartre argued that the Soviet Union was a purely defensive power faced with destruction by the men of the

Pentagon. He began a series of trips to Russia and to brother Socialist states, such as popular democratic China and Cuba, once it had become Communist. He abandoned his work on ethics, which he had promised in *Being and Nothingness*, and turned his attentions instead to the impossible marriage of existentialist phenomenology to collectivist Marxism. The work nearly killed him, and it shows; *The Critique of Dialectical Reason* is a truly impossible read.

We can be even more precise about the moment of Sartre's slide. In May 1952 he was in Rome enjoying the company of his Italian Communist friends when he heard that a Communist demonstration in Paris had been repressed and the Party's rotund, voluble leader, Jacques Duclos, had just been arrested. Sartre went on record later as saying that this was the instant of his *conversion* to Communism: "When I came back hurriedly to Paris, I had to write or I would suffocate." Unfortunately, a whole cohort of the Western world's best brains followed Sartre in his conversion, down that route to the absurd.

PORTE DE
CLIGNANCOURT

THE PROBLEM OF conversion turns out to be one of the defining features of the history of Paris, and it is only on the frontiers of Heaven that we can begin to define what is going on. Conversion is not a problem for a city like London for London is interested in the fabrication of material wealth and has not the slightest interest in ideas. It is too much of a problem for cities in the centre or the east of Europe—places like Berlin or Moscow—where whole populations convert at a dizzying rate to the most absurd philosophies. Compared to them, spiritual conversion in Paris, despite home-grown revolutions and foreign invasions, has always been a rather sedate affair endorsed, as the Prince de Talleyrand, the irreverent Bishop of Autun, once put it, "by a long succession of years, and I would even say by prescription of the centuries."

But there are those lines, and they are often the source of violence: on one side of the line one believes this and on the other side that. The lines may define political attitudes, one side being conservative, the other radical. Or religious beliefs: there are lines that indicate pockets of Protestantism in a sea of Catholicism; there are also lines which separate believers from non-believers. One of the most persistent lines in Paris is on the north side of town separating the city from the suburb; voting habits are determined by it, as are religious attitudes. It has long been a line of violence. With the expansion of the city the line has, over time, gradually moved northwards until reaching, in 1860, its current position. Back in 1860 it was defined by the city's fortifications. It was also reflected in the initial 1895 project for the Paris métro—in the circular line which never got built. Today it is traced by the ring road, the Boulevard Périphérique. The Boulevard Périphérique, particularly

its north side, follows an old line that divides local systems of belief, whose origin goes back to the very beginnings of Christianity in northern Europe.

It is interesting to note that Paris, which would be the first city in Europe to de-Christianize, had also been one of the first cities in northern Europe to convert to Christianity. The old Roman city of Lutetia had developed on the south side of town in what is today the Latin Quarter, while remnants of the Gallic tribe of Parisii, conquered by Julius Caesar in 52 BC, settled to the north of the Seine on that fault line, around Mons Mercurii, or Montmartre. Christianity first spread in the third century AD in that same northern area among the native Gallic people. But the distinction between the two peoples was fast disappearing in the face of a new threat, that of the Germanic invaders who would appear on the north side of town. Christianity would become the bond that held the defenders of old Gallo-Roman Lutetia together, on the north side of town, Heaven.

A pivotal figure in the early conversion of Paris to Christianity was the first bishop of the city, Saint Denis. We know virtually nothing about him beside the fact that he was decapitated by a Roman legionnaire, tradition has it, in the year 272. According to one legend he was the Saint Denis who the Bible tells us was converted by Saint Paul in Athens, which would give him an age of well over 200 at the time he lost his head. Another makes him a missionary of Pope Clement I, which would make him a youthful 150. A third describes him as one of seven missionaries sent in the third century from the Christian community in Rome to evangelize the northern provinces of Gaul—which is the most plausible of the three. Denis and two other missionary priests, Rusticus and Eleutherus, were arrested along with several Christians and brought before the Governor of Lutetia Sisinnius Fesceninus, who demanded that they submit to the authority and religion of the Roman Emperor. The three priests refused. So Fesceninus ordered their execution before the Temple of Mercury, at the summit of Montmartre (the "hill of martyrs") as an example to all the native Gallic people who lived there.

The story at this point enters the realm of fantasy. What we know is largely derived from a thirteenth-century manuscript, Jacques de Voragine's *La Vie des saints*, but this account was almost surely based on a much older oral tale. The legionnaires were apparently impatient; they decapitated their prisoners halfway up the slope at what is now Rue Yvonne-le-Tac, a few paces from the Place des Abbesses. After the execution, Saint Denis miraculously rose up, put his head under his arm and, guided by an angel, continued the walk up the hill. He washed his head in a spring of fresh water and continued his promenade northwards to what is today the town of Saint Denis—on the other side of the Boulevard Périphérique—where he finally fell at the feet of the widow Catulla; from the spot where she buried him sprouted shoots of wheat. At the same site, a century later, Saint Geneviève founded the basilica where all the kings of France from Charles Martel onwards—save three—would be buried.

The sacred nature of Montmartre, the route north, the fertile fields that would feed the city, the link between Christianity and French royalty are all in this tale. So too is the significance of Saint Denis' place of burial, just beyond the frontiers of the city: Saint Denis plants the seed of Christianity outside the city, as did Saint Paul, beyond the reaches of Jerusalem. The universality of Christianity is thereby confirmed. It does make the path of Saint Denis well worth inspecting.

To follow in his footsteps, we really ought to change from the Saint-Germain line No. 4 at Marcadet-Poissonniers, and take line No. 12 to Porte de la Chapelle. But Porte de la Chapelle, despite the ringing name, is a dismal place that will eliminate any thought of Christian sanctity. Two high concrete apartment blocks guard the gate. And a gate it is, blocking one world from another. "Nobody visits the towns on the north side of the *périphérique* these days unless they are unfortunate enough to live there," said a wicked reporter in November 2005 after two Arab youths, fleeing the police, got electrocuted in their hiding hole, a powerful transformer. The news of their deaths spread like fire with fire: every town beyond that urban border— Clichy-sous-Bois, La Courneuve, Bobigny and Saint-Denis—exploded into a three-week auto-da-fé; night was brighter than day.

Those northern towns, across the *périphérique*, can no longer be

called the *ceinture rouge*, the fiefdom of the Communists; the administrative term for this forsaken suburb is "sensitive urban zone," *zone ur-*
baine sensible (ZUS). The two towers at Porte de la Chapelle warn you
that you are approaching a ZUS. Next to one of them is a Supermarché
Alibaba, selling oriental wares. The African women have colourful
headdresses. Old men wear turbans and other exotic garments. Urban
blight is all about. At the bus stop you may see the advertisement for a
live concert by the black gospel singer Frère Clovis Makola—a name
worth noting. At Porte de la Chapelle you may be forgiven if you forget
for a moment that you are in the capital of France.

If it is pleasure you are seeking, you would do better to stay on line
No. 4 until it reaches its terminal at Porte de Clignancourt. Here you
can still get a sense of that urban frontier, while there are some lovely
surprises awaiting you. The crooked old streets by the métro stop ex-
cite curiosity. What goes on in that narrow Passage Penel off the Rue
du Ruisseau? On the corner of Rue Esclangon is a Café Espe run by
Monsieur Ngulu; an African flag is pasted to its window above the
phrase "Ô Nama—chez—Pris et Nov"—which possibly refers to what
is on the menu. Two minutes' walk north, in a Denisian direction across
the frontier of the *périph'*, will take you into the world of the Marché
aux Puces.

Every class of every nation comes here every weekend; it is a genuine
melting pot of peoples. The Marché aux Puces claims to be the largest
flea market in the world. Its origins go back to the Siege of 1870 when
rag pickers set up barracks and tents on the Plaine des Malassis, an
abandoned slab of land between the Fortifications and the first line of
houses of Saint-Ouen, held by the Prussians. The Marché aux Puces
consists of pavilions, each one of them having a name. At the market of
"Malassis" you will find pieces of seventeenth- and eighteenth-century
furniture going at a good price, though you should make a comparison
with the markets of "Vernaison" and "Dauphine." The market of
"Michelet" contains inviting little cafés that serve food to the sound of
live accordion music or of guitars that have the rhythm of Django Rein-
hardt. "Serpette" specializes in *art-nouveau* objects.

As in the *quartier* of Saint-Germain-des-Prés, commerce and religion play with one another on an old urban boundary. Those ethnic barriers, so present in one's mind as one treads today in the steps of Saint Denis, have always been there. The people on one side of the urban boundary—whether it was the Farmers General Wall, Adolphe Thiers' fortifications or the Boulevard Périphérique—have always been different from the people on the other. Those differences go back one and a half thousand years—to the days when the Christian Gallo-Romans faced the invasion of the original barbarians. What happened at that time would affect religious thought in Paris and right across Europe, Africa and the Middle East. And it would leave its mark on those urban lines you cross today.

LUTETIA'S ESCAPE FROM the worst of the barbarian violence owed much to the early Christianization of the city and the fifth-century conversion of Germanic tribes in the northern parts of Gaul. It was around Christmas-time in the year 406 that the most terrifying of the barbarian invasions occurred. Suevi, Vandals, Alani and Burgundians crossed the frozen Rhine near Coblenz and swept across the northern plains in an arc that took them down through Aquitaine and into Spain. Some continued across North Africa and from there mounted operations into southern Italy. In 410 the Emperor Honorius refused the Visigoth Alaric I the right of settlement in Noricum, a province covering roughly today's Austria. Alaric, whose tribe had entered Italy through the Alps, marched on Rome and, for three horrifying days, put the city to pillage and rape. Roman authority was shaken to the core. The sack of the imperial city would inspire Saint Augustine of Hippo to write his most famous work, *The City of God*, which appealed to its readers to regard the spiritual domain of Christ, the city of our hearts, as a higher authority than the toiling, cruel city of men as represented by Rome.

The invasion of 406 was part of a huge movement of peoples across the Eurasian continent that had begun three or four centuries earlier. It may have been caused by a change in the climate, a "little ice age," that can be verified through various odd means of measurement, such as the movements of glaciers or the thickness of the rings on California's bristle cone pine trees. The fact that the River Rhine froze in the winter of 406 at the level of Mainz—never witnessed in the last thousand years—suggests that it must have been mighty cold.

Oxford's polyglot historian Norman Davies has described the pattern of migrations and invasions westwards into Europe in the form of a shunting effect, similar to the way in which a small movement at one end of a train, standing in its shunting yard, propels the last wagon at the other end from its resting-place at great force. The image is convincing. The people just beyond the boundaries, the *limes*, of the Roman Empire were sedentary, like the motionless wagons at the end of a train in its shunting yard. For centuries they had been trading with the cities inside the Empire and cultivating a range of different crops. The frontiers had been relatively calm. Then it all happened: the agrarian Germanic peoples just outside the Empire received the shock of migrants further to the east. Europe would never be the same again.

The massive invasions of 406 and its aftermath created a new, multicultural Gaul. The first thing the agrarian Germans sought was, naturally enough, land to settle. Sarmatians, Quads, Jutes, Burgundians, Herulians, Visigoths, Ostrogoths and Vandals all claimed their patches of territory. The harassed Roman administration promptly divided Gaul into two dioceses and seventeen provinces. There were three Belgiums (the unimaginative Gallo-Roman functionaries called them Belgium I, II and III), two Germanias (similarly I and II), two Aquitaines, four Lyonnaises and two Narbonnaises. Equipped with their iron ploughs the newcomers planted their seeds and taught their neighbouring Gallo-Romans the German technique of crop rotation, which allowed them all to make the most of the cold mud of Gaul. As a consequence, Gaul became not only the most ethnically diversified of regions in the fading Roman Empire, but also its most densely populated.

The Visigoths settled in Spain and Aquitaine, the Burgundians took hold of lands that lay astride the Rivers Saône and Rhône, the Bretons were a Celtic people who were driven out of Britain by the Anglo and Saxon pirates at approximately the same time as the invasion of Gaul in

406. To the south-east, beyond the Alps, there developed the huge new Ostrogoth area of settlement.

Gallo-Roman Paris, or Lutetia, lay on the arc of the invasion, so that it now faced a scattering of Germanic tribal settlements dominated by people called the Franks to the north-east, in current Belgium and the Netherlands. The barbarians never made up the majority of the population; but it was the barbarians who possessed the arms. After Alaric's sack of Rome, the newcomers became increasingly independent-minded. They forbade all Gallo-Romans from bearing arms. Like the defeated Greeks centuries before, the Gallo-Romans were ordered to do the boring administrative work in the conquered territories — because they were the only people who knew how to write. The Germans thus introduced into the Roman Empire a caste system that separated German warriors from Roman functionaries. Gallo-Roman Paris was part of a thin sliver of territory — all that remained of the Roman Empire in Gaul.

In a sense, it was the Roman functionaries who turned out to be the winners in the initial conflict. By the middle of the fifth century nearly all of the warrior elite was Christian. They were Christian, but they were not Catholic — or rather, one should say, not Chalcedonian, after the Council of Chalcedon held in Greece in 425 which affirmed the doctrine of the Holy Trinity: "I believe in one God, the Father Almighty, Maker of Heaven and Earth. And in Jesus Christ, His only Son, our Saviour, Conceived by the Holy Spirit . . ."

Three gods in one! All this was far too complicated for illiterate military commanders to understand, so they adopted the simpler message of the missionary German monk Ulfila, who borrowed his heretical ideas from the Egyptian priest Arius. Arius made the Christian doctrine so much more understandable: since there was only one God, Jesus Christ could not possibly be his equal. Most of the Germanic military caste became Arian, while virtually all the Gallo-Roman churchmen — who administered the provinces and cities of Gaul on behalf of these illiterate soldiers — remained steadfastly Chalcedonian, that is, Catholic.

The whole future of Christianity in Europe stood on this division. Christianity swayed upon a delicate balance between the Trinitarian faith of the educated administrators and the simpler Arian heresy of the powerful warriors. Catholic, Gallo-Roman Lutetia was one of the keys to the plot.

But we know tantalizingly little detail. There are virtually no contemporary documents on this critical moment of transition from the ancient Roman world to the medieval Christian world. Virtually all we do know was passed down to us by word of mouth, through myths, poetry and fables that were only written down centuries—and sometimes a millennium—later. Yet what powerful myths they were! The fifth century is the century of King Arthur, who was probably a Roman commander who stayed in Britain after the departure of the Roman army in 410, the year Rome was sacked by Alaric. The tragic tale of Tristan and Isolde has its origins in the fifth century. It was the fifth-century movements of the Burgundian court along the frontiers of the Empire that gave rise to the tales of Prince Siegfried, Brunhild, Krimhild and Hagen, which were eventually incorporated into the thirteenth-century German epic poem the *Nibelungenlied*. The fifth century was also the age of massive conversions to Christianity, eventually recounted centuries later in the medieval lives of saints. Over time, collective memory adorned these stories with dragons, sea-monsters, fairies, unicorns and angels. It is not reliable history.

All the same, we know more about multicultural Gaul than any other part of the declining Western Roman Empire. The story one can trace reveals the way in which Europe, and Paris, turned Christian. Around Eastertide, 451, there occurred a second major invasion of Gaul, led by Attila the Hun, the "Scourge of God." The Huns, so often identified with the German aggressor in twentieth-century world wars, were not actually German. They have been traced to the Hunnic Empire, destroyed by the Chinese around 35 BC, and they may well have been the cause of the initial collision on the eastern end of Eurasia's train that would send the Germans tumbling into Gaul. Attila crossed the Roman frontier at Metz with an assorted collection of German tribesmen as allies. Metz was flattened, and from there the vast army of horsemen headed straight for Lutetia, where there was absolute panic. The Christian faith of the Parisians (the Parisii) was put to the test—and they passed with flying colours. The year 451 is one of the most heroic moments in the city's history.

The strong voice that united the Catholic Trinitarian Parisians was that of a woman, Geneviève, destined to become patron saint of the city. Geneviève had inherited an immense fortune from her Gallo-Roman father, an administrator of landed estates who lived in Nanterre. Her mother was a Frank. The story is told that as a child she had had a prophetic vision of her religious vocation; right through the second half of the fifth century she directed the military, political and financial affairs of Lutetia, pouring her money into huge building projects, such as that of the basilica of Saint-Denis. She became one of the ablest negotiators of the age, playing one Germanic tribe off against the other. Paris under Geneviève was like an independent kingdom, a small, ordered, Trinitarian kernel of Christian life in a sea of chaos.

The representative of Roman authority—very much on the wane at the time of Attila's invasion—was Aetius, Master of the Cavalry, an honorary title bestowed by Rome. Through Geneviève's good offices, Aetius was able to mount an alliance of Germanic tribesmen equal in strength to Attila's forces. Attila was thus turned back. Outside Châlons his army was cornered on the Catalaunian Plains. It was a battle of the nations, one of the bloodiest in late Roman times, where as many as fifty thousand men on either side fought to the death. Attila was the loser. He fled across the Rhine and led a new army into northern Italy, where, in bed with a piece of female loot, he burst an artery and died in 452. Jealous little Emperor Valentinian III in Rome had Aetius murdered the same year. Roman authority had never looked so petty: in 455 Rome was again sacked, this time by the Vandals. But during all this time the Trinitarian Parisians stood tall, proud of the stunning defeat they had inflicted on Attila at the Catalaunian Plains.

The prestige of Paris and the weakness of Rome obviously had an effect on the balance of power in Gaul: the north, for the first time since Julius Caesar's conquests in the first century BC, had more power than the south. The vacuum left by helpless Rome had to be filled. The powers in the north shifted south. It was that shift south which determined the whole future structure of Christianity—even in the Byzantine east.

The dominant people in northern Gaul were the Franks, who, during the preceding century, had been spreading into Belgium II. The Franks—*Freie Ranken*, literally "free men" but more frequently translated as "wild ferocious men"—gave their name to "France." They were a very special people. They seem to have been a confederation of different tribes. In the fifth century a distinction was still made between the Salian Franks of Belgium II and the Rhenish or Ripuarian Franks who had settled astride the Rhine in the area around Cologne. The Rhenish Franks had fought on the side of Attila on the Catalaunian Plains, and they paid the price; the Salian Franks fought for Aetius and Geneviève, and they reaped their reward.

None of the Franks were Christian. It made them quite distinct from the other Germanic warriors. Even after the war against Attila they continued to worship the old German gods of Wotan and Thor. Would they convert? The question was critical. If the Franks had become, like their German brethren, Arian heretics, the religious history of monotheism in the Western world would have been very different. In all likelihood, the Catholic Trinitarian faith would have disappeared. Islam, a simplification of the theology of one God—reducing Christ incarnate to the status of a prophet—shows certain similarities to the old Arian heresy, which like Islam was tailor-made for a warrior caste. Without the concept of the Holy Trinity, the relationship of Christianity to Islam would have been very different; one can even posit the possibility that the rise of Islam would never have happened at all—for there would have been no need.

But that, of course, is not what happened. The bishops of Gaul, vestiges of a Gallo-Roman aristocracy, far preferred to deal with a pagan power than with armies of Germanic Arian heretics. When Clovis was elected King of the Salian Franks at Tournai in 481, he found himself courted by all the bishops, from southern as well as northern Gaul. "The men who follow me do not wish to abandon their Gods," he is supposed to have stubbornly retorted to the saintly Bishop of Reims, Remi.

All the kings of France trace their ancestry back to Clovis. There are enough books on him to fill a library. And yet we know very little about him. There are no more than half a dozen contemporary documents from his reign of thirty years (481–511). Nine tenths of what has been written about Clovis is derived from the *History of the Franks* by Gregory of Tours, who only began his work in 576, sixty-five years after Clovis's death. The six surviving documents contradict Gregory on several major points, such as the dates of battles and, most significantly, on the place and time of his Christian baptism, which could have occurred at any moment between 496 and 508. In 1996 French Catholics organized a mammoth fifteenth centenary at Reims, attended by Pope John Paul II and the President of the Republic, Jacques Chirac. But nothing could be less certain than either the place or the timing. Those illiterate "Dark Ages" remain for us very dark.

We know next to nothing of his origins. Most of the Arian kings had developed a fairly elaborate genealogy by the end of the fifth century, many of them claiming ancestors, through marriage, among the emperors of Rome. Poor pagan Clovis could pretend to none of this. His real name, in fact, was Chlodweg. Transcribing it into Latin was no simple task; it became Chlodovens, Clodovecus, Hlodevecus and Clotovecus; say these terms aloud and a rich variety of sounds flows forth, from which one may detect the roots of Hlodwig, Lhodovicus, Lodewijk, Ludovicus, Luduinus, Lodoys, Loys and Loïs. It is doubtful that his murderous family ever referred to him as "Loulou," but it is certain that eighteen French kings and even more princes of the line were baptized "Louis" because they claimed the Christian convert Chlodweg to be their ancestor. Even Emperor Napoleon laid such a claim.

Since Clovis had no forebears he did what most kings do in such circumstances: he invented a descent from the gods. Clodion the Hairy— or Chlogion, or Chlodobed—is the first human being to be recorded in the Clovis genealogy, and that only went back to the 440s when Aetius, King of the Romans, referred to him as King of the Franks. The seventh-century group of monkish scribblers, known collectively as "Fredegar," elaborated on the story. They told how his wife used to go to the beach (possibly the Frankish resort of Le Touquet) and enjoy a roll in the sand with a man of her pick. One day a dragon emerged from the waves, cast an eye on this curvaceous young queen and, without so much as a flick of a serpent's tail, possessed her. From this union was born the legendary Mérovée, or Merovech, the grandfather of Clovis and father of all the Merovingian kings.

Absolutely nothing is known about him. The medievalist Michel Rouche holds the plausible thesis that Clodion the Hairy died around 450, for which there is some evidence, and that it was over the division of the Frankish kingdom between brothers that Attila intervened, launching his terrible invasion on Metz in 451. As already noted, the Franks were divided at that time. Merovech could well have fought on the side of Aetius, and it seems that he died, possibly of the same gory cause, at the time the latter was murdered. His son and successor was Childeric, Clovis's father. In the 470s he got into a quarrel with Geneviève of Paris. In a demonstration of strength, he blockaded the city; Geneviève built her own fleet and sailed upriver to Troyes, where she loaded her boats with wheat and, at her own expense, brought the grain back safely to her city, ground it and made the flour into bread, which she distributed free to the Parisians. Geneviève was always the saint, and Childeric's son Clovis, very wisely, would always treat her as such. The link between Catholic Geneviève and pagan Clovis was forged in Frankish iron.

We have no idea what Clovis looked like. His hair must have been long. Julius Caesar referred to the northern half of Gaul as *Gallia Comata*, "Hairy Gaul," because the military commanders of the Germanic tribesmen in those parts wore their hair long as a sign, like Samson, of their strength. Among the Franks the tradition never died. The greatest shame for a Frankish king or prince was to have his head shaven—a ritual Clovis frequently performed before having his rivals put to death, frequently by his own hand. His followers shaved the back and sides of their heads save the crest which they dyed red, like punk rockers. They wore neither moustaches nor beards. They passed on into history the scents of the forest—sweat, blood, onion and beer.

Clovis, elected King in the area that is now Belgium, looked south to the sun and the warmth of the Mediterranean. All the northern kings looked without benevolence upon the power vacuum developing in the south. A game of diplomacy and war was launched at that time which, already, is recognizably European.

Roman power in Gaul had been reduced to Paris and its surroundings—though there were legions of Roman administrators spread throughout Gaul, many of them now leading figures of the Trinitarian Church. Syagrius, the grandson of Aetius, called himself "King of the Romans," a title he justified through a series of campaigns he had fought against the Saxons and Bretons in the area around Angers; he kept a civilized court at Soissons, famous for its arms industry, while remaining on close terms with Geneviève and her Parisians. Paris itself was sandwiched between the pagan Franks to the north and, to the south, the extensive domain of King Euric's Arian Visigoths, who kept their royal court at Toulouse.

The grandest court of the time—the envy of all in Germanic Europe—was that of the Burgundians. But, like many kingdoms in the south, their house was divided. When Chilperic was King the greatest writers of the age used to attend his court at Lyon, including the poet Archbishop Sidonius Apollinaris of Clermont and the future saint, Avit, bishop of Vienne (just south of Lyon). Chilperic may have been an Arian heretic, but his wife, Caretena, and her children, Clothild and Sedeleube, pronounced their creed in the Chalcedonian manner. Caretena, wrote Sidonius Apollinaris, "purged the ears of her husband when they were infected by the poison of insinuations"; her beautiful daughters burned with the faith of Catholic missionaries. Gregory of Tours tells us that it was Gondebaud in Vienne who had his brother Chilperic's throat slit and Caretena thrown down a well; the two pretty Catholic daughters were obliged to live in Gondebaud's new court in Lyon until they eventually moved to Geneva and the court of another murderous uncle, Godgiselus.

"Fredegar" tells how Clothild, the elder of the girls, used to bend down and wash the feet of delighted pilgrims, among them ambassadors sent by Clovis. Their engaging tales, reported to their King, inspired Clovis to demand the hand of fair Clothild, though he was married at the time to a Thuringian princess. The deal was struck and an important alliance was forged in the wedding bed. The pagan king—married to a Catholic Christian and linked, through the good work of his diplomats, to the Catholic saint in Paris—now felt confident enough to begin his march south to sun and civilization.

Besides Visigoths in Toulouse and Burgundians in Lyon, Clovis knew he also had to contend with Theodoric the Great's Ostrogoths, who extended across the whole of northern Italy. Theodoric had built up an alliance with all the other Arian kings in Western Europe. He also represented the crucial Christian link with the important Byzantine Empire to the east, with its emperors at Constantinople.

For a German king, Theodoric was a most civilized man. He had enjoyed the benefit of being held hostage as a child by Zeno in Constantinople, where he learned the Greek and Roman classics, so that he would become one of the few German patrons of writers. Zeno had not appreciated the overthrow in 476 of the last Western Roman emperor, Romulus Augustulus, and so let loose his hostage, learned Theodoric, in northern Italy. A long war of attrition between the two German kings of Italy ended with Odoacer's defeat at Ravenna. How relieved Odoacer felt when he was thereupon invited with all his commanders to a great banquet held by Theodoric. The chance for a little collusion between the clans? Odoacer sat down next to the scholarly Theodoric, who pulled out a dagger and nimbly slit his neighbour's throat—a sign to his followers to slaughter all the other guests. Thus did Theodoric become Great, the new master of Italy and the wise man of Europe.

Theodoric bears some resemblance to Napoleon. After murdering all of Odoacer's men, he arranged a network of conjugal alliances with his German cousins, all of them Arian Christians save pagan Clovis; Theodoric himself married Clovis's sister, Audofleda. Theodoric thus created a ring of Gothic heretics, from the Adriatic to the Atlantic, that left the Catholic bishops of Gaul and the lonely Emperor in Constantinople with the distressing impression that Arian Christianity was triumphant.

Clovis bears a resemblance to Hitler. He was far too astute to arouse the fears of Theodoric's mighty marital network that could be arrayed against him with the snap of a Gothic dagger. He took careful note of the chaos developing in the two southern kingdoms of Gaul— King Euric of the Visigoths died in Toulouse in 484 and his son, Alaric II, had his hands full defending his throne against other claimants; the Burgundians of Lyon were divided by the rivalry between Gondebaud and Godgiselus. In these southern realms, he leaned on the support he managed to get from the Catholic bishops. They were being harassed by their Arian kings, especially those under Alaric the Visigoth, who did not stop at murder. A long missive from Sidonius Apollinaris to the "Lord Pope Remi,"* the Catholic Bishop of Reims and adviser to Clovis, gives an idea of just how flattering these southern churchmen could be. Sidonius Apollinaris and his learned colleagues fell in love with Remi's Latin sermons. "We have learnt most of these works by heart and have transcribed them all" writes the Archbishop of Clermont. "The feeling is unanimous. It has been declared that there are few capable of writing thus. In effect, there are few authors like this, that is to say, none." This sort of praise was the early medieval equivalent of a Nobel Prize from a committee of judges swayed by politics. The glory reflected, naturally enough, upon the sovereign.

Like Hitler, Clovis made his first move not against his main rivals, the Visigoths and the Burgundians to the south, but against his neighbour, the "King of the Romans," Syagrius in Soissons. Soissons, with its rich churches untouched by Attila and factories churning out siege ballistas, shields, swords and axes, was too much of a temptation for a pagan warlord; Syagrius, a Roman without an emperor, was too weak to resist. The last Roman army in Gaul was swiftly crushed outside Soissons and Syagrius took political asylum in Toulouse. But he had overlooked the force behind Theodoric's grand marital alliance, to which Clovis loyally appealed. Honest King Alaric bowed his head and handed Syagrius over, his arms bound, at a checkpoint on the River Loire. Syagrius was promptly thrown into a dungeon where his throat was discreetly cut. Not a single Catholic bishop is recorded as having defended this last Catholic king in Gaul; they were all watching for Clovis's next move.

Clovis moved house to the old Roman palace in Soissons. In a courtyard he assembled all his war booty, collected into neat piles that

---

* All bishops were "popes" in those days. The primacy of Rome over the other bishoprics became a reality only in the eleventh century. See Julia M. H. Smith, *Europe after Rome* (Oxford, 2005), Ch. 8.

were to be distributed to the soldiers in accordance with Germanic custom. Bishop Remi of Reims had noticed that one of his prized porcelain vases was missing; he asked Clovis to have a look in his courtyard and, sure enough, there it was shining like a lantern. Clovis would never displease the Catholic bishops. He demanded that the vase be returned to Remi. The soldier in question, claiming his war rights, smashed the vase with his axe. Clovis, though humiliated, remained silent. A year passed. As Gregory tells the story, it was only at the following spring assembly of warriors when Clovis spied the same soldier. "Nobody is ill-equipped as you," he exclaimed before him. "Your helmet, your sword, your axe, nothing is right," and Clovis seized the man's axe, throwing it to the ground. As the soldier bent to pick it up, Clovis with a swipe from his polished axe sliced the man's head off. "That's what you did to the vase at Soissons!" cried Clovis. His alliance with the Catholic Trinitarian Church was now sealed in blood.

With the defeat of the last Roman authority in Gaul the story becomes hazy. The few surviving documents of the age contradict themselves and the subsequent histories, written by churchmen, are designed to show the providential hand of God at work. They are decorated, like the manuscripts themselves, with miracles and prophetic words worthy of Camelot and other founding myths.

In Gregory's account Clovis is invited by the Franks on the Rhine to stem an invasion of Alemanni. At the foot of the fortress of Tolbiac (or Zülpich, near Cologne), he is cornered by the enemy and he appeals, "Jesus Christ! Thou who art Son of the living God, save me in my distress. If thou givest me the victory, I shall believe in thee, and I will be baptized!" It sounds like Emperor Constantine's sudden conversion on the Milvian Bridge—"In this Cross shalt thou conquer." The battle certainly took place. A letter from Theodoric the Great pleads for Clovis's moderation with the defeated Alemanni; but the letter proves that the battle occurred just before Clovis's great offensive against Alaric's Visigoths in 505 and it makes no reference to either Clovis's conversion or baptism.

There is also a problem of location. Gregory places Clovis's baptism after Tolbiac in Reims, presided over by Remi. Saint Vaast, writing over a century later, elaborates on the King's entry into Reims by having Clovis, first, making a saintly and triumphant tour of Alsace and Lorraine in the company of his Catholic Burgundian spouse Clothild. By the time we get to Hincmar's *Life of Saint Remi*, written in 875, the story has entered the realm of the marvellous, with a dove descending from the skies of Reims, bearing to the King a phial of ointment scented with "the sweetness of heaven." That potent image of the dove descending from Heaven was still used at the last coronation of a French king in Reims, that of Charles X in 1824. And it was in this tradition of a sacred baptism at Reims that the fifteenth centenary was celebrated before representatives of a most Republican government in 1996.

The baptism of France? One could as well say that it was the baptism of the Holy Roman Empire, or of Germany—the whole German line of princes, kings and emperors can be traced back to Clovis. Why not call it, for that matter, the baptism of Europe? European Christian kingship, aligned to the Trinitarian Church, also had its origins in Clovis.

But perhaps the baptism did not take place at Reims. And what evidence is there that it occurred in 496, besides Gregory's tale? One is forgetting the role of Geneviève's Paris in Clovis's subsequent conquest of southern Gaul. Clovis continued to get support from the bishops of Gaul, who were faced with terrible repressions in the south. The elderly Geneviève was not about to abandon her Trinitarian faith or ignore the plight of the Catholic bishops there. Did Geneviève make an appeal to Clovis? In Gregory's account Clovis does make a pilgrimage to Tours, the burial site of Saint Martin, whom many consider the founder of Christianity in Gaul. Several historians have argued that it was here that Clovis was baptized, perhaps in the presence of Geneviève herself. It is plausible. Geneviève was a frequent pilgrim to Tours and, for Clovis, accepting a Catholic baptism would have been the sensible thing to do before setting off for his southern offensive. When Geneviève died around 502 he ordered that a second Parisian

basilica be built where she lay buried—today's Pantheon on the Mon-
tagne Geneviève—and he declared his formal residence to be in Paris.
He and Clothild would eventually be buried in tombs next to that of
Geneviève.

In 498 Clovis launched his first offensive on the Arian south with an
attack on Burgundy. Godgiselus joined his son-in-law by sending troops
in from Savoy. They met outside Dijon, where they inflicted a crushing
defeat on the tyrant Gondebaud, who took refuge in Avignon.
Theodoric, in his Italian kingdom, was beside himself with despair; the
Arian brotherhood was breaking down. He urged his son-in-law, the
Visigoth king, Alaric, to send in troops to save Gondebaud. Clovis, always avoiding the wider conflict, withdrew, leaving Godgiselus and his
followers to be massacred outside Lyon. Clovis then drew up an alliance with Gondebaud, who in a classic piece of barbaric ingratitude,
turned with the Frankish host on Alaric. Theodoric screeched in dismay. "You are both united with me by blood," he wrote to Gondebaud
and Alaric. "Would I want to sacrifice one or the other?" To Clovis he
wrote, "I am astonished that such slight causes can lead you to engage
in a cruel conflict with my son King Alaric. You are both powerful
kings, both in the vigour of life. Do not expose your realms to ruin so
lightly and beware what you will bring upon your fatherlands!"
Theodoric arranged a meeting between Clovis and Alaric the Visigoth
on a raft moored in the middle of the River Loire, near Amboise. It was
not unlike Napoleon's encounter with Tsar Alexander on the River Nie-
man thirteen hundred years later, with the same result. The two sovereigns shook hands and then went to war; ties of blood did not count,
for this was a religious war that pitted an old Arian against the newly
converted Trinitarian king.

There was civil war in Aquitaine in 505. Catholic bishops and
priests were no longer prepared to put up with Alaric's brutalities;
they awaited their saviour, King Clovis. He was welcomed as a liberator in the area around Tours. Clovis prevented his barbarian converts
from pillaging the farms by hanging transgressors from the nearest
trees. But further south the war turned dirty. In the spring campaign

of 507 whole villages were wiped out, women were raped, children were roasted on fires. And accompanying the whole business were the inevitable miracles and marvels: outside Poitiers, a huge halo appeared above the Église Saint-Hilaire; a saintly she-goat showed Clovis the way across the flooded River Vienne. Finally at Vouillé, not far from Poitiers, the armies of Clovis and of Alaric met at close quarters. The battle lasted three hours. The Visigoths scattered and the Franks gave chase; Alaric was cornered in a copse and dealt the mortal blow by Clovis in person.

Things were not going too well for Theodoric himself. He had started his own little war in the Balkans and had driven the new Byzantine emperor, Anastasius, crazy by invading the province of Pannonia II, wiping out a Roman legion in Belgrade on the way. Anastasius riposted by sending a fleet of Byzantine pirates under the command of Counts Romanus and Rusticus to maraud the east coast of Italy. Theodoric was a much diminished man by the time the heralds arrived in his court, in the summer of 508, to announce that the war in Aquitaine was finished, his son-in-law dead.

But how nice all this was for Emperor Anastasius, who realized that Theodoric's Gothic ring of Arians was broken. He immediately packed in a suitcase a purple robe, a crown and a batch of decrees which he sent off to Clovis, declaring him Consul and Patron, the new Constantine! Dressed as a Roman emperor, Clovis, the converted long-haired pagan, went out on the streets of Catholic Tours to receive the cheers of the crowd. The Most Christian Kingdom of the Franks now stretched from Thuringia in central Germany to the Pyrenees.

It did not last long. Within months of his death in 511 the three sons of Clovis were at war over the fragments of land to which they all laid claim; for two and a half centuries the Merovingian kings would expose Gaul, Belgium and Germania to a regime of terror and division. The Capetians eventually pulled Christians together again when they were faced with a new threat from the south, that of Islam.

Clovis's lasting legacy was not a nation, nor even a city. What he left behind was the total destruction of the Arian heresy. The complex Trinity—three persons in one God—was henceforth the defining feature of Christianity. For those who would reduce the figure of Christ to a mere prophet, there would be a long wait until finally, in the seventh century, out of the desert there came that simple message from Islam. Today, Islam and Trinitarian Christianity face each other across the Boulevard Périphérique, where Saint Denis walked north, headless.

7

CHÂTELET–LES HALLES

THE SAD TRUTH about Paris is that it does not have a historical centre. Or to be more accurate, it is a hole in the ground. Just as all roads lead to Rome, so all métro lines will take you eventually to Métro stop No. 7, Châtelet–Les Halles, *"le ventre de Paris,"* the centre of the world as Parisians would have it, and a great big hole in the ground as every métrostopper will notice. It was where the old north–south axis of the long-haul trade met the east–west flow of the Seine, where the foodstuffs for the city were collected for distribution, where the architects and planners drew a natural cross in the soil from which the streets and the underground would derive their shape.

"Châtelet" simply meant the point of exchange; *une halle* is a covered market—a word that, applied to the vast central markets that served Paris, had to be put in the plural. Baron Haussmann designed his whole project for the rebuilding of Paris during the Second Empire from a cross he drew over the Place du Châtelet, confirming once more the centrality of this point in the city, and the centrality of the market. Residents of the area still thought they were at the centre of everything in the 1960s: "Les Halles is the geographical centre of Paris and of the French Republic," said one inhabitant in an official report made in 1968—a perfectly outrageous remark. Yet for people living in the proximity of Victor Baltard's iron and glass pavilions, which housed Les Halles, this kind of comment seemed as natural as the observation that the planets circled the sun. After all, Les Halles were the central marketplace of Paris. And, second, back in 1848 this was the central battleground in the fight to establish the French Republic.

The district of "Les Halles" was vast, extending well beyond the complex of Baltard's glass pavilions. Many of the old buildings and streets that fed off the markets are still there, and they constitute one of the most enchanting parts of Paris. When the new mayor of Paris, Bertrand Delanoë, wanted to show the Queen of England a typical quarter of Paris, he brought her here; Monsieur Duthu and his smiling colleagues at the Pâtissier Stohrer have never stopped speaking of the day, in April 2004, when Queen Elizabeth II walked into their shop to buy a cake. You can spend two days wandering around Rue Montorgueil without exhausting all the treasures it has to offer. But why is it there? All those pâtissiers, the delicatessens, the caterers, the brasseries and the little restaurants are by-products of a huge marketplace that is no longer there. In London, the old pavilions of Covent Garden were preserved. In Paris, where they covered half the district, they were destroyed. The market itself was moved out to Rungis, next to Orly airport, in 1969. In 1971 the demolitions began. Through most of that decade all that was left of the "belly of Paris" was a vast hole in the ground, *le Trou*.

Paris, since the time of the Roman walls, has always been subjected to ambitious urban plans, and change, of course, is the sign of a living city. But in the past, planners—such as those of the cathedrals or those of nineteenth-century theatres, town halls and boulevards—were supported by an army of anonymous artisans who chiselled stone, creating those alluring little details one generally attaches to a work of art; today plans are set in flat concrete. A journey from the underground of Châtelet–Les Halles to the surface brings to the eye that blunt fact.

In the 1980s the "belly of Paris" was turned inside out and upside down. The surface was transformed into a garden, while beneath one's feet there developed the largest underground railway station in the world, transporting over 800,000 souls a day. The station forms the pivot of the largest underground shopping centre in the world, the Forum des Halles, catering every year to 41 million consumers of clothes, handbags, postcards, pens, pocket calculators and laptop computers. There are twenty-three cinemas down there, set in huge concrete cells. Line 1 (following the modern east–west axis) crosses Line 4 (the old north–south axis) here. Line A of the RER, the rapid transit system which stretches into Paris *extra muros*, crosses Lines B and C: heaven help the poor English tourist who arrives at this point from Roissy airport with his heavy bags and a covey of tired children; he has a mile's walking to do down unending tunnels interspersed with three or four flights of concrete staircases. The labyrinth is so vast that the architects who designed it had to name the station after not one, but two places. Indeed, two whole *quartiers*, Les Halles and the north bank of the Seine, were ruined for good by the construction of this den, Paris's new underground crucifix, a calvary of sore feet.

In twenty years the concrete of the métro station has turned a dirty grey; in eight centuries the decorated stones of Saint-Eustache have never ceased to cause marvel. The contrast between ancient and modern is edifying—and not new—Émile Zola made a similar observation on this spot 150 years ago. It was indeed the leitmotiv of his novel *Le Ventre de Paris* which gave this district its nickname.

ZOLA, IN THE summer of 1872, was at an early stage of his research on the novel when he neatly noted down, in a bound exercise book, the view he got of the southern façade of the Église Saint-Eustache: "Rue des Prouvaires, choked: wine merchants, coal merchants, etc.; one can see, beyond the Halles, a porch of Saint-Eustache, two rows of windows at the level of the arch, surmounted by a rose window. Flying arches on both sides." That is exactly the same southern perspective of the church that one has today from the métro station—only we look through bare concrete walls. Zola ran his eyes through a cluttered covered alley framed by cast-iron pillars and glass. It must have been a pretty sight.

Zola's novel would open with a night convoy of wagons carrying vegetables from Nanterre to the central Halles; on their way they pick up Florent, a refugee from the penal colony of Cayenne, who has fallen, starving and exhausted, by the wayside just beyond the Pont de Neuilly. Half conscious, Florent is carried into the "belly of Paris," to the Pointe Saint-Eustache—just a few hundred yards from where he was arrested after the shooting on the Rue Montmartre, which had followed Napoleon III's *coup d'état* of 2 December 1851. But the place, he discovers, has been entirely transformed. The historical centre of Paris has disappeared. The old buildings have been knocked down. The streets have gone. Replacing them are "gigantic pavilions whose roofs, superimposed on each other, seemed to him to grow, to stretch out, to lose themselves in a hazy dust of glimmering light." Through slim Fish-bone pillars of iron he looks up, in the dawn's greyness, to perceive "the luminous face of Saint-Eustache," last vestige of the Middle Ages. So the mid-nineteenth century was another age like ours, a time of destruction and transformation.

On 2 June 1872 Zola had had lunch with the famous critic and novelist Edmond de Goncourt. De Goncourt noted in his diary that Zola, who was then thirty-two, looked "weak and nervy." Zola described over lunch the punishing method he had developed for writing "a novel on the Halles, an attempt to paint the plump people of this world." Every day he worked from 9 to 12.30 and from 3 to 8 p.m. First he drew up an *ébauche*, or draft, then he would make detailed notes on location—spending entire nights, as well as days, walking around the Halles—and only after a full review of the characters and their habitat would he start to write his novel. "The general idea is: the belly,—*Le Ventre de Paris*, Les Halles . . . —the belly of humanity and by extension the governing bourgeoisie, chewing and ruminating, sleeping it off, in peace with its pleasures and its commonplace honesty." At the time Zola spoke to de Goncourt, he was only four years into his vast Rougon-Macquart cycle, an epic on social and political life under the Second Empire which he would complete twenty-five years later.

Thus it was a young Zola who wrote *Le Ventre*, and this shows. Zola gets his historical facts wrong, some of the characters are a little artificial and it takes him too long to get the plot moving. Zola does not reach the grandeur of the later novels, such as *Germinal* on the northern coal mines, or *La Terre* set in the Beauce. But that is not the point. What we find in *Le Ventre* is a detailed portrayal of life in the Halles, the belly and the heart of Paris—the sights, the crowds, the sounds and the smells in and around Baltard's famous pavilions shortly after they were set up. *Le Ventre de Paris* is a priceless historical document.

When Zola takes you into a wine merchant's bar on Rue Rambuteau you are stifled by the smell of pipe smoke and gas lamps—something you could not imagine today without Zola as your guide. When you come out of the métro at the Porte du Jour you may reflect that this was the former Pointe Saint-Eustache where 150 years ago the wagons lined up to deliver their goods to the central market. We know the noise was deafening as the goods were unloaded, that the live fowl were packed in square baskets, the dead fowl in deep beds of feather, while whole calf carcasses were wrapped in tablecloths and laid out like children in baskets . . .

Baskets and more wicker baskets—there was barely a place to stand. Women carried baskets piled high on their heads. We know the "songs of the markets"—"*Madame, madame, venez me voir, à deux sous mon petit tas!*" "*Mouron pour les p'tits oiseaux! Mouron pour les p'tits oiseaux!*"— and if we are not aware that *mouron* is French for "chickweed" it doesn't matter very much. The fruit sales girl at her stand had plums wrapped in paper and laid out on flat baskets. She and her fruit gave off a whiff of orchards, while the old saleswoman next to her had pears that looked like sagging breasts and apricots with the cadaverous yellow flesh of a witch; fortunately the Allée des Fleurs lay just behind her. The new Halles of the mid-nineteenth century seemed like "a huge modern machine, a gigantic metal stomach, a people's furnace of digestion, bolted down and riveted." And we know all that thanks to Zola.

Zola faced vicious criticism in the nineteenth-century press for his graphic details, which his detractors said did not ennoble human beings but portrayed them rather as animals. Zola always retorted that they *were* animals. "You put man in the brain, I put him in all his organs," he wrote in 1885 to one of his most persistent grousers, the great literary critic Jules Lemaître. "You isolate man from nature, I do not see him without the soil from which he comes and to which he returns. I feel him stretching out everywhere, into his being and beyond his being, into the animal of which he is the brother, into the plant, into the stone." Zola's characters grew out of their environment; the slightest detail mattered, often told in a lurid manner that shocked. Zola, not surprisingly, never achieved his lifelong ambition to be elected to the Académie Française.

He was not at all romantic about Les Halles. His fascination in the natural environment led him to the study of architecture and, in the case of Les Halles, to the stark contrasts between ancient and modern styles of building. Zola was an unhesitant supporter of the modern. The character of Claude Lantier, a visionary painter, takes the positive view on contemporary art; he looks up at the face of the Église Saint-Eustache through the delicate cast-iron work of Baltard's pavilions and exclaims, "Iron will kill stone!" And he marvels. Enough of these whingers who claim industry kills poetry; look at the modern beauty of those pavilions! Today, standing at the same spot, one can appreciate how reinforced concrete kills iron.

Zola wanted to create, with *Le Ventre*, a modern, contemporary version of Hugo's *Notre Dame de Paris* (*The Hunchback of Notre Dame*). As the Gothic cathedral was the central feature of Hugo's celebrated novel, so would the iron pavilions be central to *Le Ventre*. Zola's Marjolin, found in a pile of cabbage leaves, would play the role of Hugo's Quasimodo. Marjolin grows up in the pavilions of the Halles as they are being constructed—thus providing Zola, to the delight of his readers, ample opportunity to explore every corner of the site, including its secret cellars, which few could describe today. In one of the pivotal scenes of the book the beast in Marjolin gets the better of him; he attempts, in the "black air" of the chicken cellars, to rape the curvaceous Lisa, who keeps a *charcuterie*—or delicatessen—on the other side of Rue Rambuteau. Zola sets his scene up with dead geese and rabbits hanging from the brick vaults, burning gas lamps that give off no light, and the rumbling sound of the market above; it is the thick alkaline odour of guano and rabbit urine that breaks Marjolin's timidity and causes him to "throw Lisa down with the force of a bull." Through the cellar's windows Lisa can hear the sound of feet passing by upon the covered, cobblestone street outside. The scene, predictably, offended many nineteenth-century readers.

Claude Lantier was inspired by Zola's childhood friend Paul Cézanne. Zola mixed with the Impressionists—Édouard Manet, Gustave Courbet and Claude Monet—at the Café Guerbois in the rural reaches of Les Batignolles before they were known as Impressionists.

Much of the book reads like an Impressionist manifesto. But Claude's remarks are more contemporary still; they put one in mind of a twentieth-century British artist much appreciated in Paris, Francis Bacon. Bacon was obsessed with meat dripping red. So was Lantier. It is, in fact, astonishing just how much of Zola's prose on Les Halles portends Bacon. Zola has Claude exploring the butcher's pavilion right opposite the Église Saint-Eustache, an area now converted into a garden of trellises, arcades and arbour pathways: around the pavilion flowed streams of blood into which Claude dipped his feet. At the tripe stands he saw packets of mutton trotters unwrapped, calf tongues showing the points where they had been torn from the throat, beef hearts hanging like bells; the great baskets of sheep's heads conjured up the thought of an interminable line of sheep waiting their turn at a guillotine. But the real horror was in the cellars where, in the thick atmosphere of a charnel house, the butchers broke open the sheep heads with mallets. Nineteenth-century readers were not accustomed to this kind of description, almost commonplace in our own literature.

Today's glass and steel Pavillon des Arts stands where Baltard's Pavillon de la Marée, the fish market, once stood. Florent, the hero of the novel, finds a job as a government inspector of the pavilion. Every day he walks between the *carreaux* where the fish are laid out, the glass roof above him creating a dusky light, and he hears the drone of the *criées* — the many auctions — along with the distant sound of bells. Every morning there are the same stinking puffs of air, the same spoilt breath of the ocean which blows around him "with great waves of nausea" (one might think of Sartre's famous novel, or of Süskind's more recent *Perfume*). A slight dizziness, a vague weariness. An anxiety rises in him which turns into "vivid over-excitement of the nerves." The 1968 report on popular opinion in the district of the Halles showed that there was not too much praise for this reeking market: "It is invasive, dirty, noisy, and inimical to other activities." Talk to the people who remember it. "The Halles were a bit sinister, you know," one old lady told me.

In the novel, Zola's fugitive from Cayenne discovers that his brother has opened a *charcuterie* on the north side of Rue Rambuteau, just opposite La Marée. The brother and his wife, Lisa, offer him a *chambre de bonne*, under the roof, on the fifth floor. Florent finds his job in La Marée and at night, unable to sleep, looks across Rue Rambuteau at Baltard's glass roofs. But Florent was not the only person looking out from his window. In *Le Ventre* there are always other eyes spying across the streets and the alleys, and they would combine and condemn Florent; the whole *quartier* of the Halles would in the end forge an alliance of spies, renegades and turncoats that would send him back to *le bagne*, the penal colony.

Zola incorporated the houses, the streets and the pavilions into his unfolding drama. The novel is so graphic because it was founded on a geographical reality, minutely observed by the author. When a room, a building or a street reappears in the novel for a second or third time, one knows that something significant is about to happen.

One critical frontier—in the novel, in historical reality and so it remains today—is Rue Rambuteau. It was named after a Prefect of Paris, the Comte de Rambuteau, who, in 1841, knocked a forty-foot-wide thoroughfare across the medieval city centre from the Église Saint-Eustache to the edge of the Marais; it thus presaged Baron Haussmann's massive transformations a decade later. During the 1850s, in which the novel is set, Baltard's pavilions wiped out the buildings on the south side of the road so that Rue Rambuteau became the dividing line between *Vieux Paris*, or old Paris, and Les Halles, between ancient and modern. And that is exactly what one sees there today. On the south side is the contemporary Forum des Halles, with its shopping bazaar and cinemas; on the north side the older Paris, with its food shops, restaurants and countless little treasures awaiting the visitor.

Zola described Rue Rambuteau as teeming with wagons before dawn during the moment of deliveries; the wagons and horses were then parked in the courtyards of the old houses to the north. The yard Zola described next to the Compas d'Or, on Rue Montorgueil, can still be seen, though the horse manure and clusters of chickens have gone. After the *criées*, which lasted in Zola's day until ten or eleven in the morning, an army of street sweepers moved down Rue Rambuteau to clean up the mess; the smell was appalling. Eyes look out from each side of the street. It was from here, on the corner of Rue Rambuteau and Rue Pirouette, that La Belle Lisa—Florent's sister-in-law—stared across the road, from her high counter in the *charcuterie*, into the interior of the Pavillon de la Marée. From inside that pavilion her gaze is returned, from the fishmonger's *banc*, or stand, by that of her great rival, La Belle Normande; it penetrates every floor of the *charcuterie*. La Belle Normande has romantic intentions on Florent. Other eyes peer, peep and poke across the natural barrier of Rue Rambuteau. High in an old house on Rue Pirouette, through light white curtains, the old spinster and worst gossip of the *quartier*, Mademoiselle Saget, is keeping watch.

"Does Rue Pirouette still exist?" asked Florent when he arrived, dazed by the presence of the new Halles. It did then, but you won't find it today. The underground motor expressway that extends from Rue de Turbigo put paid to that. However, the neighbouring Rue Mondétour is still there: inside the shoe shop on the corner there sits at a high polished zinc counter a striking blonde saleswoman staring out across the street—like Lisa, she can tell you a thing or two about Les Halles. Lisa's *charcuterie* was described as a "smiling place of live colours singing amidst the whiteness of its marble." It was typical of what you could find on the north side of Rue Rambuteau, and can still find today.

Many of the little alleys Zola described are still there. The spying endured and the rumour-mongering developed, and so the little alleys took on a sinister Parisian tone. Behind Lisa's shop there ran a narrow dark corridor just out of view of the pavilions; once one had stepped into it the only way out was through the back entrance of the shop: a mousetrap.

From the outset Florent, worried and nauseous, has vague premonitions of the trap closing him into the iron belly of Paris. It was one of the abiding features of the district which contributed mightily to the decision, one hundred years later, to pull those pavilions down: inhabitants of the area wanted to "get out"; they felt trapped. The moment Florent places a foot in Les Halles he wants to run away. But he discovers that the wagons have blocked the exit at the Pointe de Saint-Eustache; a potato market creates a barrier on Rue Pierre-Lescot; he follows Rue Rambuteau as far as Boulevard de Sébastopol only to come up against a great pile of carpets and huge handcarts; so he turns back to Rue Saint-Denis where he runs into a "deluge of cabbages." All the way to Rue de Rivoli and to the Hôtel de Ville there are unending queues of wheels and bridled animals lost amid the chaos of merchandise they carry. Other carts slowly roll their way back to the suburbs.

That is eventually what Florent succeeds in doing. He retreats with one of the carts to the suburbs. For one glorious day, as the gossiping and plotting within the Halles reaches a fever pitch, Florent, Claude the painter and Madame François, a market gardener, drive out to Nanterre, a rural suburb in those days. Madame François fills her cart up with old cabbage leaves from the pavilion rubbish dumps and takes the reins; Florent and Claude lie down on the leaves and discuss life. They follow the same route out of "rogue Paris"—as Madame François describes it—that Florent had taken into the city when a fugitive one year before. At the Arc de Triomphe, where "the winds blow up the avenues in immense gusts," Florent sits up to inhale the first odours of grass which arrive from the fortifications. (Try that today.) The Halles, which he had left in the morning, now appear to him as a vast ossuary, a "place of death," dominated by the smells of decomposition. The countryside, on the other hand, breathes life. In Nanterre, that May, he helps distribute the green manure on the soil. In the buzz of the insects and the cracking and sighs of the ground he hears the birth and growth of another generation of cabbages, turnips and carrots, the hum of "death repaired."

Here was the critical message of life and death that would be so essential in the works of Zola, the theme of urban entrapment contrasted to rural freedom. It upset traditionalists, who were shocked by the brutality in Zola's portrayals of daily life, and attracted plenty of criticism from the radicals, who preferred the comfortable, familiar coordinates of class analysis in a writer like Balzac; both camps thought Zola was getting too "biological." Yet all his work was based on minute observation of what he saw about him and, particularly in his depiction of life in Les Halles, contained a heavy dose of reality: the district of Les Halles is a harrowing, if in many ways beautiful, place.

After his day in Nanterre, Florent must return to the belly of Paris and cross that street, Rue Rambuteau, every day. It is at this moment of return that Claude presents his analysis of the human struggle in Paris not as one of social class but as one between the *Gras* and the *Maigres*, between the Fat, "enormous to the point of bursting, who sit down to their piggish dishes in the evening," and the Skinny, "bent by hunger, who watch from the streets with the look of an envious beanpole." A recent English edition of Zola's novel is given the title *The Fat and the Thin*—not entirely without reason. What shocked Zola at the Halles in the 1860s was the juxtaposition of a new consumer society side by side with blue, gaunt poverty, a poverty one does not see today. That, along with the feeling of entrapment, is why those pavilions went.

Claude never gets drawn into Florent's politics of the "revenge of the Skinny." He warns Florent against it, for Florent is surrounded by the Fat: La Belle Lisa, who will plot to expel Florent from her house because he threatens her tranquillity and earned wealth; La Belle Normande, who will eventually listen to her mother's advice that Florent was "*un grand maigre*," probably a murderer, so that she will instead marry Monsieur Lebigre, the wine merchant on Rue Pirouette; and in fact most of Florent's revolutionary friends are from among the "Fat," whose financial interests win out in the end. The Fat are found on both sides of Rue Rambuteau. They populate the stands, the auction markets and the stinking cellars. They are the profiteers of the food chain, the retailers, both large and small. They dominate the ancillary trades on the north side of Rue Rambuteau; they sell the sausages and the *andouillettes*; they collect together the leftovers—broken sugar almonds, shattered sweet chestnuts, sweets not fit to be sold in jars—and flog them off in paper cones for a sou. In the mid-nineteenth century there was a popular item called *godiveaux*, meat balls made up of minced calf innards, beef kidneys and egg: the little Cadine, a prefiguration of Zola's Nana, thinks they look delicious, she puts one in her mouth and pulls a terrible face. There are cheeses in Zola's novel—the aniseed-flavoured *géromé* that "let off such a stench that flies dropped dead around its box," or the *limbourg* that had a "brusque groan . . . like a death rattle"—which you would be lucky to find in a Parisian shop today, even on Rue Montorgueil.

Today Zola could be taken to task by the "politically correct" for his mockery of the Fat. But this would be to miss the point entirely. What Zola is describing is the rapid development of a consumer society in the midst of arch-poverty. He describes what it looked like and felt like in the marketing heart of Paris. The manufacture and the tasting of the *boudin*, the black-pudding sausage, is perhaps Zola's most telling image of the way the Fat tormented the Skinny, the new rich tyrannizing the old poor. Lisa's *charcuterie*, we are told, produced most of its merchandise itself, apart from a few *terrines*, *rillettes* and cheeses that they acquired from "the most famous houses" in Paris. For the fabrication of *boudin*, everyone would gather in the large kitchen and tell stories to the noise of the cooking pots and mincers.

Using this as a setting, Zola builds up a scene of tragi-comic contrasts that typified his writing. Auguste, an assistant who will betray Florent, brings in two pitchers of pigs' blood which he has beaten into a cream. "Ah, the *boudin* is going to be good!" he exclaims — "*Le boudin sera bon!*" Round little Pauline takes the fat yellow cat Mouton on to her crossed puffy legs, looks up at a gaunt Florent and asks him to tell "the story of the man who was eaten by beasts." The skinny Florent tells the story of his own escape from Devil's Island, a story that Zola had in fact drawn from the escape, recounted in a popular autobiographical account, of Charles Delescluze, a leading figure of the Paris Commune, who was shot during the "Bloody Week" of May 1871. As the drama of Florent's story amplifies, so do the smells of the *boudin*: "Once upon a time . . ." — the brother adds the onions; Florent describes the prisoners" disgusting food — "Auguste, pass the lard," interrupts the brother; and so on. There are critical reactions to the story: Lisa cannot hide her disgust, convinced that "honest" men would never allow themselves to stoop to such humiliation; little Pauline sinks into "wondrous sleep." When Florent ends the story with his hero starving but still alive, his brother proudly announces: "*Il est bon, aujourd'hui, le boudin.*"

At the publication of *Le Ventre de Paris* in 1873 there was outrage over the graphic "bestiality" of Zola's descriptions. Paul Bourget, in the respected *Revue des Deux Mondes*, claimed that the author was somebody for whom the "interior world did not exist"; all his scenes "end up with sensual comparisons that revolt one"; there was "never a word that derived from the soul, which attested to the presence of thought." The conservative *Le Pays* reported that Citizen Zola lived in "immorality" and "sadism." More than just vicious comment was involved in the reaction; recent research has revealed that the government opened a police dossier on Zola.

The malevolence of the commentary would follow Zola for the rest of his life and beyond. In the 1930s the Hungarian critic Georg Lukacs condemned him for favouring physiological differences in his characters over Marxist distinctions in social class—and Marxists have rarely had a kind word for Zola since. Zola's detailed descriptions of his settings and the physiognomy of his characters were certainly designed to shock and move his readers. Many of the descriptions in his work were indeed bestial, though it is unjust to omit what is stirring and ennobling about them, too.

He was a precursor. Zola's evocation of the animal nature of man preceded the popularization of Darwin in France by a decade; some passages on the abuse of animals in *Le Ventre* can put one in mind of George Orwell's *Animal Farm*. The dynamism of Zola's novel is derived from dramatic, often violent, contrasts. The massacre of hundreds of pigeons in the cellar of the Pavillon des Volailles is preceded by a description of doves that Florent notices in the Tuileries Garden. Shortly after the brutal scene in the Pavillon des Volailles, Florent is arrested in Lisa's *charcuterie*; but not before he has released a finch he had picked up, wounded, on the floor of the Halles. He lets the bird fly through his fifth-floor window into the sky, opened up by the demolitions: the bird flits across Rue Rambuteau to land, for a moment, on the Pavillon de la Marée before it takes wing again, disappearing over the grey glass roofs in the direction of the Square des Innocents. As he is taken away by police, Florent hears his brother, unaware of his arrest, announce in the kitchen: *"Ah! Sapristi, le boudin sera bon . . . "*

For anyone looking at this novel as a historical source, the most striking thing about Zola's confrontation of the *Gras* with the *Maigres* is that it is founded on a kind of poverty unknown to us today in the West. Nowadays it is the poor who tend to be fat, while the rich are so slim. To be sure, it is still an assembly of "marginals" that collects by the Fontaine des Innocents, former site of the medieval charnel house and now Paris's equivalent of Piccadilly Circus. Many of the drug addicts there today are immigrants: in Zola's day they had travelled from the provinces. Hang around for a while and you are bound to see the police arrest someone, just as Zola would have witnessed 150 years ago. The neighbouring pavilion of butter, egg and cheeses has disappeared, as has the crooked Restaurant de Barratte, which so fascinated Zola. So, more importantly, has the gnawing poverty which Zola described in such detail. On two sides of the Square des Innocents there was a long, semicircular row of benches placed end to end. To escape their stifling hovels on the narrow neighbouring streets, the poor gathered here. Shivery old women with crumpled bonnets repaired rags that they pulled out of little baskets; the bareheaded younger women, their skirts poorly tied up, chattered with their neighbours— Zola had thin Mademoiselle Saget here receiving and spreading gossip. There were suspicious men wearing worn-out black hats. In the neighbouring alleys and along the Rue Saint-Denis hordes of ragged brats dragged cars without wheels that were filled with sand. There was worse to be seen in the Pavillon de Beurre, close by. On the side of Rue Berger, behind the inspectors' bureaux, were what were politely called the *bancs* of cooked meats. Every morning little closed cars, looking like boxes lined with zinc and with closed, cellar-like windows, drove up to the pavilion, having collected the leftovers of the preceding evening's feasts in the city's restaurants, embassies and ministries. Dishes of greasy meat, mangled fillets of game, the heads and tails of fish, along with cold fried vegetables were prepared in the cellars and then sold upstairs at the stands for three and five sous. Queues of small wage earners and down-and-outs—the *meurts-de-faim* of Paris— formed in the morning chill to sniff at the greasy plates which had the odour of an unwashed kitchen sink.

Such poverty endured. Old people remember it. Talk to some of the elderly residents sitting in the cafés and brasseries of pretty Rue Montorgueil. The pavilions were pulled down by people who wanted to say good-bye to all that and let the new generations live. That is why there is no historical heartland in Paris; the local residents had had enough of it. In its place has grown up pretty Rue Montorgueil.

ZOLA AND HIS wife died, asphyxiated by an open fireplace in their home in Médan, on the night of 28–29 September 1902. It is possible that they were murdered. In the early 1950s a businessman is said to have admitted to a journalist that he had stuffed the chimney. Over the last years of his life Zola had received a number of death threats.

The Rougon-Macquart novels had become increasingly popular, and increasingly contested, too. Like his artist hero Claude Lantier, Zola had kept his distance from politics, simply painting with words the poverty he saw in the streets of Paris, in the coal mines of the north, in the flat rural landscape of the Beauce. But his story of a refugee from Devil's Island, victim of injustice, came back to haunt him in the last years of his life. He learned, in the winter of 1897–98, that a certain Captain Alfred Dreyfus had been the victim of a miscarriage of justice. A righteous fury, which he had never known before, took hold of Émile Zola; in January 1898 he published in Georges Clemenceau's *Aurore* his article "*J'accuse.*" Why should a famous writer put at risk his fortune and his reputation for the sake of a Jewish officer accused of treason? "I would not have been able to live," he said.

It is remarkable how the language Zola employed to counter the anti-Semitic campaign of the anti-Dreyfusards so resembled the language of Zola in his *Ventre de Paris*. If there were a single ideal behind his article "*J'accuse*"—which would spark off the whole Dreyfus Affair—it was not one of class or of race: it was the struggle of life against the forces of death. It was the ideal Florent realized when out in rural Nanterre. "Death to the Jews! Death to Dreyfus! Death to Zola!" cried the dockers at Nantes, the workers of Rennes and of Marseille; effigies of Zola were hanged in Moulins, Montpellier, Marmande and Angoulême. "France saved from death by education," scribbled Zola on a piece of paper a few days before he died.

PORTE DE
LA VILLETTE

NO MOVIE DIRECTOR has yet been tempted to make a film of Zola's *Ventre de Paris*, which is surprising; it is one of the founding legends of Parisian identity and the novel easily passes David Lean's minimum test of twenty good scenes. The dreamlike colours and shades created by Baltard's glass and ironwork pavilions have, nevertheless, been the scene of many works for the cinema, the most memorable perhaps being Marcel L'Herbier's haunting wartime film, *La Nuit fantastique*. After they pulled down the butcher's pavilion in 1973, Marco Ferreri used the heaps of dirt left in *le Trou* as a setting for his *Touche pas la femme blanche*, a film about Custer's last stand. Cameras and crews descended into the controversial "hole," Marcello Mastroianni was given the role of General Custer, while Michel Piccoli, Alain Cuny and Serge Reggiani played the role of the Indians. The film was a great success: Parisians love Westerns—many drive down to the Camargue, near Marseille, to play at cowboys and Indians; the richer ones will spend a season in Wyoming riding the range. The métrostopper fortunately doesn't have to go this far. Just take Line 7 out to Porte de la Villette, where the most extraordinary Parisian cowboy story awaits him.

Where did all that meat, piled so grotesquely high in Les Halles, come from? The slaughterhouses of La Villette. In the nineteenth century the cattle were brought here in droves and the men who slaughtered them were as cruel and tough as any cowhand in the Far West. Their greatest hero had been, before he turned up in their pavilions, "the most celebrated and most shot-at man in the history of Dakota Territory," as his American biographer has put it; in the U.S. press of the 1880s he was known as the "Emperor of the Bad Lands." But he was also a Parisian, an aristocrat of royal lineage at that—and he would end his life as an uncompromising racist. When the Marquis de Morès came back to Paris he dressed up those rough butchers of La Villette in purple shirts and ten-gallon hats: "Morès and Friends" were, for a brief and disquieting moment in French history, a political force that mattered.

When they knocked down the old slaughterhouses in the 1960s President Charles de Gaulle ordered the creation of new ones; they would be the largest, the cleanest and the most efficient *abattoirs* in the world, the pride of *la Grande Nation*, something to compare with the passenger liner *Le France* or the supersonic passenger jet *La Concorde*. But the project got lost in a jungle of big deals and corruption and, instead, the powers-that-be decided—as they frequently do when confronted with a large hole in an urban space—to create a "cultural centre." Amazingly it works. It is one of the most popular corners of Paris. It was late in June 1896, when news spread through the pavilions that the Marquis de Morès had been killed; he had been felled by a bullet in the side and another in the neck after facing off, with his Colt .45, fifty desert bandits of the Tuareg and Chambaa tribes in southern Algeria. One Sunday, the following July, the Friends of Morès in cowboy outfits marched down from La Villette to the Gare de Lyon, where they were joined by the coach drivers of Grenelle, Paul Déroulède's League of Patriots, the Napoleonic Imperialist Committee, the Union of Socialist and Revisionist Patriots and a host of other small-time employees and workers of the eastern *faubourgs* in a procession to Notre Dame Cathedral, draped for the occasion in black cloth. Representatives of the Republican government were also present at the funeral ceremony. Beethoven's *Sanctus* and Fauré's *Pie Jesu* were sung by a large chorus to the accompaniment of the cathedral's grand organ. Then the coffin was carried across the Pont Saint-Martin to the Montmartre Cemetery, where a crowd of over 100,000 had gathered—one of the largest funerals of the nineteenth century. Many in the crowd wore the blue carnations of the Royalists; it was the butcher Friends who formed the long guard of honour. "One word sums up this life: Devotion. One word explains this death: the need for Sacrifice," said Édouard Drumont, editor of *La Libre Parole*. "His love of France, his *élan*—the highest of

French virtues—and his chivalry were the qualities of de Morès, for which we loved him," said Maurice Barrès of the Académie Française. Devotion, sacrifice, *élan* and chivalry neatly summed up the values espoused by this thirty-eight-year-old Parisian cowboy, gunned down in the Algerian desert.

Just as at Les Halles, it is extraordinary how much of the Marquis de Morès's nineteenth-century world one can uncover at La Villette. That octagonal stone building to your right, as you emerge from the métro, is where the slaughterhouses' veterinarians used to have their office in the 1890s. The scientific-musical park is scattered with "madnesses" or *folies—folies du théâtre, folie café, folie du canal*, even an *éclat de folie*. The first you will notice is the *folie horloge*, an ugly contemporary red iron structure on top of which is a nineteenth-century stone clock: that clock used to chime out the opening and closing hours of Paris's slaughterhouses. In the concrete wall opposite you will find the list of over a hundred butchers *morts pour la France* in 1914–18; and a long list of those tortured and who died for France under the Nazis. Stop for a while on the Boulevard Macdonald—named after one of Napoleon's generals, not the fast food chain—and look at the line of eating palaces on the opposite side of the street: the beef restaurants were there in de Morès's day. To the north you can see the *périphérique* on stilts: the cars rush by today where, in the 1890s, the steam trains for Strasbourg shunted out. Just to the north were the fortifications—and you can get a very good idea of what they looked like in the nearby Fort d'Aubervilliers. Aubervilliers, beyond the *périph'*, is another Communist fiefdom, which, like Saint-Denis, Saint-Ouen, Clichy and Courbevoie, houses people from the Third and Fourth Worlds: you lock car doors when you pass through here.

Yet pass through you must. There is something special about neighbouring Aubervilliers which points to the cause of violence in the cowboy slaughterhouses of La Villette a hundred years ago. Between Avenue Victor Hugo and Rue de la Haie-Coq, on the west side of the suburb, are rows and rows of what look like warehouses selling wholesale textiles, clocks, toys, shoes, underwear, jewellery—anything you can think of. They are the *solderies* of France, an industry which developed in the

1970s and turned this part of Aubervilliers into what may justly be described as the dustbin of the world. The products of virtually every failed industry in Western Europe and beyond, of every unwanted surplus, end up here. The principal dealers, known as *soldeurs*, buy up these rejected goods—if today it is leather boots, tomorrow it could be computers—at something less than ten per cent of the wholesale price and flog them off to whatever big buyer they can find. The *soldeurs* never commit themselves to a written contract; all their deals are made by word of mouth and a handshake.

In the 1970s the majority of *soldeurs* were Jewish immigrants from North Africa; today they are being replaced by the Chinese. As always in Paris, an old historical continuity is working its way through here, in this violent little suburban corner; though the *solderies* may be a new industry, they did not spring from nothing. This was the site of the Entrepôts Généraux de Paris, which, at the head of the Canal de l'Ourcq, used to buy up as cheaply as they could the factory produce of Paris and the provinces and then sell it off as expensively as they could to the big department stores in the capital. Good fast deals could be made with the neighbouring slaughterers, who began to resent the low prices that the *commissionnaires*, or middle men, of Aubervilliers paid. Those deals were always struck by word of mouth and a handshake; no contract was ever signed. De Morès became the hero of the meat slaughterers of La Villette by promising to undercut the undercutters, the *commissionnaires*, the vast majority of whom were Jews.

It was a whole theory, a whole programme, that had evolved out of de Morès's short but extraordinary life. Nothing had ever been typical about it. He was not even a typical French aristocrat. His Spanish ancestors, knights of the realm, had participated in the conquest of Sardinia in 1322 and, in return for their gallantry, received the Sardinian marquisates of Montemaggiore and Mores. In the 1820s de Morès's grandfather had participated in a failed Sardinian *coup d'état* and lost all his properties, so he left for France, where he married a descendant of the first French Bourbon king, Henri IV. Their son made another brilliant marriage, with a family that had conquered Algeria for France, and it was from this noble union that there was born, on 14 June 1858 in the exclusive faubourg de Saint-Germain, the boy who could claim to have royalty in his blood in addition to a very long name: Antoine Amédée Marie Vincent Manca de Villombrosa, the Marquis de Morès et de Montemaggiore. His friends called him Antoine. A childhood photograph shows him with a gun in his hand.

A turbulent child, his parents entrusted him to one of the toughest tutors of the French Riviera, where they had taken up residence in the 1860s. The Abbé Raquin had Antoine speaking English, German and Italian before he was ten, and infused him at the same time with a love of the main tenets of Catholic Christianity. At the Collège Stanislas in Cannes he defended the weak and was the terror of the strong, over whom he towered. He graduated from the officer training school of Saint-Cyr when twenty-one—a handsome man of six foot with curly black hair, dark eyes and slightly hooded, Asiatic eyes. He already wore what would be his signature in the Far West and the pavilions of La Villette, a black moustache with upward turning, needle-point waxed tips.

Saint-Cyr's class of 1879 included Philippe Pétain, the future hero of Verdun, the future anti-hero of Nazi-occupied France—but at the time too poor to be the Marquis' intimate friend. That friend was Charles de Foucauld, a bit of a dandy at the time. It was not an image that stuck. De Foucauld would become one of France's uncanonized saints, a master theologian, who took his vows as a Trappist monk in Syria in 1891 to become "the hermit of the Sahara"; for twenty years he lived among the Bedouin Arabs of southern Morocco, who murdered him in 1917. One may justly speculate as to whether or not there was some element in de Morès's complex personality—which led him to the same terrible end as his friend—that, in different circumstances, would have taken him along a similarly devout route. "You know me, you know my affection for you," wrote de Foucauld to de Morès the day before he made his vows. "Poor monk, I pray from afar for all those I love. I pray for you." After the years at Saint-Cyr de Morès, like his Christian friend, he would on many an occasion face the sun and his God alone.

Life in the barracks of the French Army, following its defeat in the Franco-Prussian War, was anything but an adventure. To satisfy the ancient cravings for honour and chivalry aristocratic officers used to resort to hunting with horses and duelling with swords. It was not enough for an elegant, royal marquis. Having slain two men with his sabre, de Morès resigned his commission in 1881 and turned his talents to the world of high finance.

Many of the big capitalists of the nineteenth century were men of blue blood; the door that opened on these two worlds was marriage. De Morès's eye fell on a small German-American lady with a huge fortune, Medora von Hoffmann, whom he married in the Church of the Stained Glass Windows, Notre Dame de l'Espérance, in Cannes in February 1882. After a few idyllic months in Provence, the young couple took a steamer for New York and the banking enterprise of Louis von Hoffmann, de Morès's new father-in-law. Von Hoffmann had built up an empire of international trading, buying and selling currencies and securities in the foreign exchanges at the right time; he pioneered the system of arbitrage, as it came to be known. For de Morès it provided a practical lesson on how wealth could be generated from narrow margins on a large capital base—watch those margins and cut out the waste. It would become a moral imperative for this Catholic French businessman: "My birth confers no privileges on me," he used to repeat; "it gives me great responsibilities." Cutting the waste was soon translated into a battle to rid the market of the army of middlemen de Morès saw growing around him—rich bourgeois parasites who added nothing to the production process save their commissions and obstruction of trading forces. De Morès spent the rest of his life attempting to put the poor, honest producer directly in contact with the poor, honest consumer: it was the economics of Billy the Kid.

This is a point worth emphasizing. De Morès's initial struggle in business was with the middleman. Nothing in his behaviour or in the many interviews he granted in America gave a hint of the rabid anti-Semitism he later came to espouse. De Morès's particular interest in the cattle business began when he met Commander Henry Gorringe, a land promoter, who had brought one of Cleopatra's needles to New York during his service in the U.S. Navy. After passing through the Bad Lands of Dakota Territory one summer Gorringe had set up the Little

Missouri Land and Cattle Company with a tough local Scotsman, Gregor Lang, settling a small herd of cattle on a plot of land to prove his ownership. De Morès bought an option in Gorringe's property. Little did he know that the only property to which Gorringe's title laid claim was a set of cantonment buildings the U.S. Army had used during the Indian wars. Nor did he know that Gregor Lang was a spokesman for commercial hunters of buffalo, bear and deer—the natural enemies of cattle herdsmen.

In March 1883, de Morès set out in one of the Northern Pacific Railway's 4-4-0 steam express trains for Dakota. As soon as he discovered the fraudulent nature of the title, he informed Gorringe's agents that he was not going to exercise his option and, instead, founded a new town on the far side of the Little Missouri, naming it after his wife, Medora. Through the U.S. government he purchased around 4,000 acres of land and within a month he was building a huge brick slaughterhouse, corrals for the cattle, a railway spur that connected to the Northern Pacific and, high on a riverside bluff, a wooden château for himself and his wife. In May 1883 he registered the Northern Pacific Refrigerator Car Company in Saint Paul, Minnesota, and then committed the unforgivable sin of fencing in his land. With his refrigerator cars, de Morès aimed at cutting out the middlemen: "From the ranch to the table" was the Frenchman's appealing slogan.

There is evidence of a link between the commercial buffalo hunters of Little Missouri and the middlemen in New York, who took exception to the red painted storefronts of de Morès's new meat shops in the city. The shops were organized as cooperatives, whose stockholders were to be the common people of New York. De Morès, thanks in large measure to his father-in-law, had mustered considerable support, including that of New York's mayor W. R. Grace, New York bankers such as Eugene Kelly, and the famous labour economist Henry George. All of them were seduced by the Frenchman's message: cut out those parasitic middlemen.

But trouble developed in the Bad Lands. Gregor Lang's son, Lincoln, spoke up for the hunters' "inalienable rights" to roam the territory—without barbed-wire fences. Frank O'Donnell, a hunter, told the elder Lang he would shoot de Morès on sight. Less than one year after the gunfight of OK Corral in Tombstone, Arizona, the gunplay began on the banks of the Little Missouri. Nearly every night shooting broke out at the château. O'Donnell had organized a gang of vigilantes; in the daytime they shot up the town. The Marquis called in a sheriff's posse from Medan, 130 miles away. The O'Donnell gang disarmed them as they stepped off the train. But the outlaws did not know that Morès and friends, equipped with lever-action Winchester rifles, were waiting for them in the gully. In the gunfight that followed, one of O'Donnell's men was killed: "His horse was shot from under him, and it was really a sight to see him fight. He was very nervy," reported de Morès to the New York press. O'Donnell and another man were taken into custody. De Morès was indicted three times for murder, but on each occasion the charges were dismissed, despite the howling mob of buffalo hunters in the courts as well as outside his loghouse gaol.

But the meat-packers of Chicago and New York—Armour, Swift, Hammond, Nelson Morris and Schwarzchild & Sulzberger—were associated in a price-fixing trust that was getting its support from a very bitter Commander Henry Gorringe in New York and his men on the ground in Little Missouri, the "Lang crowd" as they were known. They organized a nationalist press campaign. In the *American Nonconformist* of Tabor, Iowa, a columnist wrote: "Counts, marquises, dukes and any other foreign aristocrats shall not establish ranches in Dakota or in any other part of this country. The soil of America belongs to American citizens only." De Morès was finished; he and von Hoffmann lost several million dollars in their Dakota enterprise.

Back in France, de Morès was quoted as saying in 1886, "I am twenty-eight years old. I am strong as a horse. I want to play a real part. I am ready to start again." He left for Indochina in pursuit of a railway scheme designed, once more, to cut out the predatory middlemen.

De Morès wanted to build his rail as a link between the landlocked Chinese province of Yunnan and the Gulf of Tonkin, thereby destroying a trade that had for the last thirty years been controlled by the Black Flag Pirates. The Pirates manipulated the local governments of

Tonkin, as North Vietnam was then known, and terrorized the population. They came from southern China, which they had poached for decades. And they were the main enemy of the French Army, which
viewed itself as a liberation force that had lost, since the 1870s, thirty
thousand men in the borderland jungles of Tonkin and China. Vicious
debate over these losses in 1885 had brought down the last government
of Jules Ferry, a Moderate Republican and educational reformer, whom
the métrostopper in Paris will recognize because so many streets and
schools are named after him. The elections of that year brought in a
number of Royalists, whose avowed purpose was to destroy the Republic, and also a number of deputies of the extreme left, who called themselves new men. They were nothing of the kind; they were the old men
of the barricades, many of whom had returned from exile following the
suppression of the Commune of 1871. As the Marquis de Morès prepared the next stage in his business career, the French Republic moved
in the direction of the two extremes, left and right.

There was still nothing in de Morès's language to suggest he was a
racist, though his experience in the Bad Lands had certainly increased
his passionate aristocratic sense of mission for France. He had learnt
directly of the terrible conditions in Tonkin when returning to France
from a tiger hunt in India on a French ship that happened to be transporting several of his old classmates from Saint-Cyr back home from
service in Indochina. The scheme to build a railway from Lang Son, on
the Chinese border, to the Gulf of Tonkin was born at that moment, in
spring 1888. By summer he had gathered enough capital to fund the
project, which he presented to the new Radical government in Paris in
August. "I don't share your political views," he told the Foreign Minister, "but politics stop at the frontier. Therefore, you can use me or not."
The Foreign Minister was convinced of his use and gave him the go-
ahead—but not without fierce opposition from a certain Ernest Constans, then an obscure Under-Secretary of the Navy, who had, however,
been for six months Governor General of French Indochina.

In December 1888 de Morès was in Haiphong to discuss his project
with the new Governor General, Étienne Richaud. Richaud was
attracted to this polite but ruthless marquis who had stood up to the

outlaws of the Far West; Richaud revealed what a scoundrel his prede-
cessor, Constans, had been—huge sums of government money had
been diverted to his private use while he had left the administration in
chaos. De Morès set off on his long march north to Lang Son satisfied
that he had found a very useful ally. Day and night he and his column of
coolies trudged by foot through a tepid jungle drizzle until they eventually arrived at the Chinese border where de Morès was astonished to
discover how eager the Chinese were to trade with them. He noted in
his diary: "The colonization of Tonkin will not be accomplished with
rifles, but with public works. We must take the position of being associates of the people of Tonkin." It was the same old economic philosophy again of building direct links between producers and consumers
through an efficient transportation system, and cutting out those pi-
ratical middlemen.

From Lang Son, de Morès's columns set out south along what is now
Route 4 in North Vietnam. They crossed a heavily wooded country,
peppered with emerald pools, climbed the mountain pass of Deo Co
and then descended into a stifling valley where the villages lay
devastated—the Black Flag Pirates had just passed through. On 11 January 1889, after four days of marching across 120 miles of jungle, they
entered Tien Yen on the Gulf of Tonkin. With Richaud's authorization,
de Morès immediately began work on docks for this sea port. But
events in Paris caught up with him.

One of the last acts of the Ferry government had been to revise the
voting system so that a single candidate could run for several constituencies. Ferry's purpose had been to encourage the development of
parliamentary parties—which did not yet exist in France. But he had
not counted on the rising popularity of General Georges Boulanger, a
new Napoleon on horseback, who ran for all political extremes and in
constituencies stretching across the country. In the provinces he was
supported by the Royalists. In Paris he had the support of the old revolutionaries and Communards—where he won with a landslide. France
was on the point of being taken over by a Boulanger dictatorship when,
through a dainty piece of parliamentary manoeuvring, a new Republican government was established—with its new Minister of the Inte-

rior, Ernest Constans. Constans had no qualms about legality. He threw many of Boulanger's supporters in gaol. In April 1889 Boulanger, realizing he was next on the list, fled to Brussels, where, in 1891, he shot himself on his mistress's grave.

De Morès was back in Paris in March 1889, for what reason one cannot be sure. It seems that the government had tempted him back with the promise of a grant; he also appears to have been attracted by the virile new politics of the Boulangist cause. At any rate, he immediately launched an attack on Constans for his corruption in Indochina, using Richaud's dossier as evidence. Richaud was ordered back to France. But he never got there: the Governor General and his cabin boy were found dead in their cabin and were buried at sea.

De Morès's denunciations of the Minister of the Interior ended when he drew a gun on Constans's gang of thugs during a by-election in Toulouse. De Morès thought it a good time to withdraw for a few months in England, where he read Édouard Drumont's popular book *La France juive*. He suddenly saw the light, the reason for all his losses: his meat cooperatives in New York had been scuttled by Jewish butchers; the Tonkin project had been blocked by a Jewish engineer to whom he had refused to pay a commission; the Toulouse campaign had turned into a farce because the department prefect was a Jew. He returned to Paris in the New Year, 1890, and arranged a meeting with this Édouard Drumont, editor-in-chief of *La Libre Parole*. Drumont invited him to a political rally in Neuilly for a Boulangist deputy who had gained a following with the slogan: "War on the Jews!"

France was entering a new age of vehement protest, and de Morès found himself at the head of it. At Neuilly the Marquis, dressed in a dark suit and a gardenia in his buttonhole, was the star of the show. The rally was held in a popular dance hall. Disgruntled workers, shopkeepers and small-time merchants drawn from the outskirts of Paris—along with the proud butchers of La Villette—provided the applause and the cheers. But there were also the elegant of *Tout Paris*: Prince Poniatowski, the Prince de Tarente, the Comte de Dion, the Marquis de Breteuil, the Marquis de Peyronnet and the Duc d'Uzès. "The rich, the aristocrats, are ready for all the necessary sacrifices," intoned the Marquis de Morès.

"As for myself, I am ready to sacrifice my life in the struggle against the financial feudalism that is supported by the government forces." It was a call for revolution.

In Paris's municipal elections that spring he ran for the down-and-out district of Les Épinettes, in the Seventeenth, with Gaston Vallée, a locksmith from La Villette. "I am above all a socialist," he told the electors; he attacked the middlemen, the bourgeois parasites. "The producer should have the maximum possible return for his work," he said; his revolution was against the *accapareurs*, the monopolists—the Jews.

De Morès lost the election to a former Communard. His next campaign was to gather support for his "socialist" cause at the "Festival of Labour" on 1 May. "I invite you all," he told his disappointed supporters at Les Épinettes, "to come and lunch with me on the Champ de Mars. Each of you will receive a cudgel, and at the end of this cudgel there will be a basket containing a loaf, a sausage, a litre of wine and a whistle." The cudgel and whistle were enough for Constans to have de Morès arrested on the charge of "provocation of crowds, provocation of murder, pillage, fire . . ." The Marquis spent the next three months in gaol.

De Morès was getting a lot of coverage in both the French and the American press, which continued to be fascinated by the "French cowboy." When he got out of prison he turned to his old skills as a duellist. The Jewish reporter Camille Dreyfus—no relation of Alfred Dreyfus of the famous affair—met with the Marquis in the Belgian town of Commines with pistols at dawn. Dreyfus received a bullet in the elbow. He was lucky. In France's Gay Nineties you did not sue an opponent for libel in the press; you killed him. De Morès's cool and elegant manner of dispatching an enemy engrossed newspaper readers in Paris and New York. Some of the Jews who were challenged by de Morès refused to be provoked, like the great Joseph Reinach of *La République Française*. But Captain Armand Mayer taught fencing at the École Polytechnique. He seconded Captain Crémieu-Foa in a set piece of swashbuckling with Drumont, who was seconded by de Morés. A wretched little squabble at the end of the duel led to the seconds challenging each other with "ordinary swords of combat." A duel was arranged in a covered arena on the Île de la Grande Jatte at 10 a.m., 23 June 1892. Mayer came charging in, flailing his weapon in every direction. The Marquis, a white glove concealing his mighty right wrist, simply held his sword out: it pierced Mayer in his armpit, ran through the upper part of a lung and came to a halt on his spinal column. Mayer dropped his sword and said, astonished, "I am hit." He calmly walked over to the seconds, the wound under his arm barely bleeding. De Morès seemed equally astonished. He came over to the wounded man and politely asked, "Captain Mayer, will you let me shake your hand?" They shook hands and Mayer promptly collapsed, never to regain consciousness.

Mayer's death did the anti-Semitic cause in Paris no good. As far as the Marquis was concerned, it ended all chances of him being elected to office. That only made the Boulangists more violent. Yet, somehow, the Marquis de Morès seemed more enchanting than ever. In his memoirs, Marie-François Goron, Chef de Sûreté, has left a record of the Marquis' arrest following Mayer's death. The Marquis was found in a hiding place on Boulevard Pereire. "Great heavens, Monsieur, you have come to arrest me? And you bring no police?" "I come without ceremony," Goron replied. "I am alone with my secretary." They descended the staircase together. De Morès comforted the despairing concierges "with the airs of a prince and caresses in his baritone voice." They mounted Goron's open carriage and "off we went, chatting away, as if we had just had dinner together at the cabaret."

After six weeks in prison the Marquis was acquitted of all charges. He turned to the butchers of La Villette for help. Gaston Vallée had established the first contacts. The butchers loved the cowboy stories and admired the man's physical stamina. There was ample material here for an anti-Semite to exploit: the Jews of Aubervilliers would buy up the cattle of La Villette for a pittance; they were the detested middlemen who earned their commissions at the honest producers' expense. In the spring of 1891 de Morès's political office on Rue Sainte-Anne—just across the road from the old Bibliothèque Nationale—was tipped off that Jews were selling unhealthy meat to the brave French soldiers guarding the fort of Verdun. De Morès and Jules Guèrin, the most black-hearted anti-Semite in town, disguised themselves as cattle merchants and, in the early hours of the morning, headed off for La Villette. Out of

the 3,200 cattle marketed that day, around forty head had been separated for health reasons. They were purchased, noted the investigators,
by Messieurs Wormser and Salomon. De Morès, in the company of two
butchers, followed the sick beasts out to the Porte de Pantin, where
they were loaded onto a train bound for Verdun. De Morès boarded a
very fast stagecoach and, so he claimed, managed to watch the same
train come into Verdun, where the beasts were taken by wagon to the
city's slaughter-houses; two of the beasts collapsed before they arrived
there. When the *Journal des Débats* reproduced the de Morès report, the
Ministry of War ordered the establishment of a new military slaughterhouse at Verdun. De Morès was now the hero of the butchers of La Villette, a much needed battalion for his cause: he dressed them in cowboy
clothes and called them "Morès and Friends."

In the winter and spring of 1892–93, no Jew could sleep tranquilly
when Morès and Friends were in the neighbourhood. No political enemy of the Marquis could hold a political meeting in town without it
ending in a brawl. De Morès had brought the terror of the Far West to
Paris. But it all came to a sudden end when the Marquis took on a man
who proved his match: Georges Clemenceau, leader of the Radicals,
the Tiger of France.

Clemenceau had been, perhaps unjustly, implicated in the biggest
financial scandal of the century, the bribing of politicians and other
public officials by the Panama Canal Company, which would face a
spectacular bankruptcy before as much as a dozen miles had been dug
across the mosquito-infested American isthmus. There is some evidence that Clemenceau was receiving money through Gustave Eiffel,
the man who built the tower; but this was unknown at the time. At any
rate, Paul Déroulède, a Boulangist deputy, possessed no evidence at all
when he denounced Clemenceau as head of the circle of bribery and
corruption within the Chamber. "There is only one response to be
made," replied Clemenceau: "Monsieur Paul Déroulède, you have lied!"
The two men fought it out with pistols on the Saint-Ouen racecourse
before three hundred spectators. The only damage done was the spoil-
ing of both men's political reputations. Morès and Friends went on the
rampage over the next months, screaming insults at Clemenceau and

hallowing the name of Déroulède. Clemenceau took the Marquis to court for libel and won after proving that it was he, the Marquis, who had been paid off by the canal company, not Clemenceau.

That August, 1893, Clemenceau attempted to renew his parliamentary seat for the department of the Var. Morès and Friends descended in hordes to disrupt the political meetings. They managed to oust Clemenceau from office, but only temporarily; they did irreparable damage to their own political reputations. The Tiger returned to public life as the defender of Captain Alfred Dreyfus in 1898 — anti-Semitism remained alive and well in French public life for several years to come. But Morès and Friends had long disappeared from sight and sound.

In late 1893 the Marquis left France in pursuit of a mad project designed to divide the British Empire in two. The plan was to incite the tribes of southern Algeria to march on Ghadames and Ghat, where they were to join the Mahdi on the Upper Nile and drive the British out of Sudan. The result was the opposite: the Algerian tribes turned on him. The Marquis died alone on 9 June 1896, after a long and bloody gunfight, under a cactus at El Ouatia. "Remember," he wrote in his last letter to his son, Louis, "in striving, against every obstacle, for justice and truth, you bring yourself nearer to God."

As you walk around the Cité des Sciences and the Cité de la Musique, you will notice the graffiti crying out for God and justice where others have scrawled the signs of racial hatred. It is remarkable how much remains of the old district of La Villette.

OPÉRA

LINE 7 RUNS STRAIGHT to the Opéra. While Châtelet–Les Halles is incontestably the central point of Paris, Haussmann's exercise of drawing straight lines through the western sections of the capital did create at the Opéra what many consider the most striking crossroads in town. The Avenue de l'Opéra, opened in 1870, created a direct link between the Louvre and the *grands boulevards*, behind which was struck the westward extension of the Rue Réaumur, justly named Boulevard Haussmann, where Paris's main department stores grew up. From the doorway of Brentano's bookshop on Avenue de l'Opéra, as Andrew Hussey remarks, one gets a fine view of "the 'Second Empire' at work in all its monumental and strangely impressive vulgarity." Zola would have agreed that the Opéra district was as magnificent as it was inhuman, a land of pleasures for the fat bourgeoisie. And that was precisely what the Opéra's architect, Charles Garnier, intended. "Let your eyes rejoice at the golden rays, your soul warm itself to the vibrations of colour," he wrote with the same pomposity as he built. "Mesdames, you will appear at the Opéra with shoulders naked, diamonds around the neck and silk about the body!" Garnier's opera house boasts of being the largest theatre in the world and it still draws a gasp from a visitor emerging for the first time from Métrostop No. 9.

Most Parisians, when they hear the word "Opéra," think of this huge square with its imperial boulevards stretching out in every direction. Folk memory has a lot to do with this. It was here that the wildest celebrations at the end of the First World War occurred—Marthe Chenal, wrapped in a tricolour flag, sang the Marseillaise from the Opéra steps while searchlights in red, white and blue scanned the ground, buildings and roofs. Picnic tables were laid out on the same square for a somewhat

149

soberer celebration on 8 May 1945. Strictly speaking, however, the term "Opéra" refers not to a place but to the troupe of performers whose origin goes back to the seventeenth century. The same confusion is made over the term "Opéra Comique" which most people would identify as the lusciously gaudy building a short way up the Boulevard des Capucines on Rue Favart. The "Opéra Comique" was a troupe of entertainers founded in 1714 to perform pantomimes and parodies of opera. Bear in mind, however, that all "*comique*" means in this context is French opera with spoken dialogue—it can include the most tragic plots, such as Bizet's *Carmen*.

It is worth taking that stroll up the Boulevard des Capucines from the Opéra to the Opéra Comique. The subsidiary industry to music was, of course, restaurants—a hundred years ago the restaurants straddling this boulevard were the most famous and expensive in town, such as Tortoni's, the Café Hardy or the Café Riche next door. "*Il faut être bien riche pour dîner chez Hardy et bien hardi pour dîner chez Riche*," one used to say in the last decades of the nineteenth century—"You have to be rich to dine at Hardy's and hardy to dine at Riche's." Hardiness was not, on the other hand, the principal quality of the directors of the Opéra. Over the last decades of the nineteenth century the repertoire for Garnier's bare-shouldered ladies consisted of no more than a dozen operas, four of them being by Giacomo Meyerbeer—*Les Huguenots*, *Le Prophète*, *L'Africaine* and *Robert le diable*. Mozart's *Don Giovanni* made it to the top, as did Carl Maria von Weber's *Freischütz*. But *La Favorite* could scarcely be considered Donizetti's best opera. And it is a rare opera house today which will risk a performance of Ambroise Thomas' *Hamlet*. In 1887 a frustrated subscriber wrote to the directors: "I shall not be subscribing again. Last winter I swallowed twelve performances of *Patrie* on Fridays, and I need a rest."

The Opéra Comique was altogether different. Its directors were a good deal more sympathetic to the wild fantasies of composers: they took risks. One of the most famous flops at the Opéra Comique was Bizet's *Carmen*, which was booed off the stage at its premiere in 1875. Poor Bizet died without ever knowing that he had composed the

world's best known opera. Eight years later the Opéra Comique rein-
stalled *Carmen* on its winter programme. By 1891 over 400 performances had graced its stage — "the best box on the ears the critics have
had," noted Claude Debussy, a composer destined to create, within
eleven years, another scandal on the stage of the Opéra Comique.

Some of the greatest battles over opera during those years were due
to Richard Wagner. It is difficult today to understand the total hold Wagner operas had at the time on the imagination of artists — not just opera
fanatics, but also poets, painters, novelists, playwrights, creative people
of all persuasions. Pilgrimages to Bayreuth, Wagner's Bavarian home,
were organized from every corner of Europe. Wagner had created a new
religion. But the great paradox was that, in Paris, Wagner was rarely performed. In 1861 the Opéra — then housed in a plain, neoclassical edifice
on Rue Le Peletier — put on a performance of *Tannhäuser*: the harangue of
the critics assured that it would not be played again in the French capital
for another generation. In May 1887 Charles Lamoureux, a conductor
who had launched six years earlier a highly successful series of concerts
(the Orchestre Lamoureux is still very active today), organized ten performances of *Lohengrin* at the Eden Theatre; a riot on the first night put
a prompt end to that. Wagner lovers in Paris were reduced to listening to
private solo performances accompanied by two pianos or — as in the case
of Debussy — reading in silence the orchestral scores, stupefied by their
brilliance. They could also, again like Debussy, take the crowded train to
Bayreuth.

How could a young composer break out of this operatic world so
dominated, despite the popular censure, by this god, Richard Wagner?
It was Claude Debussy who broke the spell with his opera, *Pelléas et
Mélisande*, which premiered on the stage of the Opéra Comique at the
end of April 1902. It was, by all accounts, one of the greatest events in
the history of opera.

But the first few days of *Pelléas*'s life on stage were rough. The li-
bretto was drawn from Maurice Maeterlinck's play of the same name,
which had been performed just once in Paris, at the Bouffes Parisiens
on 17 May 1893, five days after Wagner's *Die Walküre* opened, to much

applause, at the Opéra Garnier. Many at the time saw an affinity between *Pelléas* and Wagner's *Tristan*, including the Gothic-sounding names of its characters and its distant, medieval setting. A tender and naïve Mélisande is drawn into marrying the Prince Golaud. Her life, spent languishing in a bleak seaside castle, is transformed by the love of Golaud's younger half-brother, Pelléas: an incestuous quarrel is born, leading to the death of the two lovers. Something like the belligerence in the play emerged in real life after Debussy and the Opéra Comique's director Albert Carré refused Maeterlinck's mistress the part of Mélisande, giving it instead to the twenty-five-year-old Scottish soprano Mary Garden. Maeterlinck wrote an open letter to *Le Figaro* in which he expressed the hope for the opera's "prompt and resounding collapse." Maeterlinck, an expert with a sword, then challenged Debussy to a duel; Debussy wisely refused.

In the meantime the performers became totally absorbed in the beauty of Debussy's half tones. In her memoirs, Mary Garden recalls how the singers first sang through their parts in the drawing room of the conductor André Messager. As Debussy played the piano, she was taken over "by the most extraordinary emotions I have ever experienced in my life . . . I seemed to become someone else." There they sat, the singers bowed in their scores as if at prayer. "When Debussy got to the fourth act I could no longer look at my score for the tears. It was all very strange and unbearable. I closed my book and just listened to him and as he played the death of Mélisande, I burst into the most awful sobbing." By the end the whole cast was crying "as if we had just lost our best friend, crying as if nothing would console us again."

The scenery in greys and blues by Eugène Ronsin and Lucien Jusseaume—"At the front of a cave," "A well in the park," "A terrace at the exit of the vaults," "A room in the castle"—contained all the refined brilliance one has come to expect of that short-lived *belle époque*. Though the Opéra Comique appeared vast from the exterior, its corridors were hardly equipped to handle the large canvases. There was an average of three transformation scenes with each act, and Debussy had not foreseen the amount of time this would take, so he spent, between rehearsals, a large part of his time fretting away in his two-room flat at

58, Rue Cardinet, composing the wonderful interludes that have moved audiences for generations since.

The first reviews were mixed, some of them terrible: the music was "sickly and practically lifeless," Debussy sacrificed "music to vague conceptions and dangerous compromises," "rhythm, song and tonality are three things unknown to M. Debussy." Undoubtedly the poisonous atmosphere at the full dress rehearsal had contributed to this. The auditorium had been packed, while, in the reception rooms and corridors, there was a general to-and-fro of critics and musicians. Debussy hid himself in Messager's office, chain-smoking. The first two acts passed by in relative peace. But after Golaud had dragged Mélisande around the stage by the hair, trouble began. Mélisande ended the scene by chanting, *"Je ne suis pas heureuse"* — or, according to some accounts, missing her line with a *"Je suis malheureuse"* — "You can say that again!" screamed out somebody from the back of the theatre. General hilarity broke out in the last scene of Act III, "Before the castle," in the encounter between little Yniold and Golaud, which had given Debussy nightmares to compose.

Messager's precise execution and the performers' disciplined devotion — along with the fantastic spectacle of Ronsin and Jusseaume's decor — were what saved *Pelléas*. The premiere on 30 April saw an uncomfortable repetition of the screams and *charivari* among the audience. Perhaps it was just out of curiosity that the numbers increased. But as those numbers grew, so did the fascination of Paris for Debussy's opera. The critics shifted from cold indifference to a cheering endorsement. Young musicians, like Maurice Ravel, sat night after night in the auditorium mesmerized by the opera's beauty. "Third performance," noted Henri Büsser, who was directing the off-stage chorus, in his diary for 3 May. "Large audience, more responsive and sympathetic. At the end there are calls for Debussy, but he refuses to appear on stage." He remained in Messager's office, puffing away at his cigarettes. A *Pelléas* cult was developing.

By then Debussy was facing another problem: what to do after the completion of what had been his life's work. "To complete a work, is a little like the death of someone one loves, no?" he had written in 1895 to his artistic friend Pierre Louÿs (pronounced "Louee"). There was obviously a relationship here with what Debussy defined in another long letter, written to his benefactor, Prince André Poniatowski, in 1893, as the "Cult of Desire": "One has the most mad and sincere desire for an object of art (a Velasquez, a Satzouma vase or a new form of tie). What joy there is at the moment of possession; it is a true love. Then at the end of a week, nothing. The object stands there for five or six days without receiving as much as a glance. One will regard it again with the former passion only after an absence of several months . . ."

This is probably why Debussy never completed a second opera, though the operatic and theatrical projects that he embarked on went in all directions. His friends used to remark that he did make life difficult for himself: every time he had some success he had to make a complete break with the work he had just produced and slog away at something completely different. Debussy had to distance himself from *Pelléas*. "The realization of a work of art, beautiful as it may be, almost always contradicts the inner dream," he wrote in the review *Musica* one year after the opera's premiere. By then he was working on the orchestration of his three *Estampes*, beginning with "Pagodes," which played on the memory of oriental harem dancers that he had seen on the Champ de Mars during the World Expositions of 1889 and 1900; and on three orchestral "sketches" that cost him nearly two years of sweated labour, "On the sea from dawn to midday," "The play of waves" and "Dialogue between the wind and sea": *La Mer*.

Debussy was experimenting with the new sounds and rhythms he had created in *Pelléas*. And the press did not let up in its criticism of the sounds of Claude Debussy. Like the composer himself, the commentary became increasingly cerebral. Soon the country's most thoughtful writers entered the fray, most notably Romain Rolland and Marcel Proust. In January 1904 Jean Lorrain, a *fin-de-siècle* poet and columnist who passed himself off as a "dandy of perversity," began a series of articles in *Le Journal* entitled *Les Pelléastres*. Debussy, as always, wanted to send in a long reply. "Reply to him? One hundred times no!" wrote Louÿs, quite beside himself. "You do not argue with a journalist. No artist does that." So Debussy maintained his silence. But the articles went on and on, eventually appearing in book form in 1910. The main gist of Lorrain's argument was that Debussy and his followers had created a new religion much worse than the Wagnerian faith because it catered exclusively to effete and exorbitantly precious snobs. "At least the followers of Wagner are sincere," he noted. *Debussystes*, on the other hand, were "beautiful young men with long hair who skilfully turned their curls into a fringe along the forehead."

One could dismiss Lorrain's columns as a prolonged piece of journalistic nastiness. But Lorrain did hit a dissonant chord that resonated with the cultural quarrels of the day. On one side were the romantic idealists, the Wagnerians, on the other the symbolists, the Debussists; it was the difference between "German music" and "French music." It was precisely this that defined the difference between Romain Rolland and Marcel Proust in the way they approached Debussy's music.

Rolland, the pacifist, essayist, mystic and idealist, did not like Debussy. His early writings had been devoted to music and, at thirty-five, he had become the Sorbonne's first professor of the history of music just at the time *Pelléas* premiered. Rolland's basic view was that music was the one dimension of the arts which could bring all nations together; the great tragedy of his time was that all music since around 1850 had become decadent and nationalist. He had a slight preference for the ideals of German music, "strong" and thematic, but he was even critical of Wagner. French music was all too refined. Rolland's best known work of fiction is his ten-volume *roman fleuve*, *Jean-Christophe*, published between 1904 and 1912. Its hero, Jean-Christophe, is a Beethoven trying to come to terms with the disasters of Rolland's contemporary world. "To the devil with your manufactured chords!" cries out Jean-Christophe in Paris, in an obvious allusion to Debussy. Jean-Christophe and two Parisian musical critics set off to the Opéra Comique to hear *Pelléas et Mélisande*. After the first act Jean-Christophe leans over to one of the critics and asks, "Is it like that all the time?" "Yes," replies the critic. "But there is nothing there," says Jean-Christophe. "Nothing at all. No music. No development."

His private diary shows that Rolland was repeating a real experience he had had in 1907. Rolland was in a box at the Opéra Comique with

Maurice Ravel, the critics Jean Marnold and Lionel de la Laurencie, and Richard Strauss, whose German operatic version of Oscar Wilde's *Salome* premiered in Paris that year. After the first act, Strauss leant over and whispered in Marnold's ear, "Is it always like that?" "Yes." "Nothing more? There's nothing to it. No music, no development." Marnold made a long-winded attempt to explain the combination of Maeterlinck's poetical phrases with Debussy's subtle musical phrases. Rolland himself pointed out the sobriety of Debussy's art. Strauss replied, "But I *am* a musician, and I don't hear *anything*." He repeated, "I, I am a musician before all else. From the moment the music is in a work, I want it to be mistress, I don't want it to be subordinate to anything else." After the show, the group went down to the popular musicians" café, the Taverne Pousset, on Rue de Châteaudun. Strauss tried to elaborate. "Fine," he said, weighing the word. His French was not terribly good: "It is very fine, very . . ." he waved his hands, "very *gekünstelt* [artful], but it is never spontaneous; it lacks *Schwung*."

Schwung, in German, meant verve or energy, rather than "swing." For Rolland, with his preference for "German" music over "French," the great quality of the former was that it was *schwungvoll*, or energetic and stirring. This was certainly what made Strauss's *Salome* different from Debussy's *Pelléas*. But Rolland did not like that either. For those who think all contemporary music is a trial to listen to, Romain Rolland is their man.

For those who love Debussy, it is Marcel Proust. The playwright René Peter introduced Debussy to Proust sometime in the late 1890s, which would not have been difficult since they frequented the same cafés near the Opéra and had the same circle of friends. Proust, probably at this early date, must have felt the affinity of his own ideas of time and memory with those of the composer. Debussy, many times in his correspondence, writes of the pleasure of the moment and the effort to refine this through memory. "When you don't have the means to travel," he wrote to Messager in September 1903, "you have to make up for it with your imagination." And so he began, in landlocked Burgundy, composing *La Mer*—which he himself admitted was based on a childhood memory of his long holidays by the Mediterranean with his aunt. One cannot imagine a more Proustian theme. Proust wrote that the "only true voyage of discovery is not visiting different sceneries but possessing other eyes"—the whole of his huge, seven-volume *A la recherche du temps perdu* is based on that idea, an attempt, through the working of memory, to evoke the pleasure of a past instant. One could not find a better definition of Debussy's music. Proust sought to go behind the traditional plot of a novel. Debussy adventured into the back stages of melody.

Late in his life Proust told the writer Jacques Benoist-Méchin—a lover of things German—that music had been one of the great passions of his life. "Had been," he added, "for today I have little opportunity to listen to it." Proust's chronic timidity undoubtedly explained why he did not develop a closer relationship with Debussy. It was not, apparently, for want of trying. According to his English biographer, Edward Lockspeiser, Debussy used to meet Proust frequently at Weber's on Rue Royale, a smart café where many of the musical and literary world used to gather before the First World War. One evening, apparently in 1895, Proust proposed to Debussy to take him round to his home in his carriage. Debussy did not like Proust's way of speaking, with the unending sentences that characterized his writing. Proust, in his generous manner, proposed a large reception in the musician's honour. "Pardon me," replied Debussy, "I'm just a bear. Perhaps it would be best if we continued to meet by chance, as we have been doing up to now."

Proust had a horror of theatres and public concerts. According to the novelist André Maurois, he had the Quatuor Capet round to his apartment on Rue Hamelin to play to him alone at night as an inspiration for his work. They came and performed Debussy's *Quatuor*. Debussy's correspondence does indeed indicate that in 1901 the Quatuor Capet was giving private performances of his Quartet. In Maurois' account Proust insisted that no one else attend: "If there are others present I would be obliged to be polite and I would not listen . . . I need absolutely pure impressions for my book." While the musicians played, Proust lay down on a couch, his eyes closed, searching in the music for some mysterious communion. In 1911, more and more a recluse, he employed the

Théâtrephone—a telephone that broadcasted live musical and theatrical performances—to listen, night after night, to *Pelléas et Mélisande*.

"LOVE," WROTE PROUST, "is space and time made sensitive to the heart." This was not so very different from Debussy's notion of the "Cult of Desire," the joy of the moment which he had described to Prince Poniatowski. Debussy's problem is that he not only fed this into his music; he lived like that. Debussy's private life was a drama, a story fit for the composer of *Pelléas*.

One of the friends Debussy and Proust had in common was Robert Godet, a man of immense learning who made his name in the press as a Wagnerian zealot, but could speak on any subject one chose. He had travelled with Debussy to Bayreuth in 1889 and remained one of Debussy's correspondents for the rest of his life—a most unusual case. Just before their trip to Bayreuth, Godet had given Debussy a copy of his youthful first novel, *Mal à aimer: états d'âme*. Love, as Proust would have put it, was the most intense of all sensations but also the most dangerous. Godet presented his hero, a sensitive Swiss musician, like Godet himself, as being faced with two life plots: that of Wagner's *Tristan*, which concludes with the death of the two lovers, or Tolstoy's *Katia*, in which the hero puts all passions aside and marries for reason. "Does one prefer the end of *Tristan* or the end of *Katia*?" asks Godet in his novel. "One *must* choose." Godet, like his hero, chose *Katia* by marrying a dull and sensible Dutch woman. Debussy wrote ecstatically to Godet on Saturday morning, 13 July 1889: "Dear Friend, I read you all this night! . . . Don't feel wounded if I declare immediately my sympathy for your 'unhappy prose.' At places I had the rare sensation of 'Real Beings' whose sufferings were clear to me . . ." Debussy chose *Tristan*.

His friendships and his love affairs were always of the most passionate kind. And they always ended with sorrow and, usually, complete rupture. He told both Ernest Chausson, the composer, and Pierre Louÿs that he had never enjoyed such friendship; he broke with them both. His mistress, Gaby Dupont, with whom he shared a fifth-floor flat on Rue Gustave-Doré, attempted to kill herself. Debussy himself showed certain suicidal traits. 1898 was a bleak, impecunious year. "I never arrive at doing anything without some event happening in my life," he wrote to Louÿs at the end of March; "this is what gives superiority to memory, from that at least one can redeem a few valuable emotions'—a most Proustian thought. "I need something to love, something to which I can hook on to, without which I should go mad, and might as well commit suicide, which is a bit stupid." A month later he was writing again to Louÿs, "I feel alone and distraught, nothing has changed in the black sky that forms the backdrop of my life, and I do not know where I am going if it is not towards suicide . . ." Gaby moved out of the flat in December. Debussy moved to another tiny fifth-floor flat at 58, Rue Cardinet, today classified by the City of Paris as a historic monument, with its plaque inaccurately stating: "Claude Debussy installed himself here *in 1901* and composed *Pelléas et Mélisande*: it was a *disaster*, followed by a triumph."

In the 1890s Debussy, like all his friends, had been bathed in the poetry and prose of the American inventor of terror, Edgar Allan Poe, thanks largely to its able translator, as great a giant as Poe, the symbolist poet Charles Baudelaire. Prior to attending Maeterlinck's *Pelléas* at the Bouffes Parisiens, Debussy had been working on an operatic version of Poe's *Fall of the House of Usher*—he was still working on it during the First World War. It was undoubtedly because Poe was exercising such an influence on both Maeterlinck (who admitted that his play was derived from *The House of Usher*) and Debussy that the latter decided immediately to begin work on *Pelléas*. The old castle was modelled after Usher's crumbling ruin. The gloomy colours, the cold cellar, the working of events the characters are powerless to control are all borrowed from *Usher*. So too are the fateful words Pelléas utters to Mélisande: "You are strangely beautiful when I kiss you like that. You are so beautiful that one would say you are going to die."

Debussy's choice of *Tristan*, and his subsequent adoption of Poe, took him to Poe's women—innocent, sickly creatures like Ligeia or Morella. Gaby, after leaving Debussy, fell into a state of poverty. In her eighties she was seen in Rouen, under the German occupation, collecting cigarette butts in the streets to satisfy a nicotine habit she had

picked up from Debussy. More poignant still were the events that happened on the fifth floor of Rue Cardinet as Debussy prepared for the
premiere of *Pelléas et Mélisande*.

On 3 April 1899 Debussy wrote from Rue Cardinet to his editor
Georges Hartmann, "After so many bad and sad days, I believe I have
rediscovered a little moral tranquillity." On the 11th he was asking him
for 200 francs, "which I will reimburse as soon as possible"; Debussy
would always remain in Hartmann's debt, as he would with all subsequent editors.

Sometime that month he had met the beautiful Lilly* Texier, who
worked as a model at Paris's elite fashion shop right behind the Opéra,
Mesdames Sarah Mayer et A. Morhange, on the corner of Rue Auber and
Rue Boudreau. Their correspondence suggests the encounter had taken
place on a tram. "My dear little Lili," he wrote on Friday, 21 April, "If you
are really kind you will put on your pink skirt and your black hat and
come and say *bonjour* Sunday around 2.30." He noted there was no lift to
the fifth floor. On Monday, 24 April, he wrote, "My dear little Lili, Claude
is not yet cured of the bites from your dear little mouth . . . Impatient of
your mouth and your body, I love you. Your Claude."

For six months it was "*Ma Lili jolie*," "*Ma Lili aimée*," "*Lili chérie et très
adorée*" and even "*Si adorablement Lilly, si délicieusement Mimi*"—after the
heroine of Puccini's *La Bohème* (who died): "I send you my longest and
best kiss," "I alone in this huge bed look vainly for a little corner that has
not been embalmed in your memory," "I drink at your mouth" and "never
has anyone loved you with such absolute abandon." All the objects in his
two-room flat, exquisitely decorated in *art nouveau*, bore her presence;
the great old Japanese toad on the mantelpiece "looks obstinately at the
door through which he is accustomed to see you enter." She suspended
time: "You who have abolished all the Past . . . you know my insufferable
need to see into the Future." But she did not suspend his debts: two
weeks before Louÿs married Louise, the daughter of the poet José-Maria

---

* Is it Lili, Lily or Lilly? The sources, including Debussy's own correspondence, are
  inconsistent. Most of the time Debussy refers to his wife as "Lilly," and so we shall call
  her. She was baptized "Rosalie."

de Heredia, Debussy was asking him desperately for fifty francs—"I am in the blackest mess, without even mentioning my 300,000 francs of debt." He told Lilly of an anonymous letter, "*bête et méchante*," menacing him for payment. She did seem to invite on the household malady. Debussy could not attend Louÿs' marriage because he was so ill and, in September, he asked Proust's doctor, Abel Desjardins, to come round to the flat "to see my little Lilly . . . only don't damage her." There was a Mimi and a Mélisande living in little Lilly: "You have made me love you more than is perhaps permitted to a man; there is in me a need to destroy myself that almost overrides my need for joy—a tension so violent that it almost resembles a desire for Death" (3 July).

Claude and Lilly Debussy were married in a civil ceremony at the *mairie* of the Dix-septième Arrondissement, on Rue des Batignolles; five witnesses were present, including Pierre Louÿs. "Debussy is married," remarked Arthur Fontaine, a civil servant and friend, facetiously. "A pretty woman is always a pretty woman, and a great musician is a great musician."

She never opened her mouth when the couple were seen together in the cafés of musical Paris. The poet Paul-Jean Toulet, who would become one of Debussy's close friends after the premiere of *Pelléas*, called them "Saint-Roch [pronounced with a hard "ch" so that it is almost 'Rock'] and his dog."

In November, Debussy told Hartmann that "Mermaids," the third movement of his *Nocturnes*, was not ready because "Madame Debussy has been sick this night and she is still not well this morning." He added a week later, "I have furiously little money!" And a few days later: "Do you want to help me? I have piles of medicines to buy for Lilly." He tried to earn a little by taking on a student—teaching was not Debussy's greatest talent. Once more he got behind in his composition of *Pelléas*; the Opéra Comique must have "the score under its eyes" before it can commit itself, Hartmann warned him. "Can you advance me two hundred and fifty francs?" Debussy asked Hartmann in January 1900. On 12 April Hartmann wrote to Debussy: "I have been in bed for twelve days suffering like a martyr from gout in my arms, my knees and both feet! I scream and am broken with pain . . . My friend, you come banging at my

cash box at a moment when it is very empty." Eleven days later, Hartmann was dead. His family declared that all advances made to Debussy
must be treated as loans and repaid: Debussy had to carry the heavy
debt for the remainder of his short life.

In August Lilly suffered a miscarriage and during her two weeks of
hospitalization it was discovered she had contracted tuberculosis—a
killer in those days. "You see this means moral pain," he wrote to Louÿs,
"and added to that is a material side that is absolutely miserable." "We
don't count for much," he told his friend in October. "You surely think
like me that the most passionate will is feeble and how virtually useless
is this intense desire to live. How ironic it is that all we give—all the
blood we spill—is for this."

Carré announced to Debussy, on 3 May 1901, that the Opéra
Comique had finally committed itself to a production of *Pelléas* in April
1902. But the health problems of "Madame Mimi" did not abate. Worse,
boredom was setting in. In the summer of 1901 the couple spent three
months in Burgundy with Lilly's parents. Debussy had as much love of
green chloroform as would Jean-Paul Sartre. "This stay in the countryside is perfectly unbearable!" he wrote to his new editor. "The minutes
pass by without one ever knowing exactly why," he explained to his old
pupil Raoul Bardac on 31 August. Raoul took note, and when Debussy
was back in Paris he invited him over to his home on Rue Bassano to
meet his mother, Emma, who, as an accomplished soprano and the former mistress of Gabriel Fauré, had a high regard for musical talent. "Remember me to your mother," wrote Debussy in a note to Raoul three
weeks before the opera's premiere.

Henri Büsser, who took over the conducting of *Pelléas* from Messager after the third performance, recorded in his diary a visit to Debussy's flat that early spring of 1902 when the maestro was slaving away
at the orchestral interludes: "This little room we're in, with oil paintings, watercolours and drawings on the walls, radiates happiness. The
delightful Lilly [his wife] is its source. She's happy that *Pelléas* is being
produced. 'It's my work too,' she says, 'because I gave Claude encouragement when he was despairing of ever seeing his work reach the
stage.'" In fact, illness continued to haunt that little home.

In July Debussy was writing to Messager that a "cruel and ironic God, who controls our destinies, really makes us pay hard for our purest joys!" That August Debussy turned forty. He spent another long summer with his in-laws in lifeless Burgundy, from which he escaped by plunging himself in a new operatic project, Shakespeare's *As You Like It* — "art is the most beautiful of lies," he wrote in the journal *Musica* that autumn. The winter was relieved by the resumption of *Pelléas* and the bestowal of the Légion d'honneur; but "I am sadly troubled by the health of my wife," he wrote to a friend. Debussy was now calling her his "*petit être mystérieux*," his Mélisande: "we are united by ties a thousand times stronger than the traditional ties of marriage."

That June, 1903, Raoul Bardac invited Debussy over to Rue Bassano again to have tea with his mother. Debussy dedicated one of his piano scores, *Ariettes oubliées*, to her: "To Madame S. Bardac whose musical sympathy is precious to me — infinitely so." She was born Emma Moyse, from a respectable Jewish family in Bordeaux, and had married at the age of eighteen Sigismond Bardac, a rich banker who believed wealth would keep his wife by his side. In the case of Gabriel Fauré he proved right; the composer of *Pelléas*, however, was another matter.

Another summer in Burgundy, another winter. Debussy could share with Emma his musical humour as a picture postcard, dated 19 June 1904, of the Château de Dampierre with a declining scale in D and the Debussy monogram scribbled on the back shows. Lilly left for Burgundy alone that July. His letters to Lilly began to reveal the truth. "I was wondering in what state the pretty places of your poor little body could be in," he began one letter, and went on: "Don't believe it was a pleasure for me to put you so dryly on the wagon . . . But I have to find new things, under the pressure of deadlines . . ." He was now addressing her as "Lily-Lilo" as he launched into a series of lies: "If *La Mer* is prepared to let me go, I will be able to join you around 15 August." It was not the sea of his dreams that was holding him, but the real thing. Debussy had just begun the composition of *L'Isle joyeuse*, an ecstatic little piano piece, and at the end of July he took the ferry to Jersey, with his Emma, "*petite Mienne adorée*." "I am working in complete liberty," he wrote from Saint Helier to his new editor, Jacques Durand. "The Sea is very good for me, and she is showing me all her apparel." He asked Durand to keep his address secret "*from everybody*, including my charming family."

A week later Emma and Debussy moved to the seaside resort of Pourville, near Dieppe. He wrote to Lilly on 11 August that he was leaving for England with his painter friend Jacques-Émile Blanche—Blanche was not in sight. "If I have an invincible need to be alone it is because . . . I can no longer work as I wish." It was a farewell letter and Lilly understood it too well. She returned to Paris, where, in their empty flat, she uncovered the correspondence with Emma. On 22 August Debussy wrote to her, "It seems to me that it would be quite useless for us to see each other at this moment, that would be too sad."

Debussy remained in Pourville with Emma right through to mid-October. He then rented a small flat on Avenue Alphand, complaining of being "horribly short of money." Lilly hardly emerged from the flat on Rue Cardinet; Debussy showed little sympathy—she was now a "*petit être*" with the mystery knocked out. He imagined she was starving herself to death. But that was not true. On 13 October, a week before their fourth wedding anniversary, Lilly laid her blonde head on the famous white pillow and shot herself in the chest.

"IT WOULD NOT be from such a little wound as this that she might die," chants the doctor to the orchestral strings and a harp as he gazes down at Mélisande stretched out on a bed. "It's not grave enough to kill a bird." Miraculously the bullet from Lilly's revolver passed by every vital organ and lodged in her spine; it remained there for the rest of her life. She was taken to the Clinique Blomet in the Septième, where Proust's doctor took care of her. Mary Garden found her lying alone, helpless. "This young girl never knew anything else in her life but her love of Debussy," recalled Garden in her memoirs. Lilly recounted her version of the story and then the surgeon came in to dress her wound, opening her nightdress: "In my life I have never seen anything so beautiful as Lilly Debussy from the waist up. It was just like a glorious marble statue, too divine for words! Debussy had always said to me, "Mary, there is nothing in the

world like Lilly's body." Now I knew what he meant. And lying under-
neath Lilly's left breast was a round dark hole."

Lilly lived until 1932, alone on Avenue de Villiers, accepting the odd
interviews and writing notes in red ink on the back of the huge correspondence she had collected on her husband—some of it most compromising. She was not poor. According to the divorce terms
pronounced on 17 July 1905, Debussy paid alimony to Lilly of 400 francs
a month and every year had to turn over a sum of 3,600 francs for a
pension fund in her favour. It was another great debt on his shoulders.

All his friends turned against him: André Messager, René Peter,
Maurice Curnonsky, Paul Dukas and Robert Godet. "I have seen such
desertions around me!" he wrote to the music scholar Louis Laloy, who
at last broke his silence in April 1905 to become a real friend. Debussy's
estrangement from Pierre Louÿs was the cruellest of them all: "I went
to see poor Madame Debussy yesterday," Louÿs wrote with venom to
his brother shortly after the suicide attempt. "The husband has gone
off with a Jewess of forty years and more, Mme S. Bardac . . . You know
Bardac, very much accustomed to the elopements of his wife . . . *Jolie
race!*" Robert Godet and Paul Dukas would eventually rally to Debussy,
but their friendship was never the same. "Madame Lily Debussy is very
interesting and Claude Debussy a miserable wretch," Debussy wrote to
the painter Paul Robert. "I have the terrible defect of loving music for
its own sake, and not for its success . . . I shall go into exile."

And for a year that is precisely what he did. He eventually found
peace of mind in the summer of 1905 with Emma and her daughter,
Dolly, on the English coast at Eastbourne, in Sussex. "This place is peace-
ful and charming," he told Durand. "The sea unfurls itself with a most
British sense of correctness." There he put the finishing touches to his
Burgundy production of *La Mer*, completed his Jersey production of
L'Isle joyeuse and began an exotic series of piano pieces known collectively
as *Images*. Debussy was at last a happy man. He finally married Emma in
January 1908 just after, on a rare occasion, he had himself conducted a
performance of *La Mer*. "You really feel yourself to be the heart of your
own music," he told Durand.

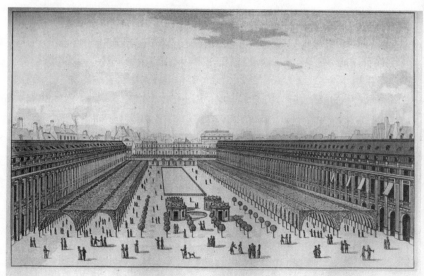

VUE DES GALERIES DU PALAIS ROYAL en 1789

PALAIS-ROYAL

FROM THE OPÉRA you can take Line No. 7 down to the Palais-Royal, which arrives in the heart of the most frequently visited part of Paris. From the west exit the Avenue de l'Opéra runs straight up to Garnier's monument; to the left is the Palais du Louvre; the Rue de Rivoli stretches in a straight line up to the Place de la Concorde. In the opposite direction lies the Arcades du Louvre, with paintings, ancient manuscripts and precious art objects for sale for those who can afford them; further down the Rue de Rivoli lies the Hôtel de Ville and, to its south, the Île de la Cité and Notre Dame Cathedral. In this small area there is practically every picture postcard scene of what the world imagines Paris to be like, with the exception of the Eiffel Tower. This is the centre of Paris's tourist trade.

But what of historical Paris? It would be difficult to imagine a more important event in the history of Paris than the French Revolution: it started right here, at the Palais-Royal.

There is not much left of revolutionary Paris. When Jules Michelet set out to write his great history of the Revolution in 1847 he walked down to the Champ de Mars for a little inspiration. The Champ de Mars, where the Eiffel Tower now stands, had been the location of the Fête de la Fédération, a tremendous show of national unity, on 14 July 1790. "The Champs de Mars!" exclaimed Michelet. "This is the only monument that the Revolution has left. The Empire has its Column . . . Royalty has its Louvre . . . And the Revolution has for her monument—empty space." It is true that Napoleon wiped out as many traces of the Revolution as he could. But there is not much of the Empire left either; when Michelet refers to the column in the Place Vendôme, he could have added that that was about all that remained of Napoleon's regime, apart from the market of Saint-Germain and a fantastic neo-Egyptian structure which serves as a market by the Place du Caire in the Deuxième. As for royalty and its Louvre, no king nor emperor in France would recognize the Louvre as it stands today. The Tuileries palace, where these sovereigns lived, was destroyed during the last days of the Commune in May 1871. On the site where the glass Pyramid now stands was a mass of hovels and stinking alleys which blocked Louis XVI's view of the Louvre. There was no Rue de Rivoli. There was no Avenue de l'Opéra. There was no thrust westward. In place of the great avenues was a maze of crooked streets, passages and urban pathways that delighted Balzac in his wanderings about town in the 1830s: "through these alleys circulate bizarre beings who belong to no world, semi-naked forms, animated shadows." Thomas Carlyle's *History of the French Revolution*, published in 1837, also took a certain pleasure in painting their obscurity: "Down in those dark dens, in those dark heads and hungry hearts, who knows in what strange figure the new Political Evangel may have shaped itself."

But out of those medieval warrens there arose, in the years that immediately preceded the Revolution, a huge complex that shone at night like a single great lantern, the new Palais-Royal, that building on your right. This is the monument of the French Revolution, the monument Michelet forgot.

Its most ancient wing had been a gift from Louis XIII to Cardinal Richelieu; the cardinal's inheritors had returned it to the King, Louis XIV, who then passed it on to the younger branch of the Bourbon family, the Ducs d'Orléans—the crucial act because there was always contention between the royal cousins. It was Louis Philippe Joseph, Duc d'Orléans, at the outbreak of the Revolution, who had decided in the early 1780s to turn his palace and its gardens into a pleasure park. He employed the architect, Victor Louis, to create the large neoclassical quadrilateral that one finds today; by 1785, when Louis Philippe Joseph's father died, the Palais-Royal had become the veritable core of Paris, or as Louis Sébastien Mercier described it at the time, "a small city of luxury enclosed in a large one."

Play and corruption were organized vertically in the Palais-Royal; the higher you ascended, the more grotesque the vice. On the ground floor, through the arcades, were the shops, which were more expensive than anywhere else in town but so colourful and bright that they "sucked dry the other *quartiers* of town, which began to take on the look of sad and uninhabited provinces." There were also the cafés, the most famous being the Café de Foy in the Galerie Montpensier. Sieur Dubuisson kept its biggest rival, the Café du Caveau, in an elegant underground gallery where some of Paris's most famous men of letters, and agitators, used to gather. On the first floors there were huge gambling houses; throughout the Revolution betting—on heads and high political stakes—was a favourite pastime. Still higher up were the nests of the debauched, male and female, of every description. No class, no rank was recognized in the Palais-Royal; courtesans looked like countesses, while countesses passed as commoners. The Palais-Royal was open to everyone—which is why the Revolution started here.

So many of the most radical debating societies met beneath its arcades. The Club des Enragés held session in the Restaurant Masse; the Abbé Sieyès's Club de 1789 was founded here in 1790 attended by the flower of the French revolutionary aristocracy—La Fayette, Talleyrand, the brothers Lameth, de Broglie, Clermont-Tonnerre. Marat used to scribble away in the cafés; Camille Desmoulins screamed out to the mob standing on one of the terrace tables.

Who was this royal duke, whose renovated palace provided the springboard for the French Revolution? Historians today have a tendency to view the Revolution as something inexorable—like Tolstoy's great locomotive of history—driving itself onwards to ever more violent, destructive phases. But that was certainly not the view at the time. Louis Philippe Joseph, the Duc d'Orléans, was the man who provided the alternative route, the hope for people at the time who sought a nonviolent solution to the political crisis, the proof for people who look back on the events that something else could have happened. The Duke could have become King, replacing his more absolutist cousin, Louis XVI, with a constitutional monarchy that would have led the movement of 1789 not towards the Terror of the Year II but to England's Glorious Revolution of 1688. It is conceivable. It was what many in the early 1790s intended. But it did not happen.

From the very outset a little grain of folly had inserted itself in the story. Perhaps it was his personality. In his youth the Duc d'Orléans assumed the figure of a light-hearted Valmont, the perverse rake of Pierre Choderlos de Laclos' *Les Liaisons dangereuses* (1782). He was stupendously rich—by the 1780s his properties covered one twentieth of France from which he culled an annual rent of over seven million livres—and he was perpetually in debt, which explained the presence of the popular new bazaars in the Palais-Royal. "To what can I aspire?" he wrote to his dear old father-in-law, the Duc de Penthièvre, in 1774 during a moment of eighteenth-century spleen. "I am twenty-seven years old and I still haven't done anything." Like Valmont, the Duke had until then devoted most of his energies to the fine strategy of seducing women, though in the Duke's case most of the women came out on top.

Two of them in particular were going to exert a lifelong influence on him, Madame de Genlis and Mrs. Elliot. The husband of Félicité Ducrest de Saint-Aubin, the Comtesse de Genlis, had become captain of the Duke's private guard in 1771. Madame had read all the classical authors; she acted in a private theatrical troupe, danced, composed proverbs and even wrote her own plays; she also played the harpsichord with an exquisite touch. And at the age of twenty-six she was incredibly beautiful. A passionate, adulterous affair immediately ensued with the Duke. Madame de Genlis, who may well have been the prototype of Laclos' Madame de Merteuil, took charge of the Duke's children, including the future King of the French, Louis Philippe. She surrounded the Duke with her own business managers and a circle of literary friends who made the Académie Française, on the opposite bank of the Seine, look small. At the head of all the business managers she imposed her own brother, the Marquis Ducrest, whose family arms portrayed a ship under full sail with the disconcerting motto: "A little wind and I will go far." It was through Ducrest that many of the writers in the Duke's circle were recruited, writers of a most radical kind. Among them figured Jean-Paul Marat of *L'Ami du Peuple* and Jacques-Pierre Brissot, future leader of the Girondins. But the writer who would play the greatest role in the Duke's developing political career was a frustrated army officer who had made a name for himself through a scandalous novel on French aristocratic *mœurs*—none other than Pierre Choderlos de Laclos. In today's jargon, we would say that Laclos was destined to become the Duke's speechwriter. More than that, it was the wily Laclos who provided the Duke's political career with its plot. But something in the plot went terribly wrong.

The second important lady in the Duke's complicated life was the resplendent blonde English divorcee, Mrs. Grace Dalrymple Elliot. Her lovers included many of the great aristocrats of her day—George Selwyn, Charles William Windham and Lord Cholmondeley. The father of her illegitimate daughter, Georgiana Augusta Frederica Seymour, may well have been George, Prince of Wales—"Prinny," "Florizel," the "Pig of Pall-mall," the "Prince of Whales" as he was variously known. Prinny and the Duke were two of a kind and they became close friends during a visit the Duke made to England in July 1782: they went careering off together across Hyde Park, riding "like madmen"; they shared the same passion for horse racing at Epsom, for the progressive politics of Mr. Charles James Fox (in opposition to the King) and for the very same woman, Mrs. Elliot. Mrs. Elliot kept a diary, a record of the plot as it went wrong.

The Duke's love of things English counted against him, both in Louis XVI's court and among the public at large. In 1784 libellous pamphlets began to appear in the streets of Paris describing his "orgies" and this "Anglomania," which was the cause of his madness for horses and racing. As for Louis XVI, he hated the English. The recent Gordon Riots in London proved to him that they were still slaughterers of Catholics; besides, they had beheaded their King. Since childhood Louis had developed an obsession with the destiny of Charles I. The advisers around the Duke, on the other hand, were enthusiastically pro-English. They saw in the Duke a new William of Orange, who would establish a constitutional peace as in England in 1688.

THEIR CHANCE CAME with the developing crisis of the French national debt. The King's ministers had made numerous attempts, each one as desperate as it was ineffective. Finally they decided to summon, in February 1787, an Assembly of Notables which had not met since 1626. The Assembly was divided into seven *bureaux*, each presided over by a Prince of the Blood: thus, it was thought, assuring the King's control. But the third *bureau* was presided over by the King's cousin, the First Prince of the Blood, the Duc d'Orléans, and it was here that the renovators of the Palais-Royal saw their opportunity to introduce a good dose of constitutional reform.

But the Duke was not a great president of the third *bureau*; he preferred galloping horses. One scandal that April nearly stopped his political life altogether. A deer had wandered into the Faubourg Montmartre and the Duke gave chase; he pursued it through the *barrières* and across Place Vendôme, knocking over several pedestrians in the process, until he finally cut it down on the Place Louis XVI—today's Place de la Concorde. Perhaps the sacrifice of that poor beast on the square where the guillotine would soon stand was a premonition of things to come; it did not help the Duke's political reputation.

An early opportunity for a French constitutional monarchy was thus lost. The quickening pace of events soon offered another. The Notables concluded that the thoroughgoing reforms demanded by the King's ministers required the consent of the people. France had no parliament so the Notables demanded the convening of the Estates General, an ancient assembly divided into three "estates"—the Church, the Nobles and the Commoners—which had not met since 1614. A second Assembly of Notables was called in September 1788 to discuss how to put it together. In the meantime the skies of Heaven collapsed on France: in July a hailstorm stretching from Rouen in Normandy to Toulouse by the Pyrenees pelted the land with stones of ice so large that they killed hares and partridge, tore branches from trees, wiped out vineyards and destroyed the wheat harvest. The kingdom was faced with the worst famine since 1709. But the peasants of the fields and the artisan workers of the towns did not lay the blame at the feet of God, they accused men—the "hoarders," the rich robber merchants, the organizers of the grain trade. Popular word spread of a "famine plot."

When it became clear that elections to the Estates General were to be held in the early spring of 1789 the radical authors of the Palais-Royal got busy penning propaganda pamphlets for their Constitutional Party. Choderlos de Laclos and the dour little Abbé Sieyès composed real little bestsellers. By the winter of 1788–89 the Duc d'Orléans was regarded as leader of the "Revolution," as people were now calling the fast flow of events. It was one of the coldest winters on record. From November 1788 to January 1789 the Seine froze over. The Duke distributed food around Paris at his own expense. He became one of the most popular men in the city. The tumult developing in his Palais-Royal was indescribable. The gardens had been converted into a circus arena, with the floor of the gardens lowered three feet—as they appear today. The crowd took on the wild appearance of spectators at a Roman holiday in the Colosseum. In the cafés inflammatory proclamations were read aloud, there was a torrent of news, false and true, and improvised speeches were made from every corner. Whether he liked it or not, the Duke was in the radical camp. Through the court at Versailles rumour rapidly spread of an "Orléanist plot."

The atmosphere in which the elections to the Estates General took place in late March and early April 1789 did not augur well for the Duke's political followers, who still sought a peaceful transition to a constitutional monarchy. The poor harvest and harsh winter had created widespread suspicion and fear which, in early spring, spilled over into violence. Throughout the country bands of peasants, many of them women, attacked grain barges, wagons or flour stores; there were cases of attacks on seigniorial property, but rarely on persons. In Paris it was worse, far worse. Up to a quarter of the adult male population had been excluded from the vote. The food crisis had ravaged the 40,000 or so artisans and workers of the eastern faubourgs of Saint-Antoine and Saint-Marcel (roughly today's Vingtième and Treizième). The frozen Seine and its stinking southern tributary, the Bièvre, had thrown a host of small traders into the pit of starvation, the most notable of the new poor being the brewers of Saint-Marcel.

At one of the electoral assemblies in Paris in early April 1789, a wealthy wallpaper manufacturer, Réveillon (who had been a poor artisan himself), demanded the deregulation of the price of bread and of wages—an idea that would have won plaudits in today's *Economist*. It was not something to advocate before the hungry inhabitants of the Faubourgs. On the night of the 26–27 April, armed with a variety of home-made weapons and holding torches in their hands, a mob from Saint-Marcel crossed to Saint-Antoine, collecting supporters as they moved. "Death to the rich! Death to the aristocrats! Death to the hoarders!" shouted the crowd of three thousand rebels. On the Place de Grève, before the Hôtel de Ville, they burnt effigies of Réveillon and one of his accomplices, Henriot, a saltpetre manufacturer. They sacked Henriot's home in the Faubourg Saint-Antoine; a line of municipal Gardes Françaises managed to halt them before they reached Réveillon's home and manufactory, on a prominent corner of Rue Montreuil.

Somehow, France would always manage to have its revolutions in the spring. Spring was also the season of sporting events. Horse racing was all the rage in 1789, thanks largely to the Duke of the Palais-Royal. On 28 April, with a mob of protestors still demonstrating in Faubourg Saint-Antoine, the racing season began in the park of Vincennes. To get there, its wealthy fans had to cross the Faubourg Saint-Antoine in their carriages.

Most of the carriages got through, though not without being exposed to the menacing taunts of "Death to aristocrats!" Carriages carrying the Orléans coat of arms were applauded, with the accompanying cry of "Long live the Third Estate!" When the Duke himself appeared, the crowd started clamouring, "Long live our Father d'Orléans! Long live the only true Friend of the People!" The Duke opened his liberal purse and threw its contents to the people. The return from the races proved a sadder tale. Several of the carriages were blocked by increasingly nervous Gardes Françaises, who were holding the crowds back from Sieur Réveillon's home. The Duchesse d'Orléans insisted, with the support of the crowd, that the Gardes let her through; they obliged, thus opening a breach for the attack on Rue Montreuil. Soldiers of the Royal Cravate cavalry regiment took fright and opened fire. In the resulting mayhem several hundred were killed. Among the bodies of the protesters were found écu coins that could be traced to the Duke. Vicious talk in Versailles about the "Orléanist plot" grew. Increasingly heated debate was heard on the streets of the "famine plot."

Prospects for a quiet "Glorious Revolution" *à la mode anglaise* were looking increasingly dim. Less than a week after the slaughter on Rue Montreuil the Estates General were opened in Versailles. For a month all business was dominated by procedural matters and for a month the First Prince of the Blood remained silent; the Duke's political position was unknown, save at a vote on credentials when he joined a minority of forty-seven liberal nobles in the call for the uniting of the three estates in a single assembly. It was finally the showdown between the Third Estate and the two privileged orders in June which forced the Duke to speak. On 10 June Sieyès, who had early gone over to the Third, declared the Third to be the "Commons" and summoned the other two orders to join them. During the next week almost half the clergy had moved over to the Third Estate, which on 17 June declared itself to be the "National Assembly."

This was perhaps the critical moment in the French Revolution, though it occurred almost a month before the popular rising of 14 July. In denying the legitimacy of the two privileged orders the declaration of 17 June closed the door to the possibility of a two-house parliament, the mark of most democracies in the Western world today. It blocked the way to a calm "Glorious Revolution." It cut the ground from beneath the Duc d'Orléans. This was lost on the Duke who, caught up in the enthusiasm of the moment, committed himself to the single-chamber parliament, though it was quite against his own interest. On that same 17 June the Duke stood up and, with his voice shaking, demanded that his fellow gentlemen join the "National Assembly"; then he fainted and had to be carried outside to recover his nerve. Only eighty-nine nobles voted for the Duke's motion. After that, the Duke retreated once again into his shell.

Later in the same week there occurred the famous Tennis Court Oath, when the Assembly vowed never to separate until they had voted on a "solid and equitable Constitution." It was the same week that the

Comte de Mirabeau addressed, from his seat in the Assembly, the representatives of the King with the words, "We will only leave our places by the force of bayonets!" At ten o'clock on the morning of 25 June the forty-seven liberal nobles left their seats in the Second Estate and entered, with huge applause, the hall of the National Assembly. The Duke was among them, though he did his best not to be noticed. "Yes, I was one of the forty-seven and all that is well and good," he told his son, Louis Philippe, in the dark days of 1792. "But do you know what the others said to me? . . . Well, they said, 'Monseigneur, do not come with us for we will look as if we *are following you*, and that will not be good.'" He added, "They were most careful to distance themselves from me and to shun me on every occasion." So the Duke's political friends had abandoned him? Nothing of the sort. On 2 July the National Assembly voted him their president. On 3 July he refused to accept the honour with the curious explanation that "I will always sacrifice my personal interest for the good of the State." Not a few in the Assembly suspected that he meant exactly the reverse.

What a dramatic period the last half of June had been. It had put France on the road to demagogy and terror; it had also shown to the world that little grain of folly in the Duc d'Orléans' personality—already known to his intimates—that would dampen hopes for an alternative, non-violent route towards reform: the Duke lacked guts.

ON 14 JULY the Bastille fell. It was the behaviour of the Duke that day which determined that the prince of the people's Palais-Royal would never be king.

On the night he joined the National Assembly, 3 July, there was a massive fireworks display at the Palais-Royal and all the houses in the neighbourhood were illuminated. On the doors to the circus in the middle of the gardens there were posters praising the Duke for his "zealous patriotism"; he was celebrated as the "avenger of the oppressed *patrie*" and compared to his ancestor, the first Bourbon king, Henri IV—"*le plus chéri des rois*." Jacques Necker, the reforming Controller-General, was acclaimed along with the Duc d'Orléans. There had never been such agitation in and around the palace. But it was not all such a pretty sight.

Bands of armed men, like those of April, roamed the streets; many of them could be seen at the Palais-Royal. The Marquis de Ferrières, a noble from the Poitou who had remained seated in the Second Estate, wrote to his sister of forty thousand armed brigands from Paris who were rumoured to be marching on Versailles. But the Marquis did not seem too worried. The man supposed to be responsible for all this, the Duc d'Orléans, "is too cowardly to be a villain."

Over the next fortnight there were armed attacks on the city *barrières*, those lovely eighteenth-century customs houses where all wagons had to stop and pay taxes for the produce they carried into Paris. For the mob the taxes were part of the "aristocratic plot" to starve the citizens. One of the reasons the twin houses of the Barrière d'Enfer can still be admired at Place Denfert-Rochereau is because that was the route to Orléans and the *barrière* was the Duke's property; none of the Duke's properties were attacked.

The Palais-Royal by the first week of July was an entrenched camp where a respectable citizen no longer dared tread. A list of "Patriots" was registered at the Café du Caveau; *discours fleuves* were pronounced by agitators on the terraces. Narrow, curving streets—the Rue de Rivoli did not exist—led down to the Hôtel de Ville, or City Hall, where the propertied men of Paris had persuaded the electors of the Third Estate to gather their sixty local offices in an assembly they called the "Commune." The Commune of Paris decided that week to organize a new bourgeois militia that would contain the mobs and the wild men of the Palais-Royal should they turn violent. The King also had his troops surrounding Paris, ostensibly to keep order. But rumour spread that he was planning a *coup d'état royal*: the forced closure of the National Assembly and the occupation of the capital. His troops, under the command of the Duc de Broglie, were not even French but Swiss and German mercenaries—it was like holding out a red blanket to the crowds.

It was rumour, for once, founded on fact. The chief fomenters of the *coup* were, it seems, the King's youngest brother, the Comte d'Artois, with support from the older brother, the Comte de Provence, the Prince de Condé and his family along with the Polignacs. The signal for action would be the dismissal of the popular reformist first minister, Jacques Necker.

Necker and his ministers were dismissed on Saturday afternoon, 11 July, and their places were taken by the Baron de Breteuil and the most reactionary nobles the King could find. The timing was obviously chosen to give the court the weekend to prepare for the use of force against the National Assembly, which would not meet on a Sunday. But the plotters of the *coup* had not counted on the reaction in Paris; the news of the dismissals arrived at the Palais-Royal on Sunday, the 12th, at midday when the number of working people present was at its maximum— the King could not have picked a worse hour of the week.

Pandemonium broke out. Chairs were upturned and the tables were transformed into popular speaking stands. The most famous speech, because it was recorded, was made by Mirabeau's young secretary, Camille Desmoulins, on a table at the Café de Foy. The crowd grabbed the busts of their heroes, the Duc d'Orléans and Necker, from Curtius's wax museum at Salon No. 7, dressed them in black crêpe and stuck them on pikes. Then they marched them in procession up and down the Rues Saint-Martin and Saint-Denis, obliging passers-by to doff their hats. In the Tuileries gardens they ran into a company of the Royal Allemand; in the skirmish that followed the man carrying the Duke's bust was dragged by a horse into the Place Louis XV (Place de la Concorde). But a defecting band of the old Gardes Françaises, in defence of the "people," drove the Royal Allemand away from the Tuileries. The battle was now on for the sovereignty of Paris.

A Swiss regiment, the Salis-Samade, attempted to regain the right bank that Sunday night, but it retreated again across the river early the next morning. King Louis XVI had lost the centre of Paris. At the same time there were running battles fought out at the *barrières*, and the monastery—the seventeenth-century residence of Saint Vincent de Paul, now a grain depot and prison—was sacked.

WHILE PARIS WAS in a state of insurrection, the "avenger of the oppressed *patrie*," the Duc d'Orléans, had spent his Sunday at the Château de Raincy fishing in the river with a party that included the liberal aristocrat, the Comte de La Marck, and Mrs. Elliot, who, fortunately for us, kept a record of their day and those that followed. They had planned on an evening of light opera at the Comédie Italienne (forerunner of the Opéra Comique). At 8 p.m. they duly arrived at the Porte Saint-Martin, where their city carriages awaited them. Mrs. Elliot's domestics came rushing up to speak of the dramatic events of the day; she proposed to the Duke that he join her in her coach to avoid being recognized. After making a few turns in the town they arrived at Monceau, another of the Duke's properties, where they found the servants in a state of panic—they had heard that the Duke had been imprisoned in the Bastille and had even been decapitated. Mrs. Elliot, a staunch royalist, took the Duke out into the gardens and, in a conversation that lasted until two in the morning, persuaded him, in a demonstration of royal allegiance, to attend the next morning the daily ceremony of the King's rising from bed, the *levée du Roi*. The Duke sent a messenger to the Baron de Breteuil protesting that "he had done nothing to obtain this popularity" among the mob and would be at the King's chamber the next morning to watch him get out of bed.

So on Monday, 13 July, as the armed boats of the Swiss Salis-Samade attempted, unsuccessfully, to regain the right bank of the Seine, the hero of the Paris crowd was in Versailles watching the King leave his bed. When the First Prince of the Blood passed a shirt to the King, His Most Christian Majesty went purple with rage and refused to say a word—a most embarrassing snub. The Duke left the palace in a state of shock. He dropped in for a moment at the National Assembly, which, in its first meeting during the insurrection, seemed to be managing very well without him. Then he rushed back to Monceau and Mrs. Elliot. He announced to her, fumbling with his coat, that from now on he was going to "cultivate friends for himself." Mrs. Elliot wrote that it was "from this moment that the Duke became his most violent in politics . . . I am sure that if one had shown him more consideration and confidence one would have been able to detach him from his detestable entourage." Talleyrand was to claim that the Duke had "already pushed himself too far forward to be able to retreat."

But retreat he did—on Tuesday, 14 July—the day the crowd took the Bastille. That was the tragedy of the Duke, and of France. On Sunday night, while the Duke was having his conversation with Mrs. Elliot in the gardens of Monceau, the Paris Commune formally voted for the creation of their bourgeois militia. Each of the sixty electoral Districts was ordered immediately to enrol and arm 200 responsible men, thereby creating a force of 12,000 men. Within three days this independent force had risen to an incredible 48,000. It had been created without consulting either the King's ministry or the National Assembly; the Paris Commune was now acting effectively as an autonomous government, encouraging the demands of the crowd in the street in order to bend both the King and the single-chamber Assembly to its will. A normal state would have considered the creation of such a militia treasonous, but nobody at the time dared pronounce the word. On Monday the crowd attacked and emptied the debtors' gaol of La Force, barricades went up in the streets and trenches were dug to repel any royalist cavalry attack.

One act could have re-established, in a single blow, the rule of law; one single deed would have covered the executive ministry, the national legislature and the new municipal government with a sheen of legitimacy: the nomination of the First Prince of the Blood, the Duc d'Orléans, as commander of Paris's new bourgeois militia. Even at this late date a decisive act by the Duke could have perhaps saved the situation. The project appears to have been under serious consideration on Tuesday morning, the 14th.

Mrs. Elliot relates that when she came to Monceau that morning she discovered that two important men had already been admitted to the Duke's chamber, the Marquis de La Fayette and Monsieur Sylvain Bailly. The Marquis, though only thirty-two, was vice-president of the National Assembly; during his youthful campaigning in America's War of Independence, he had become George Washington's adopted son and had returned to France married to "Liberty"—with a fortune of 120,000 livres a year to support him. Bailly, an astronomer, had been the first president of the Assembly and now chaired the executive committee of Electors that sat in the Hôtel de Ville. The two men to-gether had the power to name the Duke "Lieutenant General of the Kingdom," as many of the placards posted in the Palais-Royal were de-manding. Such a position would not only have given the Duke com-mand of the new militia, it would have made him King. The militia's troops were already sporting cockades of red and blue, which were the colours of Paris but also, significantly, the colours of the House of Orleans—the addition of the colour white of royalty would be the ba-sis of the tricolour flag of France. The Duke could have been King of the French under a tricolour flag on 14 July 1789.

Exactly what La Fayette and Bailly discussed in the Duke's chamber is unknown. When the Duke emerged from the meeting he saw Mrs. El-liot and asked her to join him and his two friends in an early afternoon "*déjeuner*"—"lunch" in these early days of the Revolution had not yet be-come a common habit. They were just settling down to the meal when the sound of cannon could be heard in the distance. A few minutes later the message arrived that the Bastille had just been taken by force. The Duke's two honourable guests left "in great haste." Then the Duc de Biron, a horse-racing enthusiast who received many of the leading liberal nobles in his home, and the Vicomte de Noailles, La Fayette's brother-in-law, burst into the room. Mrs. Elliot withdrew, though not without first pleading with the Duke to offer his services to the King. "He got very an-gry with me and asked if I was not in the pay of his enemies to give him such counsel, and he immediately left me."

Was Grace Elliot simply inventing the story? She had no motive to do so. She does not appear to be aware of its significance. But impor-tant it seems to be. It was the last opportunity that France had to take the road towards a constitutional monarchy. The three men who had the power to do this were together on the morning the Bastille fell ap-parently discussing that very possibility. No witnesses were left because two of them were guillotined and the sole survivor developed such a contempt for the Duke that he would hardly have admitted being with him on 14 July.

The crown was there for the picking that day. Yet, for whatever reason, the Duke never presented himself as a candidate to command the National Guard, as the new militia was called, on Wednesday, the 15th. It brought down on him the contempt of all his followers, including Mirabeau, who remarked, "People were ready to make him Lieutenant General of the Kingdom and he had only himself to blame for not becoming it." La Fayette took up the command of the National Guard himself. As of that date, the chances of France adopting a constitutional monarchy during the Revolution were virtually dead—before the National Assembly had even started drawing up a constitution.

When a humbled King, having ordered the withdrawal of his troops from the capital and the reinstallation of Necker as chief minister, went to Paris in simple civilian dress on 17 July, he was received on the steps of the Hôtel de Ville by General La Fayette and the new mayor of Paris, Monsieur Bailly. It was clear where the power now lay: in a one-chamber parliament and an autonomous Commune of Paris, both competing for approval from the mob. It was a poisonous combination.

How different might have been the course of history can be seen when, forty-one years later, in July 1830, an older and wiser La Fayette received on the same steps the new Duc d'Orléans, Louis Philippe Joseph's elder son, and proclaimed him "King of the French." It stopped the Revolution of 1830 dead in its tracks. If a similar act had been performed on the day of the seizure of the Bastille, the vicious process of revolution might have ended there and France could have avoided its mad career into terror and war. As Mirabeau bitterly put it, the fault lay in the weakness of one man. But instead of accepting the post of Lieutenant General of the Kingdom, and despite his angry response to Mrs. Elliot, the Duke did in fact follow her bad advice. He rode out to Versailles the same afternoon and sat meekly in an antechamber of the Versailles Palace waiting for one of the last sessions of the King's Council to draw to its dreary conclusion. When the door finally opened, the Duke asked the King if he could depart for England. Louis XVI, exasperated at his cousin's evident cowardice, simply heaved his shoulders and swept by.

The Duke did eventually leave for England, but only after a second occasion for kingship had presented itself during the bloody days of October 1789, when the King and his family were forcibly transferred to the Tuileries, the house next door to the Palais-Royal. Nobody has ever been able to establish precisely what the Duke's role was in this. But he was seen lurking in Versailles' Hall of Mirrors the day the crowd attacked Marie Antoinette's apartment, murdering and horribly mutilating her private guards. In England he attempted to establish an Anglo-French alliance—long the ambition of France's liberal nobility—without any visible success. He returned to Paris in July 1790 in time for the Fête de la Fédération on the Champ de Mars. The festival was presided over by La Fayette; it could have been the Duke if he had played his cards well in 1789. He and his son, the future King of the French, both became members of the Jacobin Club. In the Convention he sat as "Philippe Égalité" among the "Mountain"—the most radical wing of French revolutionary politics—and from there, on 16 January 1793, he voted for the death of the King. "This is a sad subject," he said to Mrs. Elliot two months after Louis XVI had been guillotined on Place de la Révolution (Concorde); "you cannot judge me, you must not judge me." To his younger son, the Duc de Montpensier, he had said on the night of the vote, the tears pouring down his cheeks: "Montpensier, I haven't the courage to look at you . . . I did not know what I was doing."

Philippe Égalité was arrested on 6 April of that same year on the trumped up charge that he had collaborated with generals who had deserted to the enemy on the northern war front—General La Fayette, who had never addressed a word to the Duke since the fall of the Bastille, was among the traitors. He spent the summer with two of his sons in a fortress at Marseille. In October he was taken back to Paris to face the Revolutionary Tribunal on 6 November. Philippe Égalité asked to be guillotined the same day. His wish was granted.

He died bravely. At five o'clock the following morning, his hair powdered and wearing polished boots, he mounted the tumbril with an assured air to join three unknown condemned artisans; one of them, a locksmith, refused to be guillotined in such bad company. But, one by one, all four climbed the scaffold, Philippe Égalité being—as he had often been in life—the last in the line. The aides of the executioner demanded his boots. "You can take them off easier from a corpse," he replied. The drums rolled. "Hurry up!" cried the Duke the instant before his head was chopped off.

SAINT-PAUL

MÉTRO STOP NO. 11, Saint-Paul, is the only station to serve the seventeenth-century quarter of the Marais, the most popular stalking ground in town. Jules Michelet, who was born here in 1798, loved it: its dark alleys and stove-bellied, pale yellow stone walls coloured his whole account of the French Revolution. Walking in some of its streets today you can still pick up something of the atmosphere he evoked. The station stands on the site where, in the early morning of 10 August 1792, crowds of armed artisans—"from the Bastille up to the church of Saint-Paul in *this wide and open part of the Rue Saint-Antoine*"—converged to the beat of drums and the tocsin bell of the Section Quatre-Vingts; onwards they marched to the Tuileries Palace, where, in a pitched battle, they overthrew the Bourbon monarchy. The high ornate Jesuit façade of the Église Saint-Paul-Saint-Louis, on the south side of the street, towered over them—a reminder that, before the crowds in Paris were atheist revolutionaries, they were Catholics of the most radical, fervent kind.

The Jesuits had been introduced into the Marais by the widow of the Constable of France, killed in battle in November 1569 defending Catholic Paris against the Protestant warriors who surrounded the city. At the time there seemed nothing inconsistent about inviting the Jesuits into Paris; indeed Ignatius Loyola, with François Xavier and three Spanish priests, had founded the Society of Jesus in the crypt of the Sanctum Martyrium near the summit of Montmartre in 1534. No city in France was more Catholic than Paris in the sixteenth century.

There exist a few remnants of that late Renaissance Catholic Paris in the area around here. To the west of Saint-Paul, on a black-and-white Louis Philippe wooden façade, is a sign, "The Auld Alliance, Scottish

PARIS

NAch dem die Königliche Hochzeit zwischen dem König von Navarra vnd der Princessin ... mit Dolchen vnd Wehr in Leib gestochen darauf dann das Volck bey nächtlicher Gestalt die Thüren eingebrochen zu ...

Pub," and it sells the best Scottish beers and the largest selection of whiskies in Paris, including the Dallas Dhu. On the walls hang old maps of Scotland and several historical documents, going back to the Treaty of Corbeil of 1326 between the King of France and Robert, by the Grace of God, King of the Scots. The documents prove, as the singing in the pub still demonstrates, that the ties between Scotland and France run deep — deep and religious.

The singing leads back to a sixteenth-century ballad about a soldier called Montgomery. It is one of the saddest ballads I know.

> Moy très bien les congonois
> Qui naguères estois
> De Montgommery comte.

Montgomery's ancestors were counts, starts the song in old French. In fact Gabriel de Montgomery's ancestors can be traced to Norman retainers of William the Bastard, who followed the Duke to England after the Battle of Hastings in 1066. The older branch established themselves as seigneurs in Normandy, while the younger branch had to carve out their fortune as warlords in Scotland, attached to King David I (1124–53). It was poor Scottish lords like the Montgomeries who furnished the spearhead of the French royal armies that would eventually throw the English out of France. In recognition of their service Charles VII created the Hundred Archers of the Scottish Guard in 1422; a little over a century later, in 1543, Francis I promoted Gabriel's father, Jacques, to be their captain. It was one of the most powerful positions in the kingdom and was the reason why the Montgomeries, as the song goes, became counts.

Gabriel, born on the family properties in Normandy or in the Beauce, either in 1526 or in 1530, was groomed to be a count. But fate decided otherwise.

> La France m'a cogneu,
> Chevalier bien reçeu
> Monté en fort bon ordre.

As Lieutenant of the Scottish Archers the young Montgomery cut a dashing figure in court. Then, on a sweltering Friday, in the "wide and open part" of the Rue Saint-Antoine—not far from where the métro stop now stands—King Henri II of France challenged Gabriel de Montgomery to a joust. What occurred next was one of the most tragic riding accidents in history; the whole of Western Europe would be plunged into a generation of religious war and strife as a result of it.

> Par un fatal destin
> Le Roy voulant s'ébattre
> Me dist par un matin
> Qu'à moi voulait combattre.

Not even the most talented playwright could pull together all the strands that fatal destiny suddenly combined on that day. Europe was at a turning point. The religious wars in what we today call Germany were over, the old Holy Roman Emperor, Charles V, sworn enemy of France, had abdicated. In April 1559 Spanish and French envoys had met in Cateau-Cambrésis, on the French border with the Spanish Netherlands, to sign a treaty which ended sixty years of war in Italy. The great dynastic tensions that had dominated the first half of the century ended at Cateau-Cambrésis. The year 1559 should have ushered in peace for all of Western Europe, were it not for Montgomery's jousting lance.

Two royal marriages had been negotiated at Cateau to seal the treaty. Philip II, a widower since the death of Mary Tudor, Queen of England, the previous November, was to marry Henri II's eldest daughter, Elisabeth; and the French king's thirty-six-year-old spinster sister, Marguerite, was to marry Philip's ally, Emmanuel-Philibert, Duke of Savoy. Henri II arranged a fabulous show in Paris, where the two marriages were to be celebrated in late June, the central event being a five-day jousting tournament held on the "wide and open part" of Rue Saint-Antoine, at that time the only open space in Paris, a favourite spot for *promeneurs* that stretched from what is now Rue de Sévigné to the Bastille and northwards up to today's Place des Vosges, which was then occupied by the royal Château des Tournelles. Stands higher than many of the houses were built around the periphery of the space, decorated in the colours of France, Spain and Savoy; the paving stones were torn up and replaced by sand; and the open city sewer—today Rue de Turenne—was hidden from sight by a huge wooden cross. Elisabeth married Philip II, who had sent the haughty Duke of Alba as his proxy, on Thursday, 22 June, and on Wednesday, 28 June, the jousting began. The weather got hot and sultry.

The heat had made the crowds uncomfortable and nervous on Friday afternoon—not morning as in the ballad—when King Henri was due to joust. At the centre of the royal box, dressed in bejewelled garments, sat his queen, Catherine de Medici; to her right was her eldest son, the future Francis II, with his recent wife, a tall lanky adolescent, Mary, Queen of Scots. Queen Catherine had passed a difficult night in the Château des Tournelles; she had dreamt of her husband lying on the ground in agony, his face covered in blood. Medieval superstition, magic and prophecy was never far from the surface in this late Renaissance world. The accumulating signs of the approaching catastrophe had a Shakespearean tone: Nostradamus, the King's seer, had written in 1555 in quatrain XXXV of his *Centuries* that

> The young lion will surmount the old
> In battle field in single duel,
> In a golden cage, his eyes shall be holed,
> Two wounds in one, then a death most cruel.

The stars foretold a violent death by iron or by fire at the age of forty— Henri II was in his fortieth year; Bishop Luc Gauric, famous in Italy for his accurate predictions, had warned Henri to avoid all combat at the age of forty because he could suffer a wound in his head that might render him blind. It was the Habsburg emperor, Charles V, who had told Admiral de Coligny that the young Gabriel de Montgomery, to whom he had just been introduced, had a mark between his eyes that signified the death of a prince of the *fleur de lis*. Catherine, like her husband, was aware of all these tales, and would rather have been with the King on the banks of the Loire.

But not King Henri, who carried the black-and-white colours of his mistress from Anet, Diane de Poitiers, when he rode out on to the field of contest. "Squeeze tight at your knees!" he shouted out at his first challenger, his future brother-in-law, Emmanuel-Philibert, "For I shall give you a good shaking, whatever our alliance and fraternity!" Henri wanted to show who was King. The two chargers raced towards each other, there was a crash, Emmanuel-Philibert tottered awhile — but remained in his saddle. Then it was the turn of François, Duc de Guise, one of the most powerful men in the kingdom. The chargers sped across the sanded course; another shock: neither man showed a sign of trembling. Henri was bitterly disappointed in his own performance. Against whom could he prove his royal virility?

His eye alighted on the Lieutenant of the Scottish Archers, blond, athletic and ten years his junior. Trumpets and bugles brayed and they charged; the sound of the collision echoed around the square—but both men held fast to their mounts. By the rules of the game, the King's jousting for that day should have ended there. But his Valois blood was up. He demanded his challenger to play again. Montgomery refused, invoking the heat and the late hour of the day. "It is an order!" shouted the King. Queen Catherine sent a messenger begging him to stop. The Chief Marshal was called in to place the golden-coloured helmet on the King's head; as he lowered the visor, the Marshal said, "Sire, I swear by living God that for the last three days I have been dreaming that something terrible will happen to you, that this last day will be for you Fatal."

Montgomery prepared himself. For some inexplicable reason his team forgot to replace his lance, as the rules required; he went into the field with the lance that had been cracked by the last rude encounter. As the King entered the course one report writes of a young boy running out screaming, "Sire, don't go!" The trumpets, strangely, did not play. Instead, there was a hush. A rumour spread like a menacing wave through the crowd. The horsemen faced each other, then set off at a gallop; there was a loud report as Montgomery's shaft shattered.

The King swayed to left and right. Grabbing his horse's neck he managed to hold himself in his saddle. He slumped forward. The

Queen, at her tribune, stood up; the crowd gasped. The Constable of France, Montmorency and Marshal de Tavannes rushed out and allowed their sovereign to slip into their arms. On the ground, they carefully removed the helmet; blood poured into the sand.

What happened next is the subject of 450 years of debate. Some witnesses claim to have seen Montgomery beat a way through the throng that had gathered around the prostrate King and, beside himself with grief, ask for a pardon—which the King granted. Other contemporaries claim the King was already unconscious, which seems likely. What probably happened is that Montgomery was among the men who carried the King to the Château des Tournelles. At the entrance, despite the splinter in his right eye emerging from his temple, the King had regained consciousness sufficiently to mount the steps himself, with aid. Montgomery was at his bedside that evening and it was perhaps there that the King said to him: "Do not concern yourself, you have no need of a pardon. You obeyed your King and acted as a good knight and valiant man of arms."

For a sixteenth-century chevalier like Montgomery that verbal acquittal was the equivalent of the voice of God. But the tension in the court, particularly in the vindictive sobbing of the women, was unbearable. Catherine de Medici never would forgive him—he was a regicide, an outcast. Montgomery fled Paris that night. The King died in agony on 9 July.

A strong monarch like Henri may have held the kingdom together, though it would have been a repressive age for the Protestants because Henri had never been tolerant of the reformed faith. Catherine de Medici, on the other hand, though the niece of a pope, as Queen Dowager initially showed a surprising degree of indulgence. But the ultra-Catholic family, the Guises, managed to seize control of the government. Protestant circles spoke of a *coup d'état*. Their leaders, in February 1561, met at the port of Hugues, near Nantes, to discuss what to do. They decided that the best course of action was to capture the main members of the royal family and set up a regency in their favour. The plan went seriously wrong and fifty-two of the ringleaders, singing psalms as they queued up for the block, were beheaded in front of the

royal family at Amboise in March. For France it was the beginning of
civil war. In fanatical Catholic Paris it gave rise to a new derisive term
for these treasonous heretics: the conspirators of Hugues became the
"Huguenots"—a name soon applied to all Protestants in France.

The regicide Montgomery had been on the run. First he had fled to
his estate at Ducey, in Lower Normandy, by the Baie de Saint-Michel.
Obviously he was not safe there, so he set sail for that haven of liberty
and latter-day adulterers, the island of Jersey, recently annexed to the
diocese of Winchester, though there was nothing very English about
the place in those days—its inhabitants spoke a Norman dialect that
made Montgomery feel at home. Diplomatic correspondence proves
he was in Venice in December 1559. By the following spring he was in
London at the court of Queen Elizabeth I.

There he acquired a fine command of English; befriended Sir
William Cecil, the brilliant humanist and now the Queen's Secretary of
State; established an excellent rapport with Sir Nicholas Throckmorton, shortly to be named ambassador to the Valois court; and earned
the respect of the Queen herself. He also converted to the reformed religion, though exactly how this happened is not known. Montgomery
became a Calvinist, the radical branch of Protestantism which was
hardly in the spirit of Cranmer's Book of Common Prayer that guided
Elizabeth's resplendent court. But it was the strain that was spreading
fast through his native lands of Lower Normandy. Most likely, what
prompted the conversion was an appeal he received in November 1561
from François de Bricqueville, Baron de Colombières, "to come to the
assistance of the Protestants [les réformés] of Lower Normandy, who are
persecuted and envisage taking up arms."

Montgomery landed in Lower Normandy in December 1561 and began his career as a liberator of the Protestants; his new seigniorial arms
were proudly emblazoned with a helmet pierced by a lance. Montgomery seized Avranches, in Lower Normandy, killed all the local nuns
and priests and shipped the cathedral's gold and silver off to the island
of Tombelaine, by Mont-Saint-Michel. He then marched his little army
into the Loire Country, up the course of the river, to the cathedral town
of Bourges, which he took without a fight. By late spring of 1562, the

Huguenot armies—the soldiers dressed in white surcoats and chanting psalms as they went into battle—controlled the Loire, Saintonge, Poitou, Lyon, Dauphiné and the valley of the Rhône. But in June and July plague broke out in the towns and the Duc de Guise's Catholic armies began to make progress. Montgomery conducted a brave defence of the Norman city, Rouen; Queen Catherine, knowing this, participated in the battle. The city was taken, the inhabitants slaughtered—but Montgomery made his escape by boat down the river.

An English fleet arrived in Le Havre on 29 October subjecting the town to such a vigorous occupation under the Earl of Warwick—many inhabitants were forced to leave their homes, Frenchmen were excluded from government, the English pound sterling was the only acceptable currency—that even the Protestants were shocked. At Amboise, in March 1563, a peace between Protestants and Catholics was patched together and they joined forces to throw the English out of Le Havre on 30 June.

Protestantism in France was still winning hordes of converts, many through contact with the Spanish Netherlands. In August 1567 Antwerp rose in rebellion, and from there the violence spread through the country, spilling over into France. In the Netherlands, King Philip II, not a tolerant Christian, used the vilest means of repression. In France, religious civil war broke out once more. Montgomery participated in the siege of Paris at which Montmorency, the Constable of France, was killed. Another peace was cobbled together at Longjumeau in March 1568, but as Throckmorton noted gloomily in a dispatch to Queen Elizabeth later that year, "there are more Protestants who have perished during this peace than during the preceding war."

There began, in the summer of 1568, a huge exodus of Protestants from all parts of the country to the fortified port town of La Rochelle, on the Atlantic coast. It was known at the time as the "Flight from Egypt." The fulcrum of French Huguenot power in France thus shifted south-west. The Protestant spirit was further galvanized by the arrival at La Rochelle on 28 September of Jeanne d'Albret. Her mother had been the elder sister of Francis I; her late husband, Antoine de Bourbon, was head of the Bourbon family, direct descendants of Louis XI, and thus heirs to the French throne should Catherine's unhealthy Valois children have no issue. Jeanne was Queen of the small Protestant kingdom of Navarre, in the Pyrenees, which was at that moment overrun by Catholic forces. She was accompanied by her fifteen-year-old son, Henri—the future Henri IV. Every Huguenot saw in this athletic figure their true sovereign, while his widowed mother acted as an excellent counter to the black-gowned Catholic dowager queen, Catherine.

Catherine de Medici was becoming increasingly intolerant of heretics. In April 1569 the Spanish ambassador came to her chamber after learning that she had fallen ill. He told her that the time had come for *la sonoria*, the "death knell." This delightful image of *la sonoria*—annihilating all her main Protestant opponents with one ring of the bell—brought new life to the Queen Mother; she was soon on her feet again. The ambassador's sweet words of mass murder also encouraged her already pronounced tendency for the occult, her irrational "medievalism" one could justly call it. Catherine collaborated with an Italian sorcerer who kept his shop, Vallée de Misère, on the Quai de la Mégisserie in Paris. His spells seemed to work particularly well when poison was added to the menu. Several Protestant leaders died of spasms in the month of May 1569. On 11 June Prince Wolfgang of Bavaria, who was bringing across France an army of German *Reiters* and lansquenets to the aid of the Huguenots, dropped dead after quaffing a goblet of wine.

That was the month Jeanne d'Albret summoned the saviour of the Protestants, Gabriel de Montgomery, to La Rochelle. She named him Lieutenant General of the Kingdom of Navarre and ordered him to bring her subjects back "under the obedience of Her Majesty [herself] and punish the rebels, who had revolted and pillaged the reformed churches and imprisoned their ministers." It was the sort of job for which the merciless Montgomery was ideally suited.

Montgomery, dressed entirely in black with a glacial look in his mournful blue eyes, led an army into the little kingdom of Navarre, covering over 150 leagues in ten days. By August he had restored the lands to their Protestant sovereigns. It had been a brutal campaign.

Montgomery's handling of the Carmelite monastery at Trie was typical: all the monks were slaughtered and their bodies chucked into the wells. The prior claimed to be a distant relative of Montgomery's. "Very well then," replied the regicide; "I shall render you the honours due to your birth and you shall be hanged from the main gate." The sentence was executed without further delay.

In Henri de Navarre, the Huguenots now had at their head a powerful contender for the French throne, while the future looked increasingly bleak for Catherine's sickly litter of children. The reign of Francis II had lasted barely a year. It was no secret that Charles IX, aged nineteen when Montgomery recovered Navarre, lay at death's door. He cut a poor figure for a warrior king.

By the following spring, 1570, Henri de Navarre was advancing on Paris, with Montgomery at his side. In Paris, a mood of nervous foreboding developed. Catherine dispatched her top diplomats to La Rochelle and another peace was finally signed at Saint-Germain-en-Laye on 29 July 1570. Both sides were exhausted by war. The terms were much the same as the Peace of Amboise several years earlier. But there was a secret clause which created some novelty: Henri de Navarre was to marry Catherine's only healthy offspring, Marguerite, who would be remembered in history, fiction and film as the tragic Queen Margot.

There was, in fact, around 1570, a spate of dynastic marriage proposals throughout Western Europe. Though no guarantee, it remained in a world that was still in many ways medieval the surest route to peace: marry the leading opponent and, in the good feelings generated by the feast and the princely honeymoon, old rivalries could be buried. In 1570 the Spanish and German Habsburgs were busy arranging marriages into French, English and Scottish royalty. The Guises hoped Margot would marry Henri, the young duke—who was caught in her bedroom one morning in spring. The most hopeless project of the time was between Elizabeth of England and Catherine's youngest son, the Duc d'Alençon. When negotiations began in 1572, the Queen was entering her fortieth year while the mad, pockmarked duke was exactly half her age. The Montgomery family enjoyed greater success. Shortly after the Peace of Saint-Germain was

signed his wife, Isabelle, travelled to England and negotiated the marriage of their daughter, Roberte, to the Vice Admiral of the English
Fleet, Sir Arthur Champernowne, who also happened to be Governor
of Jersey. The wedding was celebrated on 15 December 1571 in the
Royal Chapel of Greenwich before the Virgin Queen.

The marriage in December 1570 of King Charles IX to the exquisitely beautiful Elisabeth of Austria, daughter of the Emperor, enchanted
the crowds in Paris and guaranteed the peace between the houses of
Habsburg and Valois. But the critical marriage between Catholic and
Huguenot, Margot and Henri de Navarre, did not look at all promising.
Margot was revolted by the idea. She had been severely beaten up by
her elder brothers, the King and the Duc d'Anjou, for her flirtation
with the Duc de Guise. Henri de Navarre may have looked athletic but
Margot had scented that, unwashed, he smelled of the southern sun
and garlic.

The events leading to the marriage did not augur well either. Jeanne
d'Albret died in Paris on 4 June 1572 after exhausting herself in the
preparations. There was talk in Paris of poisonings and murder; and
thoughts of *la sonoria* were not far from the minds of those who governed. Others were worried. Paris, with its narrow unlit streets, its
dead-end alleys, its walls and moats, along with its fanatically Catholic
population seemed a perfect trap.

The Huguenots rode straight into it. Henri, whose mother's death
would make him King of Navarre, left his seat at Pau on 23 May 1572.
On his way north he gathered around him all the major Protestant leaders of France. News of Jeanne's death did not delay the procession's
progress. Montgomery left his estate of Ducey around 20 June and
joined Henri at Blois from where a retinue of nine hundred Huguenot
gentlemen, all dressed in black, headed directly for Paris. At the Porte
Saint-Jacques the entire corps of the city's militia were there to greet
them. They rode up a street called Hell to join Catherine's court at the
Louvre. For the Catholic denizens this black procession must have
been an awesome sight. For Montgomery, who rode immediately behind Navarre, the stifling summer's heat must have carried a few memories.

There can be no doubt about Catherine's plans to murder the Huguenots, though just how extreme was her first intention will never be known. Her most recent biographer, Leonie Frieda, attempts to shift the blame for what followed to the bellicose Huguenot leader, Admiral de Coligny, who not only encouraged King Charles to invade the Spanish Netherlands but sent in a preliminary force of 5,000 on 17 July. The Spanish trapped and slaughtered most of them at Mons; only a few hundred escaped to tell their tale. In Catherine's view, a war with Spain would have destroyed her kingdom and delivered what remained to the Protestants. Blame a warmongering victim for the atrocities committed by the murderer: historically, this has never been a good argument— every modern tyrant has used it.

An emergency meeting of the Royal Council on 10 August voted against an invasion of the Netherlands. Coligny's was the only dissenting vote. That is what sealed his fate. The next day Catherine and her soldier son, the Duc d'Anjou, were plotting his assassination. They decided to turn to the Guise clan, experts in such matters, for help.

Catherine's original project seems to have been simple: first the marriage and celebrations, which were to last until Thursday night, 21 August; then the murder, Friday morning, as Coligny stepped out of the first Council meeting after political business had been resumed. The Guises selected for the job their favourite murderer, a Gascon captain named Charles Louvier de Maurevert, who had shot his own tutor in the back. Anne d'Este, Duchesse de Nemours, whose first husband had been the assassinated Duc de Guise, selected the house from where the shots would be fired: a nice quiet little place just north of the Église Saint-Germain-l'Auxerrois, overlooking Rue des Pouillies, which Coligny would take to get back to his palatial lodging on the corner of Rue Béthisy (today at the level of No. 144, Rue de Rivoli). The Guise family tutor lived there. According to the memoirs of the Duc d'Anjou this simple plot had been hatched several days before the marriage. But history is never simple.

The rituals of marriage were pushed through with great haste. Margot became the King of Navarre's fiancée in a betrothal ceremony held at the Louvre on Saturday afternoon, 16 August. On Monday morning she was his queen.

Montgomery had been refused the right to be present at court, so he took up residence on the left bank in the Faubourg Saint-Germain-des-Prés. Site of the greatest fair in Paris, Saint-Germain had become the *quartier* of the Huguenots, many of whom were recruited from the commercial classes. Indeed, this was where Calvinism had been invented before its master, Jean Calvin, took flight for Switzerland. Heretics lived here (it was not perhaps a pure accident that, four hundred years later, this would be the birthplace of Existentialism). It was the one part of town where Huguenots felt safe.

Temperatures soared during that third week of August. The atmosphere was oppressive, muggy. In the churches Catholic priests denounced the royal wedding and the presence of the anti-Christs within the city walls. There were fights in the streets, duels in the alleys. Montgomery, forbidden to attend court festivities, reported to Coligny all that he heard and saw in the streets: this was no town for gentlemen in black to go walking. Coligny thanked the Lieutenant General, replying that his presence in the city was required to avert another civil war. But as a precaution he did ask Montgomery, on Thursday night, to accompany him to the King's Council the next morning. The alleys around the Louvre were very narrow.

Coligny was still intent on pursuing his war in the Netherlands, but he got no support in the Council; the King, his only potential ally, was attending mass. The session ended a little before 11 a.m. Montgomery, with other attendants, was there at the exit. On their way across the courtyard they met the King on his way to a match of tennis; there was a bowing and a swirling of caps. Then they proceeded along Rue d'Autriche, down Rue des Pouillies to where it turned into Rue des Fossés-Saint-Germain. Maurevert was waiting with his twin-barrelled harquebus. He squeezed on one trigger—at that very instant Coligny bent down to tighten a leather lace that had loosened on one of his boots. Then he squeezed at the other—the second bullet nearly severed Coligny's left index finger and ran up his arm to lodge in his elbow. "You see how one treats decent men in France!" screamed the Admiral. "The shot came from that window. There's the smoke!"

Montgomery and his men, after checking that the wound was not fatal, raced over to the house. They found the gun, still smoking, and two servants; but the culprit had made a quick getaway out the back by horse. They returned to their master and carried him to his home on Rue Béthisy. At his bedside Montgomery proclaimed that he would put every Guise in town to death—he had little doubt who was responsible. Coligny calmed him down.

The Spanish ambassador Diego de Zuñiga was present at the meal which Catherine had just begun when the news was brought of the attempted assassination. She remained expressionless, though secretly she must have realized that she and her whole family were now in mortal danger; she calmly got up and retired to her chamber. King Charles, unaware of his mother's intrigue, was still playing tennis. On hearing the news he squealed, "Am I never to be left in peace? More trouble! More trouble!" He decided to go and see Coligny himself. When Catherine heard this, she hypocritically suggested that all the senior members of the court go over to Rue Béthisy that afternoon.

Huguenots were already on the rampage. All the Guise properties were stoned. There was skirmishing in the streets and a murder or two. The court arrived at Rue Béthisy shortly after the royal surgeon Ambroise Paré—the same surgeon who had attended to Henri II's fatal wounds— had succeeded in cutting off Coligny's finger, with scissors that "were not well sharpened," and retrieving the bullet from his elbow. Montgomery diplomatically took leave and Coligny stoically received his royal visitors. "You, Admiral, must support the pain while I, I have to support the shame," said a distraught King Charles bending over the bed. The King returned to the Louvre and ordered an immediate enquiry into the affair; by Saturday the complicity of the Guises was evident. The Queen Mother meanwhile determined, in the words of Anjou, to "finish the Admiral by whatever means we could"; on Saturday afternoon a "war council" of plotters met in the Tuileries Garden and determined to put an end to all the Huguenot leaders, so conveniently gathered in Paris. That evening the gates of the city were closed, chains were laid in the river to prevent boats from crossing the Seine and the Prévôt des Marchands ordered the city militia to collect at the Hôtel de Ville to prevent pillaging should the mobs run amok that night.

King Charles could not be kept out of the picture forever. Catherine asked the Comte de Retz to go to his study to explain. The King's dismay was great. He burst into tears, protesting that the Admiral loved him as he would his own son, but after Retz had noted that the lives of him and his family were in peril, he cried out, "Then kill them all! Kill them all!" The number of Huguenots to be murdered increased with every hour.

Assassins were selected for specific victims. The young Duc de Guise was responsible for putting Coligny to death. Captain Claude Marcel of the bourgeois militia had the task of killing Montgomery. The slaughter was to begin at 3 a.m. with Coligny's death and the sound of the grand bell at the Palais de Justice, the death knell, *la sonoria*. Sunday was 24 August, the day dedicated to the memory of Saint Bartholomew, one of the twelve apostles, the one flayed alive by the Armenians.

On Saturday evening Montgomery, having supped in Saint-Germain, crossed the river to visit Coligny at Rue Béthisy. The Admiral was cheerful and seemed to be recuperating well from his wounds. Montgomery suggested that he and some of his soldier friends guard the building that night, for the assassins were still at large. One of the Huguenot captains assured him that there were already enough guards in the house. So Montgomery returned to Saint-Germain. He took his time. It was a beautiful summer's night when one could stare in wonder at the stars of heaven and down through the empty, quiet streets. A few of the Paris militia were on patrol; Montgomery noticed for the first time that they had white scarves tied around their left arms — no doubt to identify themselves, he thought. At Saint-Germain he paid a short visit to the English ambassador Sir Francis Walsingham, who lived in the neighbourhood. Walsingham was pleased with the rapid progress being made by the King's enquiry and was sure the guilty men would soon be rounded up. Montgomery got back to his own lodgings by the

Tour de Nesle at around midnight. He was anxious and had difficulty sleeping.

He was wakened at three or four in the morning by a stranger in his room. He reached for his sabre. "The whole town is in commotion," came a haggard reply; "they're Protestant bashing, I only escaped by diving into the river." The man ran to the window: "Sound the alarm! Sound the alarm!" Montgomery heard a bell tolling—it was actually Saint-Germain-l'Auxerrois—the screams of men and women and the pattering bursts of harquebus shot. His first thought was to get to his colleagues on the other side of the river. He and a few friends managed to find a small dinghy and get out to mid-river where they were turned back by a rain of gunfire. Many of his colleagues, he realized, must already be dead. It was a question of saving his own skin.

Coligny had died bravely. Hearing the commotion below as Guise's men forced their way into the house, Coligny knew his time had come. He told the men about him, "For a long time now I have been preparing for death, save yourselves for you cannot save me." And pausing, "I will commend my soul to God's mercy." The door, blocked by a chest of drawers, was forced open; a rough Swiss guardsman thrust his sword into Coligny's breast, beat him on the head and then threw him through the window. Coligny's fingers were seen grabbing at a ledge before he fell two storeys at the feet of the Duc de Guise, who kicked the corpse with delight. The Duke then galloped about the Louvre—where Huguenots were dragged into the courtyard and impaled on Swiss pikes—until he heard the bad news: Montgomery had got away. Guise joined the pursuit.

Montgomery and his companions had charged through a line of militia blocking the road at Vaugirard and continued west through the countryside, passing Issy-les-Moulineaux, Saint-Cloud and the Versailles Forest. Guise and his men gave up the chase at Montfort-l'Amaury. Montgomery and company were hiding among the trees. At the forest crossroads of Bel-air they separated; country ramblers today will find a stone monument there, known as "Montgomery's Cross."

In Paris the slaughter continued for at least three days. As many as three thousand perished, many of them not even Huguenots. Mass murder spread into the provinces, finally petering out in Provence in October. How many died in those three months will always be one of the mysteries of history; estimates vary from ten thousand to thirty thousand. "But yet the King to destroy and utterly root out of his Realm all those of that Religion that we profess," grieved Queen Elizabeth of England, "and to desire us in marriage for his brother, must needs seem unto us at the first a thing very repugnant." All the senior officers of the Huguenot forces had been wiped out, save one, Sieur Gabriel de Montgomery.

Just as he had done after the jousting accident, he fled to Jersey. But this time he did not get the support of Elizabeth. The Queen, despite the "thing very repugnant," not only maintained relations with Catherine's court but, incredibly, continued to negotiate a marriage with Catherine's revolting youngest son, the Duc d'Alençon. At home she had started to move against Puritanism and "prophesyings." Abroad she had to deal with the consequences of Catholic terrorism, not in France but in the Netherlands, which the Spanish were subjecting to a regime of mass starvation and slaughter. An unexpected offshoot of this was a rapid rise in Protestant piracy in the Channel and the Atlantic; William the Silent's "Sea Beggars" were using fifty- or sixty-ton man-o'-wars to rob boats of their cargo and murder their crews—and unfortunately many of their victims were English. Elizabeth closed all English ports to the Dutch privateers and threatened to form an alliance against them with Philip of Spain, the Holy Roman Emperor, Maximilian, and the German princes. So the pirates had to go elsewhere for support. And it was obvious where: the French Huguenot ports. And who would be their principal collaborator? Sieur de Montgomery at his base in Jersey.

There was another "Flight from Egypt" on to La Rochelle. Charles IX declared war on the port on 5 November 1572 and sent his brother, the Duc d'Anjou, with an army of 5,000 to introduce its inhabitants to a little Spanish treatment. After five months of siege the town showed no sign of yielding so Anjou attempted a frontal assault, which cost his army many lives. Then, in April 1573, Montgomery and a fleet of international pirates appeared on the horizon; they took on Anjou's naval

force and nearly lost their flagship, the *Primrose*, in the process—
Montgomery did not make a very talented buccaneer. But he did manage to seize the offshore islands of Belle-Île and Île d'Yeu, which made
it impossible for the French royal fleet to supply their army: it was Anjou's army that was starved out of action, not La Rochelle, which,
thanks to Montgomery, received ample food and booty estimated at
two million gold écus. Catherine sued for another peace, granting the
same religious liberties as all the previous ones. Montgomery set sail
for the Isle of Wight, where he anchored on 26 May.

But in England he was now *persona non grata*. Montgomery spent
several weeks negotiating with the French ambassador the right to live
in Normandy. Then he returned to Jersey, where, with the help of his
pirates, he amassed enough money and arms to seize Normandy. In
early spring 1574 he almost succeeded. "We hold the whole country in
subjection," he boasted on 24 March to his old friend Lord Burghley, as
Sir William Cecil was now known.

Catherine sent reinforcements to Montgomery's erstwhile foe, the
Comte de Matignon, who began a huge pincer movement into the
bocages, or bosky country, of rebellious western Normandy. By a series
of zig-zag manoeuvres Montgomery managed to get away each time
Matignon thought he had cornered his prey. He got away until he
reached the medieval fortress of Domfront, where, because of an argument he had with the Huguenot captain who held it, Ambroise Le
Hérice, the "Scarface," he was delayed a fatal twenty-four hours.

TRAVELLER OF THE Paris métro, if you have the chance, take an
excursion to Domfront in "Norman Switzerland." It is one of the
most impressive medieval citadels in France, though the fort itself
was blown up by gunpowder in 1610 on the orders of Henri IV's minister, the Duc de Sully. The town was the site of Allied aerial bombing
during Hitler's Mortain offensive in August 1944, but the medieval
quarter survived. The cafés serve *poiré*, the local pear cider; the remaining walls and turrets, often shrouded in mist, inspire thoughts of
medieval legend and terror—the parapets were designed for pouring

burning oil on the attackers; you get a grand view across the Norman *bocages*; and a stroll along the surrounding defences and the steep cliffs will give you an idea of the drama of Sieur de Montgomery's last stand.

Matignon's first troops arrived early on a Sunday, 9 May 1574. Within hours they controlled all roads of access and by afternoon his pioneers were felling the trees on the south side of the fort, in preparation for a massive bombardment. Montgomery attempted a *sortie* the following morning at dawn, but Captain Mouy de Riberprey's royal cavaliers put an end to that within yards of the portcullis.

The largest cannon available in Normandy were dragged in by horse and hauled up the surrounding heights—a feat worthy of the Pharaohs. From the artillery park of Caen, Matignon had transported a five-yard long, thirty-three-inch calibre monster called "Mad Marguerite," possibly after Henri de Navarre's Queen. It was placed on the summit of Le Tertre Grisière. On the hills of La Rouge Mothe there were six culverins, each one of them over fifty hundredweight and ready to fire after mass was sung on Sunday, 23 May. At seven o'clock that morning Mad Marguerite crashed out at the curtained fortifications of the main castle; the cannon of La Rouge Mothe strafed the battlements. Matignon had under his command six thousand infantry and two thousand cavalry. There were just seventy Huguenots inside Domfront; they sang psalms as they went into action.

In the old castle fortress of Vincennes, just outside Paris on the east side of the Bastille, King Charles IX was dying. He was not yet twenty-four. "I can give death, but you can give immortality," he had whispered to the court poet Pierre de Ronsard. Tormented by his role in the Saint Bartholomew massacre, torn between loyalty to his mother and a will to be free, he lay sweating and coughing in blood-stained sheets. Catherine could be heard singing in a nearby chamber—for she had heard that the regicide had been cornered. When the news was announced to Charles he replied, "Human things no longer mean anything to me." Yet he revived to sit up and announce, "My cure will come with the capture of Domfront and the surrender of Montgomery."

The steep river valleys around Domfront echoed to the sounds of bombardment and crumbling walls that Sunday, 23 May. Around midday two gaping holes had been blasted out of the curtain defences on the south side of the citadel and in the wall of the castle itself. Matignon's infantry clambered up the southern bluffs only to be met by Huguenots wielding their swords and sabres; Montgomery himself appeared in a white doublet braided in silver, as if dressed for a banquet, except for the axe in his right hand. His foe of yesterday, "Scarface," fought by his side. With the sun disappearing over the horizon, Matignon ordered a retreat. He had lost over two hundred men. Montgomery had won a brief respite.

Monday and Tuesday were limited to further bombardment. On Wednesday night Matignon sent in a messenger, the Baron de Vassé—one of Montgomery's own relatives—but he was peremptorily dismissed. Yet only fifteen men were left in the castle; they had no water, no food, no powder. De Vassé returned three times on Thursday. The situation was clearly hopeless. Between one and two o'clock Friday morning, 28 May, Matignon himself accompanied de Vassé to summon the surrender. Montgomery appeared in the reception hall, this time dressed "in a high hat and a short leather doublet." He received all the honours of his rank; he kept his sword and his dagger. He was even promised his life.

King Charles IX lived just long enough to receive news of the capture; it arrived at Vincennes on Saturday. On Sunday, 30 May, he lost consciousness. Queen Catherine sat at his side, holding his hand. Then suddenly he exclaimed, in a voice so clear that it could be heard by all in the room, "*Adieu ma mère! Eh, ma mère!*" —and died.

Montgomery was escorted to Paris where he arrived on 16 June. He was imprisoned in the Conciergerie. On 26 June the Paris Parlement sentenced him to "be decapitated and his body to be cut into fourteen quarters." The sentence was carried out on the Place de Grève the same afternoon. "*Quand songerey à moi*," concludes the ballad,

> jugez, seriez vous vrai
> qui vous donne à cognoistre
> qu'il ne faut point vouer

encore moins se jouer
jamais contre son maître

—do not ever, even in play, set yourself against your master.

In his lovely essay *Homo Ludens*, "Man the Player," written on the eve of the Second World War, the medievalist Johan Huizinga argued that there had always been a play element in war. "Young dogs and small boys 'fight' for fun, with rules limiting the degree of violence," he commented, and then noted that the level of acceptable violence in war games did not necessarily stop at the spilling of blood or even killing; he gave the example of jousting. Sieur de Montgomery of Normandy was a player to the end.

PÈRE LACHAISE

IDEALLY, A TRIP to the last of the métro stops, Père Lachaise, should be undertaken on a chill, clear autumn morning, when the golden leaves of the maple and the sycamore are falling, when the sky is an empty, radiant blue, when the horn of a distant car sings in the air like a bugle. They named Père Lachaise, the largest of the city's cemeteries, after Louis XIV's staunchly anti-Protestant Jesuit confessor, François d'Aix, Seigneur de La Chaise, who established a retirement home for his brotherhood on the hillside of Mont Louis, as Belleville was then known; the cemetery expanded rapidly during his own lifetime.

It has always enchanted visitors. In autumn your footsteps on the cobbled pathways echo against the ornate tombstones that tower to either side; some of the avenues at Père Lachaise seem like Lilliputian versions of Paris's boulevards. The atmosphere is always reverent. Twice in November—on All Souls' Day and Armistice Day—pilgrims from Paris carry carnations and everlasting flowers, yellow and dark blue, to the graves. Their faces reflect the season's melancholy. But there is often a glimpse of hope in their eyes: one soul may be gone, but another is always born. Balzac painted that foretelling little smile into his *Père Goriot*. An ambitious student, Eugène de Rastignac, comes to the cemetery one sad, wet evening to attend the funeral of Père Goriot. He stares down into the grave and "buries there his last tear as a young man"; then he raises his head up to notice the whole of Paris stretching out before him just as the lights in the web of streets below flicker into life with the approaching night: "Between the two of us now!" Rastignac exclaims—and Balzac's drama takes off.

Over a million men and women have been buried here since Père La Chaise opened the land to the dead. A full day is needed to wander

around these tombs. Héloise finally joined her lover, Pierre Abelard, in a grave that was laid not far from the main entrance. "The love which united their spirits during their lives," one reads in the inscription of 1701, "united their bodies in this tomb." There are not many grave robbers around today; but poor Bizet lost his head in December 2006 to what was believed to be a gang working for an art collector; the busts of several other dead celebrities disappeared at the same time.

People of every age visit Père Lachaise. In one of the alleys you may well run into a group of giggling girls, rings in their ears and noses, their hair tinted yellow, orange and blue—like the flowers. "*Monsieur, Monsieur*," they cheerily salute you, "*pouvez-vous nous dire où se trouve la division six?*" You know exactly where they are heading: after he was found dead from a drug overdose in his hotel bathtub, Jim Morrison of the Doors ended up under a flat marble stone in the northern corner of Division Six. Strange night-time rites have taken place in Division Six; a security guard who hides behind the neighbouring high tomb will tell you with a grin that at least the graffiti have gone.*

The most extraordinary tomb in Père Lachaise is occupied by one of Britain's writers who died in poverty in a small Paris hotel at the turn of the last century. There are always people milling around it, about a hundred yards south of the Colombarium, as the local crematorium is known. The square-cut stone is one of the earliest pieces by Sir Jacob Epstein, the American-born British Expressionist; it clearly shows the influence of Antoine Bourdelle. But there is one little difference: the lipstick—the lower half of the monument is covered with red lipstick kisses. Love letters are stuffed in its interstices. The graffiti, written in every colour of the rainbow, are kind and gentle. "Ah *there* he is," sighs a new visitor after clambering up the whole side of the hill. Yes, there he is: beneath the stone and the lipstick lie the remains of Oscar Wilde, Oscar Fingal O'Flahertie Wills Wilde.

Paris, and the world, is having a love affair with Oscar Wilde: "I love you," "Lucile and Elena love you," "To you," "Libertad siempre," "Keep charming." There is nothing that shocks in the popular slogans written

---

* So, in fact, has the body. Jim Morrison's remains have been removed to California.

on Wilde's tomb. Every two years or so the stone is given a scrubbing; then the slogans and the kisses start up all over again. The flowers are always fresh. No security guard stands by. The tomb at first sight puts one in mind of some pleasing *pointilliste* abstraction under the sun; the marks of the lips look like rose petals or shiny coloured stones in a mosaic fantasy. As you gaze upon all the kisses this stone has received, it is worth recalling that Wilde's own favourite in his first published collection of poems was "Charmides," in which a young man is caught making love to a statue of the goddess Athena. It earned Wilde the censure of the Oxford Student Union. Nobody, on the other hand, wants to restrain the young who make love to Oscar Wilde's stone. Just compare the lovely atmosphere you find around this tomb to that of Victor Noir's, a few paces from here. Noir was a radical journalist shot dead at the age of twenty-two by Napoleon III's cousin; the reclining figure on his tomb represents the youth as he was in death, his shirt torn open and his trousers undone. For over a century women seeking aid in love and fertility have performed so many lewd acts on the tomb that Noir's lips, nose and the protuberance in the genital area have been reduced to smooth shining bronze. In contrast, there is nothing faintly lewd in the popular worship that takes place at Wilde's grave: all is gentleness.

Perhaps the charm lies in the "*libertad siempre*" scrawled in ink under his name. Wilde was a part of that two-pronged struggle for freedom that developed in the last years of the nineteenth century; one prong untangled us from the prejudice of race, the other from mad taboos concerning sex. It is a remarkable fact that the Dreyfus Affair—the false accusation of a Jewish captain in the French Army and his imprisonment on Devil's Island—coincided exactly with the conviction of Oscar Wilde for "indecent acts" and his imprisonment in London. Paris and London were rocked by these two infamous legal battles. Paris had its racial scandal, London its sex scandal. It is another tale of two cities.

❧

IN LONDON WILDE was an outsider or, at least, that is what he thought himself. Paris presented more than a haven for Wilde; it influenced his whole artistic enterprise, turning it—and, many would argue,

Wilde himself—in a very dangerous direction. In London, Wilde had identified himself with an "English Renaissance," the aesthetics of the Pre-Raphaelites, the craftsmanship of William Morris, the art history of Walter Pater. When Wilde first moved to Paris, in January 1883, all that changed. He discovered poets and writers who had taken a step away from the acceptable norms of behaviour into "decadence." Wilde no longer spoke of a "Renaissance" after that date. He developed a fascination for the kingdom of the wicked.

And then it happened. Wilde was hoist with his own petard. Why he should have been attracted to as nasty a creature as Lord Alfred Douglas, when there were so many more talented and less temperamental young men about him, has always been something of a mystery. It could only have been his good looks—the alabaster face and blond hair, which seemed to be drawn directly out of *Dorian Gray*. It was Douglas who forced Wilde to take his father, the eighth Marquess of Queensberry, to court for criminal libel. Queensberry turned the tables on Wilde. Blackmailers and male prostitutes were dragged through the courts; chambermaids provided foul testimony.

It was almost as if Wilde wanted to be in the pillory. Wilde, not a vindictive man, could easily have avoided the trials and his imprisonment by simply not initiating the case against Queensberry—over a childish insult written on a visiting card. He was drawn into the case because of the jeers of a squirt, Lord Alfred Douglas, "Bosie." The self-destructive urge in Wilde did the rest. Wilde was found guilty of "indecent acts" and condemned on 25 May 1895 to two years of imprisonment and hard labour.

That pillory proved terrible. "We who live in prison, and in whose lives there is no event but sorrow," wrote Wilde from his cell in the early months of 1897, "have to measure time by throbs of pain, and the record of bitter moments. We have nothing else to think of. Suffering . . . is the means by which we exist." Prison offered no sanctuary. "Sorrow after sorrow has come beating at the prison doors in search of me." Wilde's friend Robert Sherard, who lived near the Wandsworth gaol, visited him on 26 August 1895 and noticed how his hands, clasping the bars, were disfigured, the nails broken and bleeding, his hair was unkempt and a small straggly beard had begun to grow on his thin jowls; he was "greatly depressed" and on the verge of tears. In October one of his former lovers, Robert Ross, wrote to a friend reporting that Wilde "hoped to die very soon. Indeed he only spoke calmly about death, every other subject caused him to break down."

"HAPPY THE DEAD!" wrote Captain Alfred Dreyfus in his prison diary that very same autumn. "How much would death be preferable to this slow agony, to this martyrdom suffered at every instant." He could not sleep, he could not eat, he was overcome by waves of shivering and fever. "He won't live through this," recorded Chief Warder Lebars after Dreyfus's first three months of confinement on a tropical island a thousand yards long and two hundred yards wide at its narrowest point; "his voice is broken with sobs and he then weeps abundantly for periods of about a quarter of an hour." Devil's Island, off the coast of the small French South American colony of Cayenne, was the smallest of three volcanic protuberances in the Atlantic, known ironically as the Isles of Salvation. On Devil's Island life was worse than sparse; only mosquitoes, brushwood and a few palm trees survived on it. The victors of Thermidor, in July 1794, were the first to use the island for deported prisoners, virtually all of whom died within a year. Bonaparte kept up the tradition. It was abandoned under the Restoration, but revived again with the Second Empire—of the 7,000 prisoners sent out to Cayenne in 1856 (Zola's fictitious hero Florent was set among them), 2,500 were dead by the end of the year. The Third Republic would have nothing to do with Devil's Island until Captain Dreyfus was convicted of treason in December 1894; a special law had to be voted in parliament, on 31 January 1895, to prepare the solitary stone hut that would house him for over three years—sixteen months longer than Wilde's imprisonment.

It is remarkable how similar the symptoms of suffering were in the two men—the weeping, the sleeplessness, the foul indigestion and an almost religious sense of martyrdom—although it is clear that Dreyfus went through more than Wilde. In his "Journal of My Sad and Appalling

Life," Dreyfus describes in detail the twelve-foot square hut, the miserable food, the irons into which he was clamped every night for two months. It is a relentless, monotonous text which repeats, from one end to the other, the same obsessive thought: "My body must not yield until honour has been rendered to me." "I speak to you as if from a tomb," he wrote to his wife, Lucie, on 29 October 1896, "from an eternal silence that pushes me down and down below everything." Dreyfus lived beneath Hell—a theme one can find in Wilde's prison writing.

The grounds of conviction were, of course, utterly different, though the cultural origins of both injustices lay in that very Parisian, *fin-de-siècle* movement which so influenced Wilde's thought: *la décadence*. Many of the Parisian decadents were openly homosexual; and unhappily several of them—as one may note among some of Debussy's friends—were rabid anti-Semites. All this formed an integral part of Parisian culture in the 1890s. It would not be inaccurate to describe it as a culture of hatreds. A common sight in the streets of Paris at that time, at the horse races of Auteuil, in the theatres and even in the Chamber of Deputies, were men sporting blue carnations in their jacket lapels, the blue carnations of the anti-Semites.

Both the Dreyfus Affair and the Wilde trials occurred at a time of spreading war rumours; in the autumn of 1898 France nearly went to war, not with Germany but with Britain, over disputed territory at Fashoda in the southern Sudan. France, defeated by Prussia in 1870, was a land consumed by jealousies, rivalries and the search for revenge; it was a place where traitors, spies and scallywags seemed to lurk in every café, whorehouse and army barracks. An archivist working for the Army's artillery section was condemned to five years' imprisonment in 1890 for corresponding with the German military attaché in Paris; at the same time, five men in the Ministry of the Marine were condemned to up to twenty years' hard labour for espionage. But hypersensitive documents, like the maps outlining the emplacements of frontier artillery, continued to disappear. The press called for action. The Army's commanders were embarrassed. The General Staff became touchy and defensive; any doubt cast on the word of the generals was considered a threat to their capacity to defend the country, a challenge to the honour of the Army. Candour and truth were not nourished in such an atmosphere.

General Ernest Mercier became Minister of War in December 1893. He was a republican and never went to church, so he was regarded with some suspicion by people of traditional values on the political right. At the end of September 1894, he was shown a handwritten note—it became known as the *bordereau*—picked up in the German military attaché's office in Paris by a charwoman who worked for the Section de Statistique, the French Army's intelligence agency. The *bordereau*, composed by a French officer, listed documents that he was handing over to the German military attaché.

Mercier at once realized that if he caught the traitor he would be able to silence his right-wing critics. The range of possible suspects was quickly narrowed down to officer trainees working within the General Staff in Paris; in less than a month the chiefs of the Section de Statistique were focusing on the case of Captain Alfred Dreyfus—there were vague similarities in the writing, he had been described as an "*officier incomplet*" by his superior, and he was Jewish. "At first glance," as Mercier himself put it, Dreyfus's guilt was established. The unfortunate captain was called in to the Ministry of War early Monday morning, 15 October, interrogated by a delirious Commandant Armand du Paty de Clam and locked up in the Cherche-Midi military gaol that night. He was offered a service revolver with which to shoot himself. "I am innocent; you can kill me if you like," he riposted. "I want to live to establish my innocence!" Dreyfus's guilt was confirmed at a court martial that December; the judges had been shown a secret dossier crammed with false documents that the Section de Statistique had made up. The press mounted a violent, anti-Semitic campaign against "the traitor." The Socialist leader Jean Jaurès called for his execution. The Army could never retreat on a judgement of a court martial, "*la chose jugée*"; that would have brought into question the competence of the nation's military defenders, the honour of the French Army.

If Captain Dreyfus had died on Devil's Island there would have been no Dreyfus Affair to divide Paris between its two warring camps, the defenders of the Republic and defenders of the Army, the defenders of the

Rights of Man and the anti-Semites. If the inmate of Wandsworth had died that same autumn in the gaol's infirmary there would have been no cult of Oscar Wilde. Both affairs were blown up by the new mass media. The French Army was drawn into a rearguard action to save its honour. Dreyfus stayed alive for the sake of his honour. And, in London, the Marquess of Queensberry pressed his case against Wilde to defend his honour. In the decadent world of the 1890s there was much talk of honour.

RICHARD BURDON HALDANE, later Viscount—who ordered the famous army reforms in Asquith's 1905 Liberal government—had visited Wilde in June 1895 as a member of the Home Office prison committee. It was he who arranged Wilde's transfer to Reading Gaol. It was he who eventually got him books, pen and paper. In January 1897, five months before his release, Wilde began writing a long letter.

His biographer Richard Ellmann speaks of it as a love letter that must rank "as one of the greatest and the longest, ever written." Addressed to Alfred Douglas, much of the text is indeed a lover's rant about Douglas's infidelities, his intellectual inconsequence and particularly his responsibility for Wilde's arrest—beautifully composed, but a rant all the same. Fortunately for posterity the other half of the text is far more than a love letter; it is a work of philosophy, of theology and even, one may not inaccurately claim, a piece of holy scripture.

Wilde wanted it published as *Epistola: in Carcere et Vinculis*; it seems it was Robert Ross who came up with the title *De Profundis*, drawn from the 130th Psalm, the terrible psalm.

In *De Profundis* lies the mystery of Oscar Wilde, his secret, the origin of the cult one witnesses today at Père Lachaise. Wilde examines a glorious past, assesses the dismal present and waits hopefully upon the future. To establish the depths to which he has fallen, Wilde celebrates the summit of his former success. Then he embraces the awfulness of his fall. Upon that anguish, weeping and sorrow he builds his hope. Wilde was borrowing directly from Dante's *Inferno*, which he had been reading in gaol in Italian, though his interpretation certainly goes back to the ideas of one of his early masters at Oxford, Walter Pater. The lowest and most damnable in Dante's hell are those who have wilfully lived in sadness, those who have worn a perpetual grimace on their faces. When Pater had introduced the idea to Wilde in his youth he thought it ridiculous, "just the sort of sin, I fancied, a priest who knew nothing about real life would invent." But sadness became his own sin. At first it was an immediate aim, then a determination to commit suicide the moment he left gaol, then something more vague, an aim never to smile again, to make everyone around him miserable, "to wear gloom as a king wears purple." Then he read Dante. Dante opened his eyes and gave his life new direction: "I must learn how to be happy." Wilde would read beautiful books. He would say beautiful things. After that, "I hope to be able to recreate *my creative faculty*" (my emphasis).

So he would leave gaol with an aura of happiness about him, and he would read and he would write. But when? In *De Profundis* Wilde spells out in some detail how he would go about this. But he never actually wrote an extensive piece of prose again. There was the long and famous poem *The Ballad of Reading Gaol* completed within three months of his release. Over the same period he wrote a lengthy letter to the *Daily Chronicle* about children in prison, and very moving it is, too. And that was it. Wilde died penniless and in agony in the Hôtel d'Alsace, on the Rue des Beaux-Arts, on 30 November 1900 — without a further verse or paragraph to his name, silent. So did he fail?

MANY OF DREYFUS'S most fervent supporters would be exasperated by their hero's silence. He did not seem to join in their enthusiasm for the great cause of justice. "What was tragic, even fatal, about the whole business was that he [Dreyfus] did not have the right to be a private man," wrote Charles Péguy in *Notre jeunesse*, certainly the most thoughtful, eloquent memoir to emerge from the Affair. "The man who is chosen must march, the man who is called upon must answer. It is the law, it is the rule." France was divided in two by the Affair. After almost a year of political polemic, Dreyfus was brought back from his island; his supporters were horrified to discover a stiff and silent captain, who, if he had not been called Dreyfus, would probably have been an anti-Dreyfusard.

He was put on trial again at another court martial in Rennes—and found guilty again. What saved him from further imprisonment, and yet another deportation, was a presidential pardon—hardly a sign of faith in French military justice. The Dreyfusards, heroically, called on the captain to refuse the offer and be a martyr for their cause; Dreyfus and his family wisely accepted the pardon. He was then denounced by his own camp. Georges Clemenceau, when he met him on one rare occasion, said he looked like a "a pencil merchant." But in a moving encounter at the Ministry of Justice in September 1899, between Dreyfus's brother Mathieu and the leading Dreyfusards, the Tiger of France admitted privately, "If I were the brother I would accept the pardon."

Dreyfus never did understand the "mystical" enthusiasm of his supporters. The passions the case had aroused were not his. Dreyfus remained forever the artillery engineer he had been trained to be, gauging the range of fire in the trials he attended and assessing their impact—as if he were observing from a distant hill. When lawyers complained of his absence of emotion at the review of his case before a civilian court in 1904, all Dreyfus could muster up in reply was: "I am stupefied; I believed in reason, I had faith in reason in such affairs, I thought the dragging in of matters of the heart would have no bearing whatever on the final judgement." Dreyfus's feelings could not be aroused. He would never breathe a word on his Jewish origins, though the anti-Semites screamed around him. He never complained of the rough conditions he had known on Devil's Island—just treatment, he remarked, if he had been a genuine traitor. He never scowled. He never even smiled—except once, just slightly, when he was decorated with the Légion d'honneur in 1906. "All his protestations of innocence sounded false," remarked the high-ranking diplomat Maurice Paléologue after attending Dreyfus's public degradation at the Ècole Militaire in December 1894; "one felt no warmth of soul; it might have been the voice of an automaton." By 1906, many Dreyfusards would have agreed with Paléologue.

Only a handful of people knew why Dreyfus was so silent. The truth was revealed to those who observed him at close quarters. When his wife, Lucie, first saw him on his return from Devil's Island, she found a man "distant, huddled up, incapable of expressing anything." Mathieu met him a couple of weeks later in Rennes; he was very thin, he spoke only slowly, and when he did speak there was a slight whistling sound due to the loss of several teeth. A shy and solitary person even in childhood, Dreyfus was the victim of his imprisonment: the courts martial had effectively condemned Captain Dreyfus to silence.

THE OLD BAILEY in London had likewise condemned Oscar Wilde to silence, though the nature of that silence was not exactly the same. Wilde, unlike Dreyfus, never even pretended to be innocent. But if he was guilty, he was guilty of what? The charge levelled against him in court had been "indecent acts"—the charge of sodomy was dropped for lack of evidence. Like Dreyfus on his Jewish roots, Wilde, in *De Profundis*, never mentioned a word on his sexuality, though this was the obsession of the London press at the time. Wilde judged himself guilty not of homosexuality but, by associating himself with the unimaginative Lord Alfred Douglas, he avowed that he had "soiled and shamed my life irretrievably." He had committed a sin of the imagination, not of sex. He had been the "spendthrift of my own genius," basking in glory and ignoring sorrow and the essential lessons sorrow had to teach. Now, in prison, he would learn the hard way, sinking beneath Hell to the common foundation of human suffering, upon which he would build his new "creative faculty."

Only one man in the world understood why he did not do this, why Wilde would remain silent. André Gide would dominate the Parisian literary scene until Sartre's existentialism. He must be one of the most cultivated men who has ever walked this planet; he steeped himself in the Latin classics, the French classics, English and German, both ancient and modern. At seven he was playing on the piano the symphonies of Haydn. Bach, Chopin and Schumann pervade the pages of Gide's work as much as the thoughts of Plato, Spinoza, Schopenhauer, Homer or Dante. Born into a family of Protestant manufacturers and lawyers, he was one of the richest men in France. So he had no concern about his earnings; for the first forty years of his life he would consider the sale of thirty copies of any one of his books, printed at his own expense, a sovereign success. André Gide devoted himself entirely to his art.

Gide first met Wilde in 1891; he was only twenty-one. Over the following six years Wilde would exert a powerful influence on Gide, which Gide would feel for the remainder of his long and productive life. But it would not be straining the truth to say that young Gide would also have an appreciable influence on Wilde. Indeed, Paris's gift to Wilde was not just decadence; it was also Gide.

One feature of his life coloured all Gide's art, his homosexuality. In Gide it could not be separated from a religious sensibility fostered by his Huguenot parents, particularly his mother. Though he eventually rejected God, he never passed a day without a reading of the Bible. His pederasty—as he termed it himself—seemed to open the way to a new form of godless religion. It was as if a sexuality experimented without women invited a spirituality lived without God: every major affair in his life brought on an intense religious brooding, most notably in the case of his unconsummated marriage in 1895 to his cousin Madeleine Rondeaux—one of the mystical turning points in his life. It would have a direct impact on Wilde.

Gide's attraction to his cousin Madeleine was triggered by a sorrow, a secret sorrow from which she seemed to suffer. Just before Christmas, 1882, when Gide was thirteen, he discovered what it was: her mother was having an affair. By chance, he had come upon the mother with her lover on a settee in their drawing room; he climbed the stairs to find the fifteen-year-old Madeleine kneeling by her bed, weeping. This critical event in the life of Gide can be pieced together from his journal and his autobiographical novel, *La Porte étroite*. "I remained standing beside her," he writes; "she remained kneeling; I could find no words to express the new rapture in my heart . . . Drunk with love, pity and a vague mixture of enthusiasm, abnegation, virtue, I called on God with all my strength and offered myself . . . I finally knelt down beside her; my heart full of prayer." Gide's adolescent love was indistinguishable from his first teenage feelings of religious fervour—and the gradual revelation of his homosexuality, the "hell of the flesh." Madeleine became an ideal, an object of religious exaltation. They were married in the Protestant chapel at Étretat, near one of the Gide properties, on 8 October 1895, four months after the death of his mother—and four months after Wilde went to gaol.

What Gide brought to Wilde was this passionate, Christian sense of pity which permeates the whole text of *De Profundis*. Wilde indeed refers to Gide in the text, and the reference is not just random: it occurs at the moment Wilde is portraying the artist, the perfect artist, in Christ. Gide, too, is present in Wilde's analysis of the role of imagination in love. Both are rare gifts, beyond ordinary mortals, argues Wilde; "nobody is worthy of love." Gide would have said as much. And it is astonishing how close Wilde's acceptance of love resembles Gide's early experience at Madeleine's bedside: "Love is a sacrament that should be taken kneeling, and *Domine, non sum dignus* ["Lord, I am not worthy"] should be on the lips and in the hearts of those who receive it." The passage immediately precedes Wilde's long outline of how he intends to rebuild, from beneath Hell, his "creative faculty."

The relationship between Wilde and Gide went two ways. What Wilde brought to Gide was knowledge of what it was to be homosexual; he was—as Gide's biographer Alan Sheridan notes—a Mephistopheles to Gide's Faust; Wilde was always, as Gide put it himself, "trying to insinuate inside you the *authorization of evil*."

Gide cut all references in his journal to his encounters with Wilde in 1891, save one entry on New Year's Day, 1892: "Wilde, I believe, has only done me ill. With him I had unlearned how to think." Two articles Gide published in the *Mercure de France* shortly after Wilde's death in 1900 tell what happened. There was no sex; Gide is very clear that his first experience with boys, as well as girls, was in North Africa in October 1893. Wilde proved much more perverse; he told tales. Every day, for weeks on end, Gide would join Wilde in a Paris café and listen to Wilde's fantastic stories. "You listen with your eyes," Wilde said on their first encounter at a restaurant in the company of Stéphane Mallarmé's circle of friends. But a week later he told him, "I don't like your lips; they are straight as if they had never lied." He would have to learn how to lie, said Wilde; it was the secret of art; nature was always repeating itself, whilst each work of art was unique because it was a lie.

The story told by Wilde that touched Gide most was that of a village *raconteur* who drew crowds with his tales of prancing fauns in the forest and mermaids swimming in the waves. One day the storyteller went out to the seashore and he really did see three mermaids rolling in the waves; then he turned round to discover at the edge of the wood a faun playing on his flute: "Tell us, what have you seen today?" asked the villagers on his return. "I saw nothing," the storyteller replied. Truth had reduced the artist to a paralysing silence.

It may not yet have been the silence of Dreyfus, but the sequence of events over the next few years would bring the silence of Wilde dramatically close to it. In January 1895, the month Dreyfus was shipped out to Devil's Island and three months before the trials opened in London, Gide was travelling through Algeria in the grip of one of his mystical depressions; he had just completed his fourth book. He was leaving the Grand Hôtel de l'Orient at Blida to catch a train to Biskra when he noticed on the blackboard list of guests the names of Wilde and Douglas — "that terrible man, the most dangerous product of modern civilization," accompanied by his friend, "*cette folie de dépravation*." He scrubbed out his own name and left. But on approaching the railway station he had second thoughts, and returned to the hotel.

Gide had changed; he was no longer a virgin. More significant was the change in Wilde. The stories had dried up; his laughter was husky and forced. He told Gide that he was fleeing thought. "I want to worship only the sun," he said. "Have you noticed how the sun hates thought? It makes thought retreat and take refuge in shadow." Thought had retreated from Egypt and Greece, and was now only found in Norway and Russia. "I hope you are like me," interrupted Alfred Douglas; "I hate women. I like only boys. Since you're with us this evening, I'd rather tell you straight away." "Here begin the tragic memories," noted Gide.

Later in the day Gide was sitting in a café with Wilde when Douglas burst in and, with "a hissing voice," upbraided Wilde on some minor subject. Wilde was visibly shocked. Wilde took Gide to a Moorish café in the neighbourhood and signalled to a boy named Mohammed to play on a reed flute, accompanied by another boy on a *darbouka*. If the account in *Si le grain ne meurt* is to be trusted, Wilde then took Gide outside and asked, "Dear, *vous voulez le petit musicien?*" Gide choked out a "*Oui.*" Wilde roared with laughter, negotiated with the two boys and, at a hotel by the docks, Gide spent the night with Mohammed while Wilde slept with the *darbouka* player. It was, according to Gide, the turning point in his life. That same year, 1895, his mother died and he married Madeleine; Wilde went to gaol.

"You go back to England and what is going to happen to you?" Gide asked before leaving for Biskra. There was something sombre in Wilde's face. "My friends keep on saying to me, Take care, take care!" he answered. "That would be to go backwards. I have to go as far forward as possible. Something has to happen." He paused and then repeated: "Something has to happen." Gide told him he ought to speak in public the way he spoke to his friends. "Why," he probed, "aren't your plays better?"—a wicked question which Gide would later regret. Wilde brusquely leant over and, taking Gide by the shoulder, he said slowly: "You want to know the great drama of my life? I have put all my genius into my life; I have only put my talent into my works." Wilde's two years in gaol would put to the test both genius and talent. The result was a paralysing silence.

AFTER HE HAD met the Parisian decadents, Wilde made a fetish of evil and lying. In "The Decay of Lying," which he first read at a Christmas dinner in 1888, he presented the liar as the embodiment of the genuine artist. "The aim of the liar is simply to charm, to delight, to give pleasure," he remarked. "He is the very basis of civilized society, and without him a dinner-party, even at the mansions of the great, is as dull as a lecture at the Royal Society." It was an attack—very *fin-de-siècle* in style—on conventional Victorian morality and reason; Wilde was reconnoitring artistic zones that lay beyond the frontiers of good and evil. It was here that he observed that "Life imitates Art," that the brown fogs of London were a creation not of the weather but of the French Impressionists. The darkness of evil, he further hinted, was much more interesting than the bright light of goodness. "At twilight nature becomes a wonderfully suggestive effect," he concluded, "and is not without loveliness."

Sure enough, within a few years the Dreyfus Affair began proving Wilde's point. The innocent man would turn out to be so dull; the guilty man so fascinating.

In July 1895 Commandant Georges Picquart replaced the dying Colonel Jean Sandherr as director of the Section de Statistique. He was as convinced as his colleagues on the General Staff of Dreyfus's guilt. The charwoman who worked at the German embassy kept on supplying the agency with packets of torn-up crumpled pieces of paper she had retrieved from the wastepaper baskets. One day in March an assistant showed Picquart a telegram—a *petit bleu* or blue form that was sent through a network of pneumatic tubes, the nineteenth-century equivalent of an email—which he had laboriously pieced together from around thirty or forty shreds. It was a note from the German military attaché asking for further details on documents supplied—obviously by some traitor in the French Army. On the other side of the form was the traitor's address (the letter had not been forwarded): Monsieur le Commandant Esterhazy, 27, Rue de la Bienfaisance—Paris. Dreyfus by this time had spent over a year on Devil's Island. Wilde had already been transferred to Reading where he was reading Dante on Hell.

Who was the Bienfaisant, as Picquart nicknamed him? Picquart would not consult his immediate seniors for another five months; strange behaviour in the Ministry of War had aroused his suspicions. Esterhazy, oddly, was sending in numerous demands to the ministry at this time for employment. In late August 1896 one of these letters fell into Picquart's hands. The handwriting seemed familiar . . . The *bordereau*! He pulled out of a drawer a photograph of the one piece of evidence that had condemned Dreyfus to his island. The writing was not similar; it was identical! Esterhazy was the author of the *bordereau*, not Dreyfus!

Commandant Count Marie Charles Ferdinand Walsin-Esterhazy was a son of the French illegitimate branch of the great Esterhazy dynasty whose domains stretched from the mouth of the Danube across

Hungary and into Austria, who imposed on Hungarian noble rebels the Habsburg imperial crown, and inspired a penniless Franz Schubert in 1824 to dedicate his Unfinished Symphony to one of their beautiful daughters. They claimed direct descent from Attila the Hun. The Commandant was born in Paris in 1847 and never spoke a word of Hungarian; but he did learn German. He failed to graduate from the Lycée Bonaparte but he did serve with some distinction in Gambetta's Army of the Loire during the winter campaign of 1870. His German got him into the Army's Service de Renseignements — a forerunner of the Service de Statistique — in 1877, where over a period of three years he got to know Colonel Hubert Henry, one of the key figures in the Dreyfus Affair. How close this early relationship was is a matter much debated to this day; Esterhazy was the kind of master liar who would have elicited the admiration of Oscar Wilde in his own time and was to confuse historians a hundred years on.

He was a gambler, a womanizer and lived in a perpetual state of bankruptcy. His marriage to Anne de Nettancourt-Vaubécourt brought him a dowry of 200,000 francs but she proved as much of a spendthrift as he. "My wife," he complained one day, "never realized for an instant, never even took a moment to understand that when you marry as poor as us you have to make economies, not buy dresses, coats and hats left, right and centre, not travel first class, not pay chambermaids sixty francs a month." In 1888 they bought a huge château at Dommartin-la-Planchette, in the Marne, without any idea how they would maintain it. He had an extraordinary circle of friends. Under a series of pseudonyms he wrote regularly for Édouard Drumont's anti-Semitic *Libre Parole*, keeping up his correspondence throughout the Dreyfus Affair and even beyond, when he was in exile. But he was also the friend of a number of high-profile Jews. Shortly after the Marquis de Morès killed Captain Armand Mayer in the fatal duel of May 1892, he put about the rumour that he had been the murdered man's second; as a result Esterhazy won the sympathies and financial support of both the Grand Rabbi Zadoc Kahn and Edmond de Rothschild. Maurice Weil was a Jew he befriended while working at the Service de Renseignements.

Weil's pretty wife was the mistress of the Paris military governor, General Félix-Gustave Saussier—and some have argued that it was through him that Esterhazy managed to pass misleading documents on to the Section de Statistique. Weil was also a very close friend of Jules Roche, former Minister of War—it was through Roche that Esterhazy passed his almost hysterical demands for employment to the ministry, one of which found its way into Picquart's office. Under the name of Rohan-Chabrol, Esterhazy ran a high-class whorehouse on Rue du Rocher which helped him through the difficult year of 1897; he had a list of over 1,500 possible clients, drawn mainly from army officers. Esterhazy's web of friends and associates reached into the highest places of government and the Army; his life was built on a long sequence of lying, trickery and deception; and he looked the part of a conspirator—thin, drawn face, straggly moustache, dark eyes sunken into deep orbits. Mathieu Dreyfus, when he first saw him in court, thought he looked like a bird of prey. Haunted by debt, he began selling his secrets to the German military attaché in Paris on 20 July 1894, and continued selling them long after Dreyfus was shipped out to Devil's Island.

Picquart proposed to the General Staff a sting operation. The Minister of War said he did not have the right to order such an act against "a superior officer." The Second Chief of Staff heaved his shoulders and asked Picquart, "What do you care if this Jew stays on Devil's Island?" He waved his hands and went on: "It's possible Dreyfus is innocent. That's of no importance. These are not considerations that should be taken into account." "What you say is abominable," replied Picquart. He saluted, turned on his heels and walked out. It was Picquart who was stung. He was first sent off on a useless mission in Tunisia and subsequently court-martialled for divulging secret documents. He was to spend a total of ten months in gaol.

Like spilt sour milk in a hamper, evil spread through every nook and cranny of Parisian society in those last years of the nineteenth century. Rural France was hardly touched, though many of the provincial cities, along with Algeria, were soiled. The corruption of one man, Esterhazy, had infected all the vital organs of a nation—government, parliament, the armed forces, the schools, the universities, the law courts along with the flowering literary and artistic creations of the *belle époque*. Everything and everyone that mattered in France was drawn into the stinking Dreyfus Affair.

Joseph Reinach, who published a multi-volume work on the Affair shortly after the events, remarked, "Because it was extraordinary one wanted it to be more extraordinary yet." He criticized writers for reading too much into the Affair, for imagining things for which there was no evidence. Perhaps Reinach leant too far in the other direction. In particular, to dismiss as a mere defence of the Army's honour the General Staff's ferocious war against Picquart's efforts to discover the truth beggars the imagination. One wants to hear more.

Once Picquart was dismissed, the Section de Statistique was transformed into a factory of faked evidence. The charwoman at the German embassy continued to supply her piles of scrapped paper. These were now studied at the Section de Statistique not for evidence against Dreyfus, but for pieces that could be cut up, pasted together and otherwise manipulated to make them look like damning evidence. Dates were changed, letters were altered, whole paragraphs were added. But the work was done in a most amateurish manner. One of the key pieces was made up of a page supposedly torn out of a square lined notebook; neither the squares matched up, nor were the lines of the same colour. Another fruitful source were the letters Picquart continued to receive at the Section after his departure. These were supposed to demonstrate his secret collaboration with the Dreyfus family and the "Jewish syndicate." To add spice to the sauce, incriminating letters, addressed to Picquart, were sent in the post and then "intercepted." The grand dossier that General Charles Gonse, the Deputy Chief of Staff, finally pulled together in June 1898 contained 365 documents, nearly all of which were creations of the Section de Statistique. "One cannot fabricate 1,500 papers!" noted the general in his covering letter: "One can swear to one's soul and conscience with the judges of the Court Martial of 1894: 'Yes, Dreyfus is guilty.'" The new Minister of War, General Godefroy Cavaignac, a no-nonsense republican, was sure he had got to the bottom of the matter when he revealed before the Chamber of Deputies three conclusive proofs of Dreyfus's guilt—all three eventually turned out to be fabrications of the Section de Statistique.

One person, and one person alone, was responsible for producing all these tampered documents, Colonel Henry, the fat and jovial officer who had known Esterhazy in the Service de Renseignements in the 1870s. That is to say, the evidence used against Dreyfus was manufactured by a man who personally knew Esterhazy. But it was even worse than that: it seems that it was Henry who put the Chiefs of Staff directly in touch with this damnable spy. In October 1897 shortly before *Le Matin* published a photograph of the *bordereau*— revealing Esterhazy's cranky handwriting to the whole world—Henry, Gonse and General du Paty de Clam (who had arrested Dreyfus in 1894) decided to send an anonymous letter to Esterhazy warning him that Picquart was planning to substitute him for the "guilty man" on Devil's Island. Secret meetings between the three officers, disguised in coloured spectacles and false beards, and Esterhazy were arranged in parks and on bridges in Paris. Esterhazy, now equipped with all the secrets of the Section de Statistique, began writing threatening letters to the military Governor of Paris, the Minister of War and the President of the Republic, Félix Faure. What did they do? Arrest the man who was quite evidently the spy? Faure maintained a discreet silence. The Minister of War ordered the military enquiry that would lead to Picquart's arrest, court martial and prison sentence. Henry and Esterhazy began to collaborate on a regular basis. Esterhazy granted a series of interviews to *La Libre Parole*, *Le Matin*, *L'Écho de Paris*, *Le Figaro* and *Le Temps*, denouncing Picquart's wicked plot which had been revealed to him, he claimed, by a veiled "lady most elegant, most fine" on the Pont Alexandre—possibly Madame Henry or Madame du Paty de Clam, or simply an invention. Esterhazy seemed invulnerable. For most of the press he was a hero, defending the nation against the incursions of the Jewish lobby. The Army, the courts, parliament and the President of the Republic shivered at each of his pronouncements.

However, the publication of the *bordereau* and the identification of the handwriting could hardly favour Esterhazy in the long run. Many of the country's leading writers, artists, academics and teachers saw in Dreyfus's case the symbol of injustice in the world. "Who is protecting Esterhazy?" asked Clemenceau in *L'Aurore*. The protectors in the Section de Statistique thought the best defence for their secret client would be for him to ask for a court martial; they could guarantee his acquittal. Esterhazy duly wrote his own demand, though it was edited by the chief of the ongoing military enquiry into Colonel Picquart. A high-profile trial opened at the military court on Rue du Cherche Midi on 10 January 1898, and two days later, after the judges had deliberated for just five minutes, Esterhazy was acquitted—to cries of "Long live the Army!" "Long live France!" and "Death to the Jews!" The following morning, 13 January, Émile Zola published *"J'accuse,"* his devastating indictment of the Army, government and courts. The atmosphere in France was one of civil war. It was Clemenceau who popularized the term "intellectuals" for thinkers engaged in the public cause of justice—a term that has stuck in France to this day.

The case for Esterhazy was bound to collapse at some point. Zola's *"J'accuse"* had provoked the Minister of War to take both the author and his newspaper, *L'Aurore*, to court on the charge of defamation. They were, of course, found guilty. But the minister's witnesses—members of the General Staff—made the mistake of producing one of Henry's forgeries; the document was an obvious fake. Even worse for the generals, the scandal brought to the forefront of the press the name of the fraudster, Colonel Henry. His fate was sealed by Godefroy Cavaignac's attempt to prove Dreyfus's guilt before the Chamber of Deputies on 7 July with the three key pieces drawn from Gonse's dossier. "These pieces are forgeries," boomed out Jean Jaurès, "they smell of forgeries, they stink of forgeries." The cat was out of the bag. The Chamber may have applauded Cavaignac's speech and voted that it be posted in every commune—so copies of the forgeries went up in the thirty-six thousand towns and villages of France. But on 30 August Cavaignac interrogated Henry, who confessed. The next day he was locked up in Fort Mont Valérien, where he cut his own throat with a razor that night. "My dearest Berthe," were the last words he wrote to his wife, "I am as if mad, a terrible pain grips my brain, I am going to bathe in the Seine . . ."

On 1 September 1898 Commandant Esterhazy took a train to London under a new name, Monsieur de Becourt.

ON THE DAY of his release from prison, 19 May 1897, Oscar Wilde applied to a Jesuit home, on Farm Street in London, for a six-month retreat. Wilde sobbed bitterly when his request was refused; he decided to take the next boat to Dieppe. He was met on the pier at four in the morning by his two most faithful friends, Reggie Turner and Robert Ross. His hotel room was filled with flowers and books, including Gide's latest novel, *Les Nourritures terrestres*, which had just been published.

It was perhaps the first book Wilde read after his release. By Gide's standards the book was a massive success, selling over 200 copies in two years and reaching 500 by 1908. After the First World War it would become a cult book among the younger generation who sought physical pleasure in nature and the flesh. For Wilde, straight out of prison, it must have been like a window reopening on the world's beauty. Typical of Gide, the book also contained a powerful religious dimension, which must have appealed to the author of *De Profundis*—or so one would have thought. But Wilde never spoke a word about *Les Nourritures terrestres*.

Richard Ellmann claims that it was his reconciliation with Douglas that was the cause of Wilde's writer's block—"a second fall for Wilde," as Ellmann terms it. By letter, Wilde offered Douglas a pardon the day he arrived in Dieppe. But they did not meet until the end of August. And Douglas only lived with Wilde, in Naples, for three months, and for a brief period at Nogent-sur-Marne, outside Paris, the following spring, 1898. This certainly caused a drying up of funds, and particularly it cancelled the life interest he had in his marriage settlement. But his writing had clearly dried up first, before his re-encounter with Douglas. As Wilde himself explained, Douglas was the only person in the world willing to keep him company.

Many of Wilde's friends, including Gide, longed for him to start writing again. A new career in writing was above all what his estranged wife wanted of her husband. She called herself Mrs. Constance Holland and lived with their two sons in Freiburg, Germany. She had found *The Ballad of Reading Gaol* exquisite and wrote on 4 March 1898 to Carlos Blacker, a journalist and a trustee of her marriage settlement, "I hope that the great success it has had in London at all events will urge him on to write more. I hear he does nothing now but drink." Unhappily, she died one month later, on 7 April, following spinal surgery. But Blacker would not give up. He, like Constance, wanted Wilde to write again. The renewed relationship between the two men, who had been intimate friends, would launch one of the most curious episodes in Wilde's already exotic life, and link him implacably with the Dreyfus Affair.

But, first, what was it that caused Wilde's writing to dry up? The two essays proposed in *De Profundis*, "Christ as the Precursor of the Romantic Movement in Life" and "The Artistic Life Considered in Relation to Conduct," never got as much as a courtesy call from their potential author—and, on the surface, they had little to do with his recent prison experience, which hordes of pressmen were urging him to write about, with good pay. Wilde had two plays up his sleeve, "Pharaoh" (a particularly Wildean vision of Moses) and "Ahab and Isabelle." But, again, that was not what was being asked of Wilde in the late 1890s. Commissions came streaming in. One of them, proposed during a meeting in June 1897 with Fernand Xau of *Le Journal*, would have solved all his financial problems. Wilde put down his pen and stared at Xau: "My former successes will suffice me," he replied imperiously. Wilde did not want to write about his prison experience. As he told one of his few genuine friends, Vincent O'Sullivan, "I would rather continue stitching sacks."

It was at this point that Gide once more turned up on his doorstep. For Gide *Les Nourritures terrestres* had been a passionate statement on the "discoveries" he had made with Wilde in Algeria; naturally, he wanted to hear what Wilde had to say about the book. He discovered that Wilde had taken up residence at Berneval, a small seaside village just to the east of Dieppe—"the sea," wrote Wilde in his conclusion of *De Profundis*, "washes away the stains and wounds of the world." It would be a substitute for the Jesuits' home in London. Wilde called himself Sebastian Melmoth after a mysterious, satanic hero invented by his maternal grand-uncle, a romantic novelist; the character bore resemblances to Gide's Ménalque in *Les Nourritures terrestres*.

Gide records that he arrived in the middle of the day "unannounced"—which is odd for a man like Gide who organized his life like clockwork. Wilde was not there to meet him. He wandered around this "lugubrious village" in the wind and rain. The hotel, populated by "second-rate people," was a "sad society for Melmoth." At eleven that night Wilde's immense profile appeared at the door. He shook the whole hotel into life, demanding a grog. He did not say as much as a hello to Gide.

But he did invite him up to his rooms, where *Les Nourritures terrestres* was prominently displayed on a bookshelf. Wilde did not say a word about it. Gide noticed that the skin of his hands and his face was red "like that of a commoner." "When we last met, you knew what was awaiting you in England," remarked Gide. "Oh! naturally! naturally!"—he had his old confident tone—"I knew there would be a catastrophe, this or another, I expected it. It had to finish like that. Just imagine: to go further would not have been possible; it just could not last." He lit up one of his gold-tipped cigarettes and went on: "The public is so terrible that they only see in a man the last thing he has done. If I were to go to Paris now all one would see in me is . . . a condemned man. I do not want to be seen there until I have written a play or two." And he added brusquely: "I was right in coming here, wasn't I?" The rain made the window panes shudder. "I did well, don't you think, to come and live here in Berneval?" he repeated.

"They call the local church Notre Dame de Liesse! Oh! Isn't that charming? And the customs officers, they are so bored! I've bought them all the novels of Dumas, *père*. And the children all adore me. For the Queen's Jubilee I held a great dinner. Isn't that absolutely charming?"*

---

* Cross-Channel travellers who get off the ferry at Dieppe and drive the short distance to Berneval will be surprised to discover that the village no longer exists. It is one of the *villages disparus* of the Second World War. In the place of the small church there is a war memorial to the Canadians who fell here during the abortive raid of 19 August 1942. Next to it, a plaque notes that on the opposite side of the street stood the Hôtel du Plage, "where Oscar Wilde spent the summer months of 1897 in exile"; it was destroyed on 3 June 1944 during one of the many air raids that preceded D-Day.

Wilde had still not said a word about Gide's novel. Gide began to feel uncomfortable. He got up and deliberately perused the bookshelf where the novel was sitting. "Have you read Dostoevsky's *House of the Dead?*" he asked. The great thing about the Russian authors, replied Wilde, was their sense of pity. "Do you know, dear, it was pity which prevented me from killing myself?" He told Gide that his favourite author now was Saint Francis of Assisi, who had relived the life of Christ. Gide turned out to know a lot about the saint. "Oh admirable! admirable! You want to do me a great favour? Send me the best life of Saint Francis that you know."

And there surely was the secret. Wilde had set himself a quite impossible task. He wanted to bring the life of Christ to his writing; he wanted to be a modern Saint Francis; but the one area where he could have applied this, the one subject that lent itself to such an ambitious project—his own drama—he refused to write about. No invented tale or piece of theatre could approach the power of his own life story. As the windswept days of Berneval passed by, without as much as a line written, a stanza composed, he came to feel this terribly—like his storyteller who witnessed something fantastic and could only say to the villagers, "I saw nothing."

The next morning Wilde spoke of his two plays, the plots of which "he recounted marvellously." But he said not a word about Gide's novel. The carriage came up to the hotel to take Gide on his way. Wilde mounted and accompanied him for a short part of the route. And at last he brought up the subject of the book.

He was full of praise—but there was still this reticence. He ordered the carriage to stop, said farewell and was about to descend when he said: "Listen, dear, you now have to make me a promise. *Les Nourritures terrestres* is good . . . really good. But, dear, promise me: never write *I* any more." Gide looked at his friend, somewhat baffled. So Wilde explained: "In art, you see, there is no first person."

That was the whole difference between Gide and Wilde. In Gide the first person was all that mattered. Most of his novels were autobiographical. His greatest contribution to literature was his *Journal*, which he kept from the age of seventeen, editing as he went along. Indeed it is the *Journal* that alerts us to Gide's lifelong obsession with Oscar Wilde. Gide constantly looks back at him. It could be the discovery, twenty-three years later, of his old hotel bills at Biskra. Or it could be some indirect reference, as in the way he noted "progressive decay of age:" "if I didn't look at myself in the mirror there would be nothing to remind me that three days ago I entered my fifty-ninth year"—there is a wink there to *Dorian Gray*. For Gide, Wilde's greatest work was *De Profundis*—Wilde's only autobiographical work. He would attend meetings at which it was read aloud, in French or sometimes in German, which he preferred. He records one particularly moving session in May 1905 when Count Harry Kessler of Berlin did the reading. There was Gide's fascination for Wilde's play of masks, Wilde's perpetual game which revealed in a half-light what could not stand the light of day: "it was the profound secret of his flesh which dictated to him, which inspired him, which determined him." "As for me," adds Gide, "I always preferred frankness."

Wilde's refusal of the *I* creates a marvellous play of masks; but Gide, for the sake of his own sanity, comes close to saying, "Let's put the *I* back into art." After the encounter at Berneval, Gide went on to produce, over the next fifty years, a series of autobiographical works. Wilde, in refusing the *I*, produced nothing. Within three years he was dead.

Gide made no further effort to contact Wilde. He did encounter him in Paris. Wilde's Christ-like colossus of a figure in the Paris cafés was not something one could ignore. Wilde hailed him one day from his seat in a street-corner café. Gide took a chair opposite. "No, sit by me," he said; "I am so terribly alone at the moment." Gide was not alone and his friend became agitated; they rose to leave. Wilde made a motion to pay, and then took Gide aside: "I am completely without resources." A few days later Gide saw Wilde for the last time. "Why, oh why, were you in such a hurry to leave Berneval; you had already promised me you would stay longer?" asked Gide, exasperated; he leant over to Wilde: "I can't say I hold it against you, but . . ." Wilde then took him by the arm and shook him vigorously: "You must not hold anything against *someone who has been struck down*."

Gide found it difficult to accept that the great Oscar Wilde had been struck down; he would even write that it was that latent element of fate in Wilde which gave his life such beauty. There lies the real secret to Wilde's silence—and Dreyfus's. Though Gide lived through two world wars, he did not fully grasp war's appalling nature. It is we, with the perspective of time, who grasp the full horror: the massacre in the trenches, the terror of the camps. The stories of Captain Dreyfus and Oscar Wilde, their imprisonment and their suffering in the preceding *fin de siècle*, seem to us so much a premonition of what was to come. The silence of their suffering is particularly striking. In the Second World War German survivors of bombardment would speak of an *Emotionslähmung*, a paralysis of the emotions, which also occurred in the camps and on the field of combat—on the Somme, at Stalingrad and at Kursk, in Auschwitz and in Kolyma. An *Emotionslähmung* is what explains the silences of Captain Dreyfus and Oscar Wilde. It seems inevitable that one of the places wiped out by bombing should have been Berneval, where Wilde's fate was decided. Wilde himself would undoubtedly have seen his story as an *artistic* premonition of war. In which case, nature's imitation of art in the twentieth century proved particularly brutal.

❋

AFTER HIS SOJOURN in Nice, where Douglas behaved with the barbarity and callous self-centredness that would always mark his personality, Wilde arrived in Paris penniless on 13 February 1898. Zola's trial was in its second week: the mood in the streets of the city was one of civil war. "If I go back to Paris without writing my plays the world will only see me as a condemned man," Wilde had told Gide. So he knew exactly what he was heading for, and it was not writing; he told Ross and several other friends that he would not live to see the new century. "I cannot bear being alone," he wrote to Ross, and Wilde was very much alone; the world was slipping away from him. "I see no one here but a young Irishman called Healy, a poet."

Chris Healy was a bohemian poet who, to stay alive, worked for Rowland Strong, a correspondent of the *Observer*, the *Morning Post* and the *New York Times*, and also an intimate friend of the terrible Douglas.

Wilde had, probably on Douglas's recommendation, attempted to contact Strong on his way out to Nice in the hope of borrowing a little travel money. He failed to find him. But when Wilde arrived in Paris the following February, Strong was the first man he contacted. That was how he met Healy. But he also made another acquaintance.

Strong, not unlike Wilde and his fellow decadents in Paris, had a certain attraction to evil. On the day following Wilde's arrival, Strong was taken by another of Wilde's old friends, Robert Sherard, to the offices of *La Libre Parole* where he was introduced to Commandant Esterhazy. In a memoir he wrote at the time, Esterhazy records being introduced by Sherard to "a little man with a red beard . . . and a ferocious enemy into the bargain of all Dreyfusards, past, present and future." Esterhazy was delighted with his new acquaintance, a man with frayed cuffs, very dirty and who stank of drink ten feet away. Esterhazy, Strong and Healy went on drinking binges together, first at a café called the Horse Shoe, where Strong would start off by tossing down fifteen or twenty whiskeys without any visible effect, and later at a bar on Rue Saint-Honoré, where Strong introduced Esterhazy to Oscar Wilde. Wilde was utterly fascinated by this unshaven, tubercular crook with his long, unkempt moustache, the villain of the world. Wilde entertained him with a "flow of his gayest witticisms," while Esterhazy riposted with his extravagant outbursts about Jews and Dreyfusards. Henry Davray, Wilde's translator, thought Wilde was going too far in his enthusiasm for this *"crapule"*; day after day their meetings went on, regular symposia between Faust and the Devil. Wilde's reply to Davray was that, since his release from gaol, he had been forced into a commerce with thieves and assassins. "If Esterhazy had been innocent," he said, "I should have had nothing to do with him."

But did Wilde know for sure—at the time of Zola's trial—that Esterhazy was the guilty man? Mrs. Constance Holland had sent the trustee of her marriage settlement on a mission to save Oscar, to get him writing again. "Oscar is or at least was in Paris at the Hôtel de Nice, Rue des Beaux-Arts," she wrote on 4 March. "Would it be possible for you to go and see him there?" Wilde was so delighted to hear that the best man at his wedding, Carlos Blacker, was coming to visit him. "I long to shake you by the hand again," he wrote. "I am living here quite alone: in one room, I need hardly say, but there is an armchair for you." But he warned his old friend, "I don't think I shall ever write again: *la joie de vivre* is gone."

Blacker was also on a second mission. Like virtually every "intellectual" in Western Europe, he wanted to get to the bottom of the extraordinary Dreyfus Affair. But Blacker had dug further than most. He had long been an intimate friend of Colonel Alessandro Panizzardi, the Italian military attaché in Paris and homosexual lover of the German military attaché Colonel Maximilian von Schwarzkoppen, the employer of Commandant Esterhazy's services and author of most of the torn-up notes the charwoman had been turning over to the Section de Statistique. As Blacker himself put it, "Three beings alone knew the whole and entire truth [about Dreyfus], namely God and the two Military Attachés." After the publication of the *bordereau* in November 1897 and Mathieu's denunciation of Esterhazy as the sole traitor in the case, Blacker developed a plan with Panizzardi that would nail him. Blacker and Panizzardi were close to realizing their project, shortly after Zola's conviction for libel, when Blacker stepped into Wilde's dingy little room in the Hôtel de Nice on Sunday afternoon, 13 March 1898.

Blacker had spent most of the weekend reflecting on what he would say. He decided to combine the two missions: get Wilde writing again and nail Esterhazy—he could do this by recruiting Wilde to the cause. So Blacker revealed all that he knew to Wilde. But a serious problem developed after he left: his wife, Carrie, was dead set against further meetings between her husband and this infamous sodomite—just the sort of attitude that had so isolated Wilde. Blacker did manage to meet Wilde on a few occasions in cafés alone; he paid his bills and even reinstated his allowance under the marriage settlement, which permitted Wilde to move to the neighbouring and more comfortable Hôtel d'Alsace—a place of pilgrimage today. But this was not enough for Wilde. "Could we dine together at some little restaurant?" he wrote despairingly, "just you and I together."

Despair turned to bitterness. On 28 March Wilde injured his mouth when the horse pulling his fiacre fell, throwing Wilde through the front window and cutting his lower lip almost in two. Wilde asked Blacker to come and see him that afternoon; Carrie would not let him go. Instead, Wilde—according to his own correspondence with Blacker—went out for dinner with Esterhazy, accompanied by Rowland Strong and, it seems, Chris Healy. One can imagine the scene: Wilde with his cut lip, Esterhazy with his drooping moustache. "We are the two great martyrs of humanity," said Esterhazy, "but I have suffered the most." "No," replied Wilde, "I have." "At the age of thirteen," said Esterhazy, brushing aside Wilde's comment, "I had a profound conviction that I would never be happy again." "And he never was," reported Wilde to Blacker. Shaken by his accident and yet strengthened by the revelations Blacker had made barely a fortnight earlier, Wilde decided it was the moment to force a confession out of Esterhazy. He succeeded.

Esterhazy plunged into his usual delirium about Jews and Dreyfusards. Wilde leant across the table and tapped Esterhazy on the arm. "The innocent always suffer, Monsieur le Commandant; it is their *métier*," said Wilde slowly and deliberately. "Besides we are all innocent until we are found out. It is a poor, common part to play and within the compass of the meanest. The interesting thing surely is to be guilty and wear as a halo the seduction of sin." The Commandant fell straight into the trap. "Why should I not make my confession to you? I will." He drew himself up: "It is I, Esterhazy, who alone am guilty. I put Dreyfus in prison, and all France cannot get him out." His dinner companions all burst into laughter.

But the smiles soon turned sour. Chris Healy, equipped with the secret information Blacker had passed on to Wilde, went to speak with Émile Zola, with whom he had been in close contact during the weeks of the trial. Zola passed the information to two young writers, Yves Guyot and Francis de Pressensé, who sat down in Joseph Reinach's home and wrote "*Lettres d'un diplomate*." The first of their series appeared in the Dreyfusard *Le Siècle* on 4 April. The letters, whose initial source was Panizzardi and Blacker, made Esterhazy's position untenable; they would lead eventually to Henry's arrest and suicide, and to Esterhazy's exile. But they also totally undermined Blacker's plan to expose Esterhazy. The anti-Dreyfusards thought Blacker was the author of the *"Lettres"* and menaced him and his family with so many death threats that he had to leave the country. Blacker was furious with Wilde; the breach between the two men was irremediable—or almost. Rupert Hart-Davis censored the Blacker–Wilde correspondence from his 1962 collection of Wilde letters on the grounds that they would still upset their respective descendants.

While Blacker descended into rage, Zola made desperate efforts to get in touch with Wilde. But Wilde would have nothing to do with Zola, on the ostensible grounds that he was a "writer of immoral romances." Wilde was basically in Esterhazy's camp.*

Strong in the meantime drafted an article in defence of the Commandant; it was dated 29 March, the day after the dinner. The article was published in the *New York Times* on 10 April and reported that "an English gentleman connected with the aristocracy named Blacker has obtained from Col. von Schwartzkoppen's [*sic*] own lips' a statement that Esterhazy had sold him documents. "Major Esterhazy," Strong added, "declares that the documents, if they exist, are forgeries."

Esterhazy continued to see Wilde. In June 1898, just a few weeks before Henry's arrest, they stayed at a small hotel, L'Idée, at Nogent-sur-Marne, where they were joined by Maurice Gilbert—one of Wilde's new young men—Rowland Strong, who employed him as his new secretary, and Lord Alfred Douglas. On 7 June, just before he left for England, Blacker came to pay a courtesy visit. According to Wilde he "enquired affectionately into my financial position—actually wept floods of tears—begged me to let him pay the balance of my hotel bill—a request that I did not think it right to refuse—and left me with violent protestations of devotion."

Chris Healy had left Paris in April; he could no longer support Strong's sympathies for the evil Commandant. One suspects he felt the

---

* Wilde's real reason for refusing to collaborate with Zola was Zola's refusal to sign a French petition on behalf of Wilde at the time of his conviction. Zola, who lived as a respectable bourgeois, had been disgusted by what the trials revealed about Wilde; Robert Sherard, author of a biography of Zola, described Zola's attitude as that of an "editor of a religious magazine, or the writer of moral textbooks." Wilde could never accept the moralizing of the Dreyfusards.

same about Wilde. But his last view of Wilde is, in justice, the image we should all retain of Wilde. He had just learnt of his wife's unexpected death. Healy found him in Notre Dame Cathedral, kneeling. "The sun streamed through the windows," he recalled, "the organ was pealing a majestic chant, and his head was bowed, almost hidden." No person at the time, or even less today, could imagine what lay within that great soul so devoted to the pursuit of beauty. "When I left him," wrote Healy, "he was still kneeling before the altar, his face hidden by his hands."

RECOMMENDED READING

Apart from those listed under General, which are ranged in order of interest, books follow the chronological sequence of the text in each chapter.

GENERAL

Colin Jones, *Paris: Biography of a City* (London, 2004)

Andrew Hussey, *Paris: The Secret History* (Paris, 2006)

Alistair Horne, *Seven Ages of Paris: Portrait of a City* (London, 2003)

—— *Friend or Foe: An Anglo-Saxon History of France* (London, 2004)

R. P. Tombs and Isabelle Tombs, *That Sweet Enemy: The French and the British from the Sun King to the Present* (London, 2006)

Jean Favier, *Paris* (Paris, 1999)

Jacques Hillairet, *Dictionnaire historique des rues de Paris*, 2 vols. (Paris, 1985)

Ian Littlewood, *Paris: A Literary Companion* (London, 1987)

Walter Benjamin, *The Arcades Project* (trans. Howard Eiland and Kevin McLaughlin, Cambridge, Mass., 2002)

Louis Chevalier, *L'Assassinat de Paris* (Paris, 1977)

David H. Pinkney, *Napoleon III and the Rebuilding of Paris* (Princeton, NJ, 1958)

I. DENFERT-ROCHEREAU

Jacques Godechot, *The Taking of the Bastille* (trans. Jean Stewart, London, 1970)

Simon Schama, *Citizens: A Chronicle of the French Revolution* (New York, 1989)

Michel Foucault, *Surveiller et punir* (Paris, 1975); *Discipline and Punish* (trans. Alan Sheridan, New York, 1977)

Louis Chevalier, *Classes laborieuses et classes dangereuses à Paris pendant la première moitié du XIXe siècle* (Paris, 1958); *Labouring Classes and Dangerous Classes in*

Paris During the First Half of the Nineteenth Century (trans. Frank Jellinek, Princeton, NJ, 1973)

Marie-France Arnold, *Paris, catacombes . . . où, quand, comment, pourquoi?* (Paris, 1993)

Patrick Saletta, *A la découverte des souterrains de Paris* (Paris, 1990)

René Suttel, *Catacombes et carrières de Paris* (Paris, 1986)

Philippe Ariès, *L'Homme devant la mort*, 2 vols. (Paris, 1985); *Western Attitudes Towards Death From the Middle Ages to the Present* (trans. P. M. Ranum, 1976)

2. GARE DU NORD

André Dodin, *De Monsieur Depaul à Saint Vincent de Paul* (Paris, 1985)

—— *Initiation à Saint Vincent de Paul* (Paris, 1993)

Fanny Faÿ-Sallois, *Nourrices à Paris au XIXe siècle* (Paris, 1980)

Danielle Laplaige, *Sans famille à Paris: orphelins et enfants abandonnés de la Seine au XIXe siècle* (Paris, 1991)

Patrick Süskind, *Perfume: A Story of Murder* (trans. John E. Woods, London, 1986)

3. TROCADÉRO

Albert Speer, *Inside the Third Reich* (London, 1970)

E. James Lieberman, *Acts of Will: The Life and Works of Otto Rank* (New York, 1985)

Otto Rank, *The Trauma of Birth* (New York, 1999)

—— *Art and the Artist: Creative Urge and Personality Development* (Foreword by Anaïs Nin, New York, 1989)

Jacques Van Rillaer, Didier Pleux, Jean Cottraux and Mikkel Borch-Jacobsen, *Le Livre noir de la psychanalyse: vivre, penser et aller mieux sans Freud* (Paris, 2005)

Anaïs Nin, *Fire: From "A Journal of Love": The Unexpurgated Diary, 1934–1937* (New York, 1996)

4. MONTPARNASSE

Jean-Paul Crespelle, *La Vie quotidienne à Montparnasse à la Grande Époque 1905–1930* (Paris, 1976)

Jean-Marie Drot and Dominique Polad-Hardouin, *Les Heures chaudes de Mont-parnasse* (Paris, 1999)

Sylvia Beach, *Shakespeare & Company* (New York, 1956)

Gaston Varenne, *Bourdelle par lui-même* (Paris, 1937)

Ionel Jianou and Michel Dufet, *Bourdelle* (Paris, 1970)

Émile-Antoine Bourdelle, *Œuvres graphiques* (Montauban, 2001)

Véronique Gautherin, *Centaures, centauresses: le mythe du centaure vu par Antoine Bourdelle* (Paris, 1995)

—— *L'Œil et la main: Bourdelle et la photographie* (Paris, 2000)

Philippe Monsel and Juliette Laffon, *Antoine Bourdelle* (Paris, 2004)

Modris Eksteins, *Rites of Spring: The Great War and the Birth of the Modern Age* (New York, 1989)

5. SAINT-GERMAIN-DES-PRÉS

Pavillon des Arts, *Saint-Germain-des-Prés, 1945–1950* (Paris, 1989)

Boris Vian, *Manuel de Saint-Germain-des-Prés* (Paris, 1974)

Jean-Paul Sartre, *L'Être et le néant: essai d'ontologie phénoménologique* (Paris, 1943); *Being and Nothingness* (trans. Hazel E. Barnes, New York, 1957)

—— *Situations, III: lendemains de guerre* (Paris, 1949)

—— *Lettres au Castor et à quelques autres, 1940–1963* (Paris, 1983)

—— *Modern Times: Selected Non-Fiction* (trans. Robin Buss, ed. Geoffrey Wall, Harmondsworth, 2000)

Annie Cohen-Solal, *Sartre 1905–1980* (Paris, 1999)

Herbert Lottman, *The Left Bank: Writers, Artists and Politics from the Popular Front to the Cold War* (Chicago, Ill., 1998)

H. Stuart Hughes, *The Obstructed Path: French Social Thought in the Years of Desperation 1930–1960* (New Brunswick, NJ, 2002)

William Barrett, *Irrational Man: A Study in Existential Philosophy* (New York, 1962)

Gabriel Marcel, *The Existential Background of Human Dignity* (Cambridge, Mass., 1963)

Gérard Streiff, *Procès stalinien à Saint-Germain-des-Prés* (Paris, 1999)

Hazel Rowley, *Tête-à-Tête: Simone de Beauvoir and Jean-Paul Sartre* (New York, 2005)

6. PORTE DE CLIGNANCOURT

Norman Davies, *Europe: A History* (London, 1997)

Chris Wickham, *Framing the Early Middle Ages: Europe and the Mediterranean, 400–800* (Oxford, 2005)

Julia M. H. Smith, *Europe after Rome: A New Cultural History, 500–1000* (Oxford, 2005)

Grégoire de Tours, *Histoire des Francs* (Paris, 1995); *History of the Franks* (trans. L. Thorpe, Harmondsworth, 1974)

Michel Rouche, *Clovis* (Paris, 1996)

Dominique Jamet, *Clovis ou le baptême de l'ère* (Paris, 1996)

Pierre Chaunu and Eric Mension-Rigau, *Baptême de Clovis, baptême de la France: de la religion d'État à la laïcité d'État* (Paris, 1996)

Joël Schmidt, *Le Baptême de la France: Clovis, Clotilde, Geneviève* (Paris, 1996)

7. CHÂTELET–LES HALLES

Émile Zola, *Le Ventre de Paris* (Paris, 1964); *The Fat and the Thin: The Belly of Paris* (trans. Ernest Alfred Vizetelly, London, 2007)

—— *Carnets d'enquêtes: une ethnographie inédite de la France* (ed. Henri Mitterand, Paris, 1986)

Henri Mitterand, *Zola*, 3 vols. (Paris, 1999–2002)

COPRAS, *Étude d'opinion auprès des leaders* [sic] *de participation à l'aménagement des Halles* (Paris, 1968)

8. PORTE DE LA VILLETTE

Donald Dresden, *The Marquis de Morès: Emperor of the Bad Lands* (Norman, Okla., 1970)

Charles Droulers, *Le Marquis de Morès* (Paris, 1932)

Alain Sanders, *Le Marquis de Morès: un aventurier tricolore, 1858-1896* (Paris, 1999)

Gordon Wright, "The Marquis de Morès," in *Notable or Notorious: Gallery of Parisians* (Cambridge, Mass., 1991)

Marie-François Goron, *Les Mémoires de Monsieur Goron, ancien Chef de la Sûreté*, 2 vols. (Paris, n.d., *c.* 1900)

Zeev Sternhell, *La Droite révolutionnaire: les origines françaises du fascisme 1885-1914* (Paris, 1978)

Gregor Dallas, *At the Heart of a Tiger: Clemenceau and His World, 1842–1929*
     (London, 1993)

9. OPÉRA

Claude Debussy, *Correspondance (1872-1918)* (ed. François Lesure and Denis
     Herlin, Paris, 2005)
Edward Lockspeiser, *Debussy: His Life and Mind*, 2 vols. (London, 1962–65)
Roger Nichols, *The Life of Debussy* (Cambridge, 2003)
Léon Vallas, *Achille-Claude Debussy* (Paris, 1944)
Simon Trezise (ed.), *The Cambridge Companion to Debussy* (Cambridge, 2005)
André Boucourechliev, *Debussy: la révolution subtile* (Paris, 1998)
English National Opera, Royal Opera, *Pelléas and Mélisande by Claude Debussy
     (Opera Guide Series)* (London, 2004)
Robin Holloway, *Debussy and Wagner* (Eulenberg, 1979)
W. D. Halls, *Maurice Maeterlinck: A Study of His Life and Thought* (Oxford,
     1960)
Mary Garden and Louis Biancolli, *Mary Garden's Story* (New York, 1951)

10. PALAIS-ROYAL

Evelyne Lever, *Philippe Égalité* (Paris, 1996)
Russell T. Barnhart, *Gambling in Revolutionary Paris: The Palais-Royal, 1789–1838*
     (New York, 1990)
Grace Dalrymple Elliot, *Journal of My Life During the French Revolution* (Lon-
     don, 1955)
Jules Michelet, *Histoire de la Révolution française*, 2 vols. (Paris, 1979); *History of
     the French Revolution* (trans. Charles Cocks, ed. Gordon Wright, Chicago,
     Ill., 1967)
Thomas Carlyle, *The French Revolution*, 3 vols. (London, 1989)
Simon Schama, *Citizens: A Chronicle of the French Revolution* (New York, 1989)
Norman Hampson, *A Social History of the French Revolution* (London, 1963)
John Hardman, *Louis XVI* (New Haven, Conn., 1993)
Jacques Godechot, *The Taking of the Bastille* (trans. Jean Stewart, London,
     1970)
Claude Quétel, *L'Histoire véritable de la Bastille* (Paris, 2006)

11. SAINT-PAUL

Alain Landurant, *Montgommery le régicide* (Paris, 1988)

Ivan Cloulas, *Catherine de Médicis* (Paris, 1979)

Jean Orieux, *Catherine de Médicis ou la reine noire* (Paris, 1986)

Leonie Frieda, *Catherine de Medici* (London, 2003)

Christopher Hibbert, *The Virgin Queen: A Portrait of Elizabeth I* (London, 1990)

Maria Perry, *Elizabeth I: The Word of a Prince* (London, 1990)

Mack P. Holt, *The French Wars of Religion 1562–1629* (Cambridge, 1995)

Emmanuel Le Roy Ladurie, *L'Etat royal, 1460–1610* (Paris, 1987)

Johan Huizinga, *Homo Ludens: A Study of the Play Element in Culture* (Boston, 1955)

12. PÈRE LACHAISE

Oscar Wilde

Richard Ellmann, *Oscar Wilde* (London, 1987)

Lionel Lambourne, *The Aesthetic Movement* (London, 1996)

Oscar Wilde, *De Profundis and Other Writings* (includes "The Decay of Lying") (London, 1954)

—— *The Letters of Oscar Wilde* (ed. Rupert Hart-Davis, London, 1962)

Alan Sheridan, *André Gide: A Life in the Present* (London, 1998)

André Gide, *Journal*, 2 vols. (Paris, 1997)

—— *Oscar Wilde: In Memoriam (souvenirs) & le "De Profundis"* (Paris, 1939)

Kazimierz Brandys, *Hôtel d'Alsace et autres adresses* (trans. Jean-Yves Erhel, Paris, 1991)

J. Robert Maguire, "Oscar Wilde and the Dreyfus Affair," *Victorian Studies*, 41:1 (Autumn 1997)

The Dreyfus Affair

Jean-Denis Bredin, *L'Affaire* (Paris, 1983); *The Affair: The Case of Alfred Dreyfus* (New York, 1986)

Joseph Reinach, *Histoire de l'Affaire Dreyfus*, 7 vols. (Paris, 1901–11)

Michael Burns, *Dreyfus: A Family Affair, 1789–1945* (New York, 1991)

Guy Chapman, *The Dreyfus Case: A Reassessment* (London, 1959)

Alfred Dreyfus, *Cinq années de ma vie* (Paris, 1982); *Five Years of My Life: The Diary of Captain Alfred Dreyfus* (London, 2001)

—— *The Letters of Captain Alfred Dreyfus to His Wife* (London, 2005)

Charles Péguy, *Notre jeunesse* (Paris, 1993)

Émile Zola, *L'Affaire Dreyfus: la vérité en marche* (Paris, 1969); *The Dreyfus Affair: J'accuse and Other Writings* (London, 1997)

Robert Gauthier, *Dreyfusards* (Paris, 1965)

Marcel Thomas, *L'Affaire sans Dreyfus* (Paris, 1961)

—— *Esterhazy ou l'envers de l'affaire Dreyfus* (Paris, 1989)

Henri Guillemin, *L'Énigme Esterhazy* (Paris, 1962)

Count M. C. F. Walsin-Esterhazy, *Les Dessous de l'affaire Dreyfus* (Paris, 1898)

INDEX